Solopreneur
Business

A Wiley Brand

Solopreneur Business

by Joe Rando, CEO, LifeStarr and Carly Ries, CMO, LifeStarr

A Wiley Brand

Solopreneur Business For Dummies®

Published by: **John Wiley & Sons, Inc.**, 111 River Street, Hoboken, NJ 07030-5774, www.wiley.com

For general information on our other products and services, please contact our Customer Care Department within the U.S. at 877-762-2974, outside the U.S. at 317-572-3993, or fax 317-572-4002. For technical support, please visit https://hub.wiley.com/community/support/dummies.

Wiley publishes in a variety of print and electronic formats and by print-on-demand. Some material included with standard print versions of this book may not be included in e-books or in print-on-demand. If this book refers to media that is not included in the version you purchased, you may download this material at http://booksupport.wiley.com. For more information about Wiley products, visit www.wiley.com.

Library of Congress Control Number: 2025944152

ISBN 978-1-394-32467-5 (pbk); ISBN 978-1-394-32469-9 (ebk); ISBN 978-1-394-32468 a (oblt)

Contents at a Glance

Table of Contents

Introduction

Welcome to *Solopreneur Business For Dummies*. If you're building a one-person business, or thinking about it, you're in the right place. This book is your road map to launching, running, and continuously improving a business that not only pays the bills but also serves your life.

We wrote this book because, frankly, the world hasn't caught up with solopreneurs. Business books tend to focus on companies with employees, funding, and long-term plans to *scale* (or grow their revenue and profit). But what about the millions of people who want to build a business that serves some greater goal? That's where we and this book come in.

Whether you're just starting out or you've been in business for a while, this book helps you do things the solopreneur way: as simply as possible (but not simpler), strategically, and aligned with the life you want to live. We've developed the Solopreneur Success Cycle, a process that guides you through every phase of imagining, building, and improving your business.

About This Book

Most business advice is written for companies with teams of employees, funding from investors, or venture capital backing. This book is different. It's designed for *solopreneurs*, people who want to build a business of one, keeping things lean, flexible, and focused on what matters most to them.

We take you through the entire solopreneur journey using the Solopreneur Success Cycle, a proven framework that helps you start, run, and continuously improve your business. Relying on this framework, you'll define your goals, design your business to fit your life, attract the right customers, and grow without adding employees (unless you want to). We've organized the content into the following seven parts.

Part 1: Introduction to Solopreneurship. Find out what solopreneurship really is, how it's different from other work paths, and how the Solopreneur Success Cycle and Solopreneur Action Plan can help you succeed.

Part 2: Starting Your Solopreneur Career. Define your goals, brainstorm business ideas, choose your business model, research your competition, and identify your ideal customers to build a business that works for you.

Part 3: Building Your Solopreneur Business. Position your business to stand out, craft messaging and marketing that connects with customers, and set up the legal, financial, and operational systems you need to launch with confidence.

Part 4: Running and Learning from Your Solo Business. Run your business with confidence while learning from real-world results, which helps you develop a list of changes to consider making to your business.

Part 5: Improving Your Business. Know how to assess what's working, choose the right changes with the PRIORITY framework, and make improvements with the SMOOTH Method so your business stays aligned with your goals.

Part 6: Living the Solopreneur Lifestyle. Protect and maintain your energy and well-being, build a business that supports your life, and stay relevant by learning, automating, and planning for long-term success on your terms.

Part 7: The Part of Tens. Get quick tips to avoid common solopreneur mistakes, strengthen your mindset, and find answers to the top questions solopreneurs ask about running and growing a business of one.

As with all *For Dummies* books, this one is designed to be easy to navigate and read in a nonlinear manner (jump to whichever chapters interest you rather than working through them in order). It's filled with actionable tips you can apply right away. You'll find hands-on tools, checklists, and downloadable templates to put your ideas into practice without needing a business degree or a team of consultants.

We also leveraged AI in the writing process, specifically using the You're Wrong tool developed by Joe Rando to critique and challenge our work. This tool helped us spot gaps, sharpen our ideas, and improve the clarity of each chapter.

Foolish Assumptions

We don't assume you've already decided that solopreneurship is right for you. This book starts by helping you figure that out, before you waste your most valuable resource: your time.

You're probably wondering whether you have the skills to be a solopreneur. Well, you need to be good at something that people will pay you for. But this book gives you the information about the various aspects of running a solo business so that you can either master the skills or outsource the job to someone who can (and no, that's not cheating).

Whether you're just getting started or you're looking to improve what you've already built, this book gives you practical tools and clear insights to help you start, run, and grow a solo business that works for your life. We guide you through a proven, easy-to-follow process, from planning to execution, so you can navigate this exciting and challenging journey with confidence.

Icons Used in This Book

Throughout this book, icons in the margins point to valuable information that calls out for your attention. Here are the icons you'll encounter and a brief description of each.

TIP

Marks helpful information and shortcuts you can use to make the task at hand easier.

REMEMBER

Highlights information that's especially important for you to know.

TECHNICAL STUFF

Denotes bits of information that are more technical in nature but can generally help deepen your understanding of a topic.

WARNING

Tells you to watch out! This icon marks important information that may save you headaches, time, and sometimes even money.

Identifies files you can download from the book's companion website at www.dummies.com/go/solopreneurbusinessfd.

Beyond the Book

In addition to the abundance of information and guidance related to solopreneur businesses that we provide in this book, you can find even more help and information online at Dummies.com. Check out this book's online Cheat Sheet: Just go to www.dummies.com and search for "Solopreneur Business For Dummies Cheat Sheet."

You also get access to the book's companion website at www.dummies.com/go/solopreneurbusinessfd, where you can download a Solopreneur Action Plan template and various templates and worksheets we discuss throughout the book.

Where to Go from Here

Not every reader of this book is in the same situation. Whether you're just starting to think about solopreneurship or you've been running a business for years, you'll find the help you need in these pages. But to save you some time, here's a quick guide to help you jump in at the best place for you.

If you're frustrated with the corporate grind or recently laid off and wondering about solopreneurship, start with Chapter 1. It gives you the real story about what it takes to go solo, so you can decide if this path is for you. If you have an idea but haven't gotten your business off the ground yet, head over to Chapter 4, which helps you start shaping your business idea into something real while making sure it actually supports the life you want to live.

If you already have a solo business but it isn't going the way you hoped, or it's going fine but you know it can be better, jump to Chapter 19 and work forward from there. You'll find out how to assess what's working (or not), and what to do about it. Of course, if you want the full picture of solopreneurship or just love a good cover-to-cover read, feel free to start at the beginning and work your way through to the end. Either way, we've got you covered.

1

Introduction to Solopreneurship

Understand what it means to be a solopreneur and what makes it different from other work paths.

Explore the Solopreneur Success Cycle and how it helps you start, run, and improve your business.

Find out how to create a living, working business plan with the Solopreneur Action Plan.

Chapter **1**

Understanding Solopreneurship

ave you ever wondered what it truly means to be a solopreneur? If you're reading this book, odds are, your answer is *yes*. Solopreneurship is more than just a career path. It's also a mindset and a lifestyle that can be incredibly rewarding, but it isn't for the faint of heart. In this chapter, we pull back the curtain on what it really means to be a solopreneur and debunk common misconceptions about running a one-person business. We talk about what solopreneurship looks like, the many roles you need to embrace, and why flying solo is both weird and wonderful.

Why Solopreneurship?

Let's be real. Traditional jobs don't always offer the same security and fulfillment they once did. With freedom and the chance to build something that matters to them in mind, people are realizing the "9:00-5:00 for 40 years" model isn't the only path to success.

With modern technology, running a company of one has never been easier. You can work from anywhere, your target audience can expand from local to global, and you can make a living while following your values and passions. Solopreneurship isn't just a trend or career choice. It's a mindset and lifestyle change that prioritizes flexibility, work satisfaction, and puts you in the driver's seat of your life.

Figuring Out What a Solopreneur Is

While the term *solopreneur* has become popular over the past few years, it isn't mainstream, even though the number of business-people who fall into this category is in the tens of millions (and counting).

For the purpose of this book, a *solopreneur* is a person that runs a company of one. They manage and grow their business independently, often bringing on contractors, freelancers, or virtual assistants to support them. What sets them apart is the intentional decision *not* to build a traditional team of employees. If you manage contractors for your business, you need to understand the legal distinction between contractors and employees. Thoroughly research rules and regulations to ensure you're classifying people correctly.

REMEMBER

The keyword in the previous paragraph is *manage*. While a solopreneur is ultimately responsible for every area of their business, you'll see that throughout the book we strongly encourage outsourcing and collaboration with others.

What often differentiates solopreneurs from traditional entrepreneurs is that instead of purely turning their passion into profits, they opt for work-life balance, flexibility, and autonomy. The following sections explain a few notable things about being a solopreneur.

You don't have any employees (except you)

Solopreneurship is a one-person show. And while being your own boss can be exhilarating, it also means that you're every employee you would hire wrapped into one. Just because you don't have a marketing, sales, or customer service manager, that doesn't mean those roles don't exist; it just means each one falls on you.

Look at solopreneurship as an exciting adventure in which you'll discover many new things, rather than an overwhelming to-do list you'll never get through. Embrace the potential chaos and roll with the challenges. Most solopreneurs don't know how to perform all the traditional jobs required to run a business, but they figure out a way to get things done, and so can you.

You are forgoing a scaling tool

You may have heard that solopreneurs lose a powerful scaling tool by not having employees, and that's true, but it doesn't mean you can't grow. You can do it in a variety of ways, including the following:

» **Artificial intelligence (AI):** If you haven't embraced AI, it's time to give it a try. Spend time on the big-picture stuff like strategy and growth, and let AI help you take care of things like market research, idea generation, and more.

» **Automation:** You don't have to do your lead nurturing (building relationships with potential customers), onboarding (welcoming new customers to your business), and invoicing manually. You can put automated systems in place to perform repetitive tasks behind the scenes.

» **Outsourcing:** Although you don't have employees, you do have the option to hire contractors and freelancers. But remember that outsourcing doesn't eliminate work; it shifts work. You'll still need to set expectations, communicate clearly, and oversee delivery of the outsourced work. That said, outsourcing gives you access to specialized expertise without the commitment or costs of a full-time staff if you manage the process well.

» **Productization:** If you're starting a service-based business, figure out a way to productize your skills, for example, by creating a video course. This way, you can have *passive income* (which requires little effort after creation) and not trade your time for money (a finite quantity).

» **Rate increases:** If you like the way things are going in your business but want more money, consider raising your rates. People are often afraid to hike prices, but charging higher rates can be a low-risk, high-reward way to increase revenue.

>> **Strategic partnerships and collaborations:** Aligning your business with complementary businesses allows you to reach new audiences, jointly create offers, and establish more credibility. You can increase your growth and exposure without a ton of extra effort.

REMEMBER

Being able to scale doesn't mean you have to. If you're happy with the direction your business is moving in, and you're bringing in your desired income, just continue running things the way you have been.

What solopreneurship isn't

Solopreneurship isn't freelancing. Sure, they're similar, but we've found that while freelancers typically go after projects or gigs, solopreneurs build a business around their product or service.

Similarly, solopreneurship doesn't always follow the rules of traditional entrepreneurship. Entrepreneurs typically want to scale with employees, expand their operations, and grow their revenue exponentially. Solopreneurs want to make a living while enjoying their life. The dollar amount on their bottom line isn't usually their North Star the way it is for many aspiring entrepreneurs.

Solopreneurship shouldn't be mistaken for a *side hustle* (something you do to supplement your primary income) because the mindset, goals, and commitment level are fundamentally different. While starting a one-person business as a side hustle is a smart, low-risk way to test the waters, the ultimate aim is to create something that replaces your current paycheck and ideally offers more freedom, fulfillment, and control over your work-life balance.

You may also hear that solopreneurship is all about bringing in passive income, and while that can certainly be an arm of the business, most solopreneurs are very involved and actively engaged with the daily operations of their business.

Lastly, solopreneurship isn't a constant struggle where you have to say *yes* to anything that comes your way to make ends meet. Top solopreneurs focus their offering, and set up systems, business models, and strategies to run a successful company.

Solopreneurship is about designing a business around the life you want, not just earning cash on the side. That long-term vision is what separates it from a hobby or gig. It requires strategic thinking, long-term planning, and a commitment to growth. It's not just trading time for money; it's building something you own and shape over time.

Why solopreneurship is weird

Although being a solopreneur is wonderful, it's also unfamiliar to a lot of people (maybe even you), so this business and lifestyle has a way of feeling, well, weird from time to time. Here's what we mean:

>> **You wear every hat.** One day you're the top dog crafting strategy, the next you're creating marketing materials, and the next you're responding to customer emails. Some of you may even scrub your office toilets! There isn't an area of the business you don't touch, and that might be a new feeling.

>> **No two days are alike.** Never knowing what the day will bring is stressful and thrilling at the same time. While you can certainly attempt to set a routine, you must be ready to pivot if need be.

>> **People won't understand what you do.** When people aren't familiar with the world of solopreneurship, they make all kinds of assumptions about what your day looks like, how many hours you work, and so on. You can try to explain your work to them but don't take it personally if they never fully understand. It's a unique world!

This is a reference to what a day in your life looks like, not what you sell. You absolutely want to make sure people understand your products and services; otherwise, you have a major problem. But, don't worry, because this book is designed to help you with that.

>> **The unknown becomes familiar.** It's okay not to know what you're doing a lot of the time. The true test of whether you'll be successful as a solopreneur is that you have the desire to figure things out. The unknown is scary at first, but if you embrace it as an opportunity to learn and grow, you'll be much better off in the long run.

>> **You have complete freedom.** This can be both a blessing and a curse. You have the ability to decide whom you want to work with, how to run your business, and how you want to spend your days, but people who need structure may struggle with all that freedom. So, know yourself, and if you fall into the latter category, try to build a routine with some buffer for flexibility so you don't get distracted too easily.

>> **It's easy to take things personally.** "It's not personal; it's just business," said no solopreneur ever. Because you are your brand, it can be easy to take any critical feedback personally, but you must figure out a way to separate your feelings from your intellect.

Solopreneurship is a wild mix of freedom and responsibility that's both rewarding and challenging, sometimes weird, and mostly wonderful.

A successful solopreneur's mindset

Solopreneurs think differently than other entrepreneurs and business owners. They're a special breed with a unique mindset and different priorities. Successful solopreneurs have a clear vision, keep their eye on the prize, and do what it takes to get it.

Veteran solopreneurs are extremely self-disciplined. While they may contract some of their tasks and collaborate with others, at the end of the day, solopreneurs are only accountable to themselves, so they need to have an innate drive to get things done and move the needle in their business.

Successful solopreneurs are coachable and willing to learn. You don't know what you don't know, and as any solopreneur can confirm, that phrase has never been truer than when you decide to go solo in business. You may be knowledgeable about your product or service, but when you begin your planning and operations, you need to be prepared to eat a slice of humble pie, and pivot and grow from each new obstacle or unknown situation you may encounter (because you *will* encounter them).

You must be resilient and able to adapt as new information and critical feedback come your way. You have to prioritize progress over perfection and make improvements as you go, knowing you don't have a grasp on everything from the outset.

Lastly, successful solopreneurs are mentally tough. You get all the glory when things are going well, but you also carry all the blame and liability. You'll have to endure the roller coaster of highs and lows that come with this type of business. For those that can ride the wave, it's all worth it, but it takes some stamina and determination. If you want to be a solopreneur long term, embrace an ownership mentality and don't waste time blaming external circumstances for setbacks or challenges. Accept any consequences and be optimistic that you can bounce back stronger when difficult situations pop up.

Debunking Common Myths About Solopreneurship

After working with thousands of solopreneurs, we've found that there are many misconceptions about the concept of solopreneurship, so we want to debunk some of the most common myths we've come across.

You need to know everything before you get started

Wrong! As a business owner, you'll never know everything, and you'll always be learning. So, if total enlightenment is what you're waiting for, we have bad news: Your business will never get off the ground. Instead, you need to dive in as soon as you think your business is good enough, release it to the public, and let real-world experience be your greatest teacher. Fail fast and bounce back just as quickly. In the world of solopreneurship, progress always beats perfection.

Solopreneurs work alone

Repeat after us: Flying solo in business doesn't mean you're alone. You'll see this reassuring phrase throughout the book because we can't say it enough. Although you won't have employees, you'll find community with other solopreneurs, work with clients, develop collaborations . . . the list goes on. Many solopreneurs say they work with far more people now than they did in their corporate job because their networks expand past the walls of their business.

You can certainly close yourself inside your home office and choose not to work with others, and if that's your preference, it's totally okay. But just be aware that many solopreneurs don't go it alone.

"Solopreneurship" is a fancy way to say "unemployed"

Don't listen to the haters! Describing solopreneurs as unemployed is simply ignorant and belittles the grit, the resilience, and, frankly, the economic impact these business owners have. To say a person who handles all the operations, marketing, finances, customer support, and every other aspect of their business without a partner or employees (*and* assumes all the risk and responsibility) is unemployed is insulting.

Anybody can be a solopreneur

While we're certainly fans of solopreneurship, we'll admit it isn't for everybody. Some people perform their best when they're working in a team environment or with a manager who holds them accountable. Here are some things to consider before deciding if solopreneurship is right for you:

>> **Your risk tolerance:** When you're a solopreneur, you don't have the safety net of a steady paycheck, you cover your own benefits, and all the responsibilities and liabilities of the business land on you. If you can stomach this, running your solo business is totally worthwhile, but it can be too much to take on for many people.

>> **Your skill set:** Although you can theoretically turn any skill set into a solopreneur business, you need to remember that the skills you're selling aren't the only ones you need to run a business. You have to know the basics of marketing, sales, operations, and finances. You can outsource some of these tasks, but you'll still want to be familiar with the basics and best practices so you know if your contractors are doing what they should. If you don't want to learn new things and adapt, then solopreneurship probably isn't for you.

>> **Your financial stability:** Solopreneurship can eventually lead to financial success and stability, but that doesn't often

happen immediately. When you start out, you want to have enough savings to support yourself as you ramp up. You should plan not just for your day-to-day financial needs but also for your start-up expenses, like equipment, technology, marketing costs, and so on.

>> **Mental and emotional preparedness:** You need to figure out ways to be resilient and persevere through adversity. Things won't always go your way, and you may feel like giving up some days, but you have to power through the tough times. Work on your mental strength and make it a priority. And, keep in mind, every solopreneur experiences setbacks, imposter syndrome (see the later section "Overcoming imposter syndrome"), and countless other obstacles, so you're far from alone.

>> **Access to resources:** Everybody starts their solo journey from a different place. Some solopreneurs have bigger networks, some have deeper pockets, and some have a dream but need to work multiple jobs to make ends meet. Figure out your barriers and how you can overcome them. Identify them, make a plan to remove them, and get started on your business. Where there's a will, there's a way, right?

It's an easy get-rich-quick scheme

This assumption is funny, yet it's a common misconception about solopreneurship. Sure, scams exist, and a select few individuals succeed with get-rich-quick schemes. But the majority of solopreneurs are among the hardest workers we know and put more blood, sweat, and tears into their livelihood than the average person.

Building a successful solo business requires time and effort, and it's certainly a marathon, not a sprint. The reality is that it can take years to hit your stride. This doesn't mean you won't find clients quickly, but it takes time to figure out what works and what doesn't, and optimize your operations to reach your full potential.

If you think solopreneurship is your ticket to making $1 million in a week while wearing your pajamas, you have some unrealistic expectations!

Knowing What You're Getting Yourself Into

Nobody can predict the future. You may have an incredible idea, a sound strategy, a solid business plan, and the necessary skills to make your business succeed. But even with all your ducks in a row, you don't know what you don't know, and you'll need to be able to handle the curveballs that will inevitably be thrown at you. Here are a few ways to land on your feet when you're tripped up by unexpected situations.

Embracing continuous learning

If you think you know everything going into solopreneurship, you're in for a rude awakening. Embracing continuous learning is one of the most important things you can do for your solo business. Not only do you need to develop new skills (sales, marketing, accounting, and more), but you also need to stay on top of current trends, know what your competition is doing, and continue to please your audience. What worked for you at one point may not work for you in the future.

If you want to stay ahead of the competition, remain relevant, and, if we're being honest, stay interested in your own business, you need to make continuous learning a priority. What this entails is different for each person and business. For some, it means adding to their long list of credentials and certifications; for others, it means reading books about their industry or their audience. Some solopreneurs may set up daily Google Alerts or attend virtual events to stay up to speed on everything they need to know for their business.

WARNING

Decide what works best for you, but don't put continuous learning at the bottom of your to-do list. If you keep moving it down the list of priorities, you risk waking up one day to the realization that your business is no longer current and it's too late to pivot because a competitor has gotten there first. We don't want to sound dramatic, but it happens all the time.

Cultivating resilience and adaptability

When you daydream about solopreneurship, you may visualize yourself on the path to success, celebrating your wins and coasting through your career. It's a lovely thought, but it isn't necessarily reality. As wonderful as solopreneurship is, you'll have setbacks and failures, perhaps lots of them. And when you're running the show, you're the only one to get your business back on track after something derails you. Are you the type of person who can handle that?

TIP

As you plan your solo business, consider all the possible setbacks you may encounter and how you'll respond if they occur. Hopefully, you won't face a lot of adversity, but if you do, you'll be mentally prepared for it because you've already thought of a solution.

Overcoming imposter syndrome

Imposter syndrome is a persistent feeling of self-doubt despite having accomplishments or qualifications that contradict those doubts. It's basically the voice in your head that makes you think you can't do something, even when you can. Imposter syndrome can be a solopreneur's most pesky constant companion. It'll lower your confidence and make you feel like you truly are all alone on your solopreneur journey. But trust us when we say that nothing is further from the truth.

Almost all solopreneurs experience this feeling from time to time. While it's annoying and unhelpful, you can use the following strategies to overcome it so you can bounce back and thrive:

>> **Get something done.** Your confidence will grow once you start accomplishing things, no matter how small or insignificant they seem. Figure out some easy quick wins to build your momentum and grow your self-assurance. This can be as simple as writing an email to a customer you've been meaning to contact.

>> **Focus on something other than your business.** Sometimes a simple change of scenery can shift your mood. Step away from your business for a few hours and get some exercise or spend time on a hobby. Some of the best ideas come when you aren't in a work setting, so get your mind off your business for a while. Who knows? Maybe you'll solve all your challenges and frustrations while focusing on other things.

>> **Talk to somebody.** The more you hold it in, the louder imposter syndrome gets. Vocalize your concerns to a friend, peer, or mentor who can provide a listening ear. Talking through imposter syndrome helps it lose its power over you.

REMEMBER

Feeling like an imposter doesn't mean you're failing; it often means you're growing. Psychologists call this the *Dunning-Kruger effect*: when beginners think they know everything, but as they gain knowledge, they realize how much they don't know. Ironically, self-awareness is a sign you're becoming more competent, not less. Next time you feel overwhelmed by everything you still have to learn, take it as proof that you're on the right track.

Asking Yourself If You Should Be a Solopreneur

We wish we had a crystal ball so we'd be able to look into the future and tell you if solopreneurship is the right career path and lifestyle for you, but that's ultimately up to you to decide. You may want it badly, but you need to be really honest with yourself about whether you're cut out for the solopreneur life. Solopreneurship can be your ticket to career freedom but not without hard work and maximum effort. You'll call all the shots but take all the blame. You'll celebrate your victories but internalize your failures. It can be a great ride, but it's not for everybody.

Listing your reasons to start a solo business

Before you get too far down the rabbit hole of business models, market research, and strategy, take a step back and ask yourself this powerful question: What kind of life do I want, and how can my business support that?

One of the biggest advantages of being a solopreneur is freedom. But too often, people leave the corporate world to build a business that ends up owning them, and they become burdened by the same stress, burnout, and poor work-life balance they were trying to escape in the first place.

In Chapter 4, we do a deep dive into creating your goals and finding your *why* as a motivation tool to start your own business. But before you do this, start brainstorming some reasons for going out on your own with a solo business. Do you want to work three days a week and travel more? Design your business around that goal. Do you need flexibility to care for family or pursue creative passions? That's the motivation you should use when you make foundational decisions.

Don't build a business that you need to survive. Build one that helps you thrive.

Keep in mind, however, that some reasons for starting a solo business don't always set you up for long-term success and fulfillment. If any of these situations resonate with you, you may want to reconsider your plan to go solo because you may not get what you're looking for:

» **You hate your boss or current job.** Running a solo business takes planning and strategy. Jumping into it because you're unhappy with your current situation seems reactive and impulsive, which isn't a good headspace to be in when you're starting a new business. Use your distaste for your current employment as motivation to leave, once you've properly planned your exit and thought through your options.

» **You want to get rich quickly.** While exceptions to the rule certainly exist, solopreneurship isn't necessarily the best or fastest way to become the next millionaire. Most people dive into this work setup for the lifestyle, not for the money.

» **You want to work less.** This is certainly the ultimate goal, and the reason a lot of solopreneurs start their business, but the reality is, you may work more (a lot more) hours when you're trying to get everything up and running. From there, your ability to reduce your hours depends on how well you automate and outsource. If you have a hard time doing that, the hours you work aren't likely to decrease.

Take time to reflect on your reasons for jumping into the solo business world. If they come from a place of purpose and alignment, you're getting started on the right foot. If you're being impulsive because you're dissatisfied with your current profession, take a step back to reconsider your plan and examine why you think solopreneurship can solve whatever problem you're facing.

Overcoming fear

Besides imposter syndrome (which we discuss earlier in this chapter), many solopreneurs experience fear. Your fears can take many forms, including these universal ones (you may experience others based on your individual circumstances; everyone does):

Fear of the unknown	Fear of making the wrong decisions
Fear of failure	Fear of letting people down
Fear of inconsistent income	Fear of isolation
Fear of judgment	

Diving into life as a solopreneur can be scary. If you're letting your fears get in the way of chasing your dreams, look to these pointers to guide you:

>> **Take baby steps.** Figure out ways to make whatever you're fearful of less intimidating and start tackling it with small actions. If you're afraid of sales, practice selling to a close friend or family member to get comfortable talking about it.

>> **Reframe the way you view failure.** Instead of fearing failure, look at mistakes as opportunities to learn and grow.

>> **Get to the root of what's causing your fear.** There's often more than meets the eye when it comes to why you're afraid of something. Identify what's behind your fear and address that first.

>> **Practice visualization techniques.** Picture yourself overcoming your fear and exceling at whatever you're trying to achieve. This helps you believe it's possible and reduces your anxiety around it.

>> **Act confident and wear a smile.** Fake it until you make it, right? Carrying yourself with confidence can trick your brain into thinking you're *actually* confident. Act like you've already conquered your fear and see what happens.

Kicking Things Off: Taking Your First Steps

So, now what? You know what a solopreneur is, but are you confident that you're cut out for this career path? Check out the Should You Be a Solopreneur Quiz (https://quizzes.lifestarr.com/are-you-ready-to-be-a-solopreneur). If you're having trouble deciding if you should travel become a solopreneur, this quiz can help you make the decision.

You may not know if solopreneurship is right for you unless you start testing the waters. This may mean starting a side hustle or freelancing in your spare time to get some experience. Although side hustles and freelance gigs aren't the same thing as solopreneurship, this experience can help you figure out if working for yourself is what lights you up.

You can also meet up for coffee with people whose opinion and expertise you value to run your ideas past them and get feedback. Or, offer your product or service to friends and family to figure out if you can see yourself developing and running a business around it for the long term. Getting feedback and real-life experience can give you a glimpse into what the solopreneur world is like.

We may be biased, but working your way through this book and understanding the Solopreneur Success Cycle is a good first step, because it provides guidance and encouragement for each part of the solo journey. We're here for you every step of the way. What are you waiting for? Get to it!

Chapter **2**

Introducing the Solopreneur Success Cycle

The *Solopreneur Success Cycle* is a process for solopreneurs to start, run, and improve their business. It's designed to operate like a *flywheel*. What's a flywheel? It's a heavy wheel that keeps moving once you get it started and goes faster and faster as you push on it. In this case, faster means better.

The idea is that as you follow this process, your business gets better and better. It becomes more successful, gets easier to run, and better suits your needs and goals over time. You'll spend less time figuring things out and more time building, launching, and improving a successful one-person business.

Before you start using the Solopreneur Success Cycle to build or improve your business, it's helpful to walk through it so you know what the process looks like. This chapter provides an overview of the key parts of the Solopreneur Success Cycle and how they work together.

At this point, you simply want to take this process in. Don't worry about starting the work until you get to later chapters. If you haven't already, take a look at Chapter 1, where we define solopreneur and solopreneurship.

Identifying the Benefits of the Solopreneur Success Cycle

When you start any business, solo or not, you have much to consider. The most challenging aspect is that you *don't know what you don't know,* so anything you do to avoid mistakes can save a lot of grief. The Solopreneur Success Cycle helps you avoid many mistakes people make when starting a solo business.

People often use a trial-and-error approach to start their business. But this can lead to a lot of wasted time and money, often resulting in failure. The Solopreneur Success Cycle lets you follow a framework that avoids many of these mistakes.

The Solopreneur Success Cycle is about starting with a business idea that fits your goals and life, building it step-by-step, figuring out what works (and what doesn't), making changes, and then regularly repeating the process of understanding what works and adjusting your business so that it continues to run smoothly and improve.

Even if you've been in business for a while, this process allows you to stay current with

>> Changes in your industry
>> Changes in the world
>> Changes in technology
>> Changes in your goals

Exploring the Phases and Steps of the Solopreneur Success Cycle

The Solopreneur Success Cycle consists of three phases, as shown in Figure 2-1. These phases highlight the major processes you go through to start, run, and improve your business: Get Started, Do, and Improve. Notice how the Do and Improve phases form a loop. This creates a continual process of improvement.

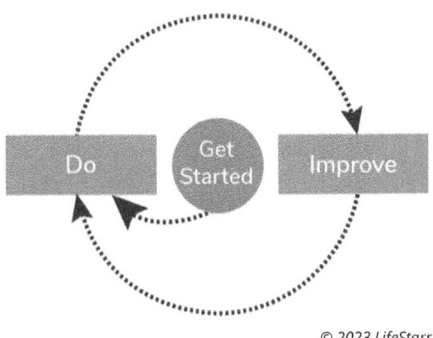

© 2023 LifeStarr

FIGURE 2-1: The phases of the Solopreneur Success Cycle.

While the phases illustrate the Solopreneur Success Cycle in an easy-to-understand way, you can grasp the actual execution better by looking at the detailed steps shown in Figure 2-2.

These steps indicate the thought processes and activities you're involved in as you work through the Solopreneur Success Cycle, which we present here in a nutshell:

>> **Get Started:** Here's where you define your goals, envision your business, do some planning, and get it all set up.

>> **Do:** In Figure 2-2,this phase has just one bubble, which reads Execute/Learn. It's a big step, though, where you execute your Get Started decisions and learn what is and isn't working along the way.

>> **Improve:** In this phase, you refine what you discovered in the Do phase, making more decisions, and then making adjustments, and the cycle continues.

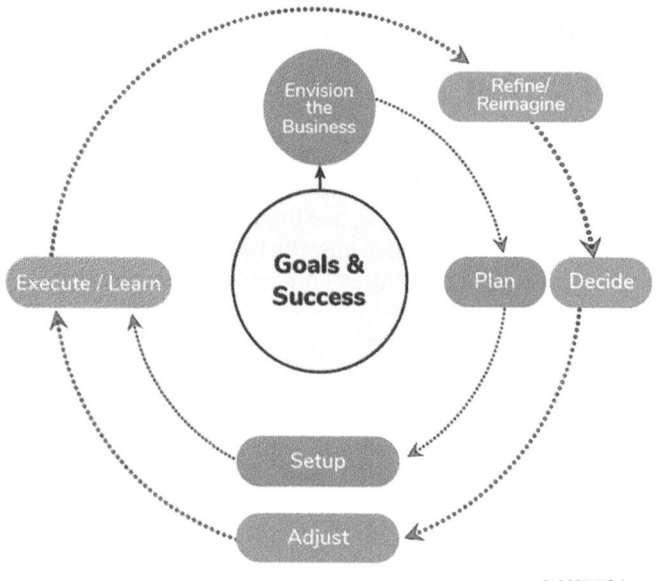

© 2023 LifeStarr

FIGURE 2-2: The detailed steps of the Solopreneur Success Cycle.

Each of these phases and steps is crafted to be appropriate for one-person businesses and avoids the complexity of employee-based businesses wherever possible while boosting the chances of a successful outcome. Before we dive deeper into the Solopreneur Success Cycle (pretty much throughout the rest of this book), we go over each phase and step in some detail in the following sections to provide you with the big picture.

TIP

You may run across terms and concepts throughout the rest of this chapter that are unfamiliar to you. Don't worry too much about that yet. For now, focus on understanding the big picture, and look for the details in later chapters (as referenced).

Phase 1: Getting started

As you launch your business, this phase helps you get underway more smoothly by doing the right things in the correct order. Working through each step in the order presented allows you to build a successful business that you want to run.

Phase 1 includes four steps: defining your goals, envisioning your business, planning your business, and setting up your business.

The next sections provide a brief overview of each. We dig into the details in other chapters as noted.

Step 0: Defining your goals and success

This is called Step 0 because few people do this, even though it's critical for ending up where you want to be in your solo business. As the saying goes, "If you don't know where you're going, how will you know when you get there?"

First, you define your *why*, that is, why you're creating a one-person business. Then, you identify specific goals you wish to achieve with your business, including

>> What you will do for the world (or at least your customers)

>> What you want your financial position to look like

>> How much free time you want

>> How much flexibility you want in your work schedule

>> Any other goals you have for your business

TIP

Everyone knows that they don't want their business to fail. But you also risk creating a successful business that you don't like running. That's no fun either. Going through Step 0, the topic of Chapter 4, significantly increases your chances of success and happiness.

Step 1: Envisioning your business

Once you've defined your goals, you can start to imagine what your business will look like, which we discuss in Chapter 5. This involves thinking deeply about the kind of work you want to do and matching that up with the types of things people will pay you for.

It also involves considering how the business matches your goals. If one of your goals is being at all your kids' ball games, then a business that requires a lot of travel isn't going to make sense.

Step 2: Planning your business

With your vision in place, you need to plan the details. Planning makes the rest of Phase 1 go much smoother. We cover this in Chapters 6 through 9. In this step, you do the following:

>> **Define your product or service:** Identify the problem you're solving and how your product or service solves it.

- **» Identify your target customer:** Specify your ideal customer and how you can uniquely help them.
- **» Analyze your competition:** Figure out who your competitors are and what they offer.
- **» Position yourself in the market:** Make yourself special in the eyes of your customer.
- **» Choose your business structure:** Decide how to incorporate to limit your liability. Also see Chapter 15.
- **» Specify all things that need to be done:** Identify all the jobs and tasks to start and run your business.
- **» Craft your messaging:** Plan what you'll say to your market.
- **» Create your brand:** Come up with creative logos, colors, fonts, product design, your tone of speaking to the market, and a name for your business.
- **» Design your marketing program:** Choose which marketing channels (such as networking and advertising) you'll use to generate leads for your business.
- **» Outline your sales process:** Map out the steps and processes you'll use to turn prospects into customers.

Step 3: Setting up your business

In this step, you do everything you planned in Step 2, which we discuss in Part 2. This involves the following tasks:

- **» Checking for showstoppers:** Identify what can stop you from getting your business up and running and address the issue(s).
- **» Incorporating your business:** Create a legal structure that will limit your liability.
- **» Implementing financial systems:** Set up your banking, accounting, and tax systems to organize your finances.
- **» Creating your website:** Build a website aimed at converting prospects to customers.
- **» Setting up your marketing program:** Shift the marketing plan you developed in Step 2 into gear.
- **» Setting up your sales process:** Identify which leads have the most potential and how to engage them, and choose the

best tools for initiating your sales process (such as a free initial consultation and free events).

>> **Managing fulfillment:** Organize your plan for delivering your product or service to your customer.

>> **Outsourcing jobs as needed:** Make arrangements with contractors to perform jobs that should be outsourced to save time or get a better result.

Phase 2: Doing (and learning)

In the Do phase (refer to Figures 2-1 and 2-2), you tackle tasks specific to your business. But don't worry, every business has some basics in common.

This phase officially has only a single step, Step 4: executing while learning. However, feel free to customize this phase by breaking it down into steps that suit your unique business needs. Think of it as creating your own version of the Solopreneur Success Cycle!

Step 4: Executing while learning

The most important thing about Step 4 is that it's where you keep track of all the things that aren't going the way you want. (Chapter 19 has an in-depth discussion of how to do this.) You need this information later to improve your business.

WARNING

Trying to remember all the things that don't go well isn't a great system. Instead, write down any issues or challenges as they happen and organize them in one place you can easily access.

This step involves paying close attention to the things that most businesses do, plus all the things you need to do to run your unique business, including

>> **Executing your marketing plan:** Make sure your system works smoothly, effectively, and efficiently.

>> **Implementing your sales plan:** Document the sales practices that win more deals as well as those that fall short.

>> **Overseeing accounting and bookkeeping:** Keep close track of financials so you know how you're doing.

>> **Maintaining working capital:** Ensure you have enough cash to keep the business running.

>> **Tracking accounts receivable:** Make sure your invoices are sent out promptly and customers pay you on time.

>> **Managing contractors:** Keep track of whether your contractors are working efficiently and effectively.

>> **Managing your time:** Note the things that are taking a lot of time but not directly generating revenue. This enables you to find ways you can reduce the amount of time spent doing these things.

Phase 3: Improving

No matter what, your business will never be perfect. Even if you make it perfect, that perfection won't last. The world changes, technology changes, and your goals change. You need a way to ensure your business keeps up with those changes. Phase 3 of the Solopreneur Success Cycle helps you do that in three steps. This section provides an overview of these steps, but the chapters in Part 5 have the details.

Step 5: Refining or reimagining your business

This step starts with reviewing your goals to see if the business is matching your expectations. Health, happiness, income, and relationships all come into play here.

If you decide to make changes, you have to determine whether you want to refine your business or reinvent it. The option you choose will depend on how well or how poorly your business is meeting your needs.

After deciding whether to refine or reinvent your business, you list all the things you can change and how to change them. This will probably be a more extensive list than you want to implement; after all, you're running a business while you're making these improvements!

Step 6: Deciding what to change

In the previous step, you came up with a laundry list of ideas for improving your business. Now, you need to decide which ones to implement. Consider your goals, strategic impacts on your business (customer perception, marketing, sales, competition, and so on), changes to your workload, and the difficulty and time involved in making each change.

You also have to consider the difficulty of rolling back any changes that don't work the way you hope. You don't want to start down a road that's a dead end without mapping out a way back. Choosing wisely about which changes to make helps keep you out of trouble.

Step 7: Adjusting your business

In this step, you make the actual changes, starting with an implementation plan. This involves reviewing the changes, grouping them together if that makes sense, and then creating a logical order for implementing each change.

Getting the Most from the Solopreneur Success Cycle

This book takes you through the Solopreneur Success Cycle from start to finish. It can be used by people new to solopreneurship or those who have been in business for a while. Your approach to the book depends on your situation and goals.

If you're just getting started

If you're new to solopreneurship, you'll benefit most by working through this book from start to finish. Doing this ensures you don't miss any critical steps in the process of building, running, and improving your business.

If you're in business already

If you've been in business for a while, the way you use this book depends on how your business is going. Consider these questions:

>> Is your business meeting your needs financially?

>> Is it serving your goals to your satisfaction?

>> Are you enjoying the work you're doing?

>> Are you working the number of hours you would like?

>> Do you like the customers you're working with?

If the answer to all these questions is yes, this book can still help you by giving you a system to keep your business current with changes in the world and in your own needs and goals. However, if the answer to any of the questions is no, you should use this book to make changes to your business.

If you're happy with your business

Start by reviewing Phase 2: Doing (and learning) and tracking issues and problems with your business and processes. Then move on to Phase 3: Improving.

If you feel your business needs changes

Start with Step 0: Defining your goals and success, if you haven't already done this, to make sure your business is aligned with your goals. Then:

>> **If your business is aligned with your goals:** Go to Phase 2: Doing and (learning) and continue through the rest of the book.

>> **If your business isn't aligned with your goals:** Continue through Phase 1: Getting started and work through the rest of the book.

If you want to reinvent your business

You should start at the beginning of the book and work your way through the Solopreneur Success Cycle. This allows you to craft a business that truly meets your needs.

Chapter **3**

Creating a Business Plan That Works

When you type "Do I need a business plan?" into a search engine, the answer is a resounding *yes*, but with a lot of different reasons to back it up: 20 Reasons Why You Need a Business Plan, 9 Reasons for Creating a Business Plan, 15 Reasons Why a Business Plan Is Right for Your Business . . . you get the idea.

Bottom line? It seems almost everyone agrees you need a plan, even if they don't agree on the number of reasons why. And they're right, you do need a plan. As you get your business off the ground, you'll be researching, weighing options, and making decisions about everything from pricing to marketing to operations. Trying to keep all that in your head won't cut it. You'll forget important details, lose track of why you made certain choices, and have a harder time staying focused. Writing things down, even in a simple, short document, helps you stay organized, see the big picture, and make better decisions as you go.

In larger businesses with employees, investors, or lenders, a *conventional business plan* does even more. It spells out your vision so everyone's on the same page, shows lenders how you'll make money and pay back loans, and proves to investors you have a clear strategy for growth. It also helps your team understand their roles and how their work fits together. In short, it's a roadmap for keeping people aligned, securing funding, and staying on course.

But as a solopreneur, you probably don't need a full-blown, conventional business plan. They're a lot of work, and you want any plan you create to be worth the effort. Your plan should be geared to your goals and relevant to how you actually run your business. In this chapter, we walk you through how to figure out what kind of plan makes sense for you and provide a general idea of what it should look like.

Deciding If You Need a Conventional Business Plan

As a solopreneur, a conventional business plan may not be your best option. This is because conventional business plans were developed for — surprise! — conventional businesses, meaning those that have employees, investors, and bank loans.

Conventional business plans are designed to achieve specific goals. They are used to

>> **Clarify the business's vision:** This helps everyone understand the big-picture goals.

>> **Inform employees:** Teams need guidance, so they know what to do.

>> **Get debt financing:** Lenders often require detailed plans.

>> **Identify risks:** This shows you've thought through potential problems.

>> **Attract investment:** Investors want evidence you're serious and prepared.

>> **Define the business's strategies and tactics:** You need to outline how you'll operate and compete.

Look at each of these items. Which do you imagine your business will need? For most solo businesses, you probably won't be getting debt financing or investment. And if you have employees, you're reading the wrong book! Removing these requirements makes creating the plan simpler. Additionally, a conventional business plan is designed to be read by others. This means it must contain a lot of detail and clarity, which increases the level of effort required to create it.

If you aren't raising start-up money from outside investors or looking for bank loans, then a conventional business plan may be overkill for your purposes. A streamlined plan tailored to the specific needs of your business is what you need. This book helps you create such a plan, what we call the *Solopreneur Action Plan*. We overview this plan in the next section and end the chapter with a few tips on how to write it.

Reviewing the Key Components of the Solopreneur Action Plan

The *Solopreneur Action Plan* is a modified version of a conventional business plan with some elements removed and others added. It's a single document that helps you start, run, and improve your business. It combines the various plans you need to run your business and leaves out the things you don't need. The following sections outline the key components of the Solopreneur Action Plan.

TIP

Don't let these components scare you at all. This book walks you through the process of creating each part of your Solopreneur Action Plan. It will require some hard work and creative thinking, but you have this book as a guide for the whole process.

Conventional companies have a lot of other plans besides their business plan — and so do solo businesses like yours, just not necessarily the same ones. All these plans are needed to set up and run the business effectively. The Solopreneur Action Plan contains various plans (detailed in this section) adjusted to fit your business and acts as your road map.

When you've created your plan, you'll have completed Phase 1 of the Solopreneur Success Cycle. But keep your celebrations to a minimum because it won't be static. You'll update it regularly as part of Phase 3 of the Solopreneur Success Cycle, where you make improvements to your business after figuring out what works and what doesn't.

Your reasons and goals

Reasons and goals are foundational to your Solopreneur Action Plan because they are your why — why you're going into solopreneurship. You need to keep them in mind as you build and change your business to make sure it will continue to serve your life the way you want. We devote Chapter 4 to these important topics.

You'll review your reasons and goals often as you build out your plan and as you improve your business. They may evolve in the future, which will require you to make changes to your business.

Details about your product/service

As you envision, plan, and build your business, many things will come into focus: your target customer, how you help them solve problems, your messaging, your brand identity, and so on. All these things will impact your product or service and how you present it. It's pretty likely that, as you go through the Solopreneur Success Cycle, you'll find that even if your product or service doesn't change, how you talk about it does. See Chapter 6 for details.

Your pro forma profit and loss statement

Although you're building a business to serve your goals, it's important to remember that all businesses need to make a profit. Starting with a plan that makes money on paper is an excellent way to increase your odds of making money for real because it helps you understand your funding needs, profitability projections, and financial goals.

Don't let the Latin term scare you. *Pro forma* simply means that you're describing your plan for the future (as opposed to reporting on what already happened). As you lay out your Solopreneur Action Plan, you'll create a financial plan that estimates your revenues and costs in Chapter 9. The goal is to ensure that you have a good business model to make money and determine how much money you'll need to get off the ground.

Your target market/personas

Chapter 8 explains how to define a target market for your business and create *personas* (also called *avatars*), which are fictional people who represent your ideal customer. You may have only one persona, or possibly just a few.

Creating a specific picture of your ideal customer lets you:

>> Tailor your messaging so it resonates with them.

>> Design your product or service to better meet their needs.

>> Focus your marketing efforts on the best channels.

>> Measure your results by persona to decide which are best to focus on.

Defining your target market and personas will make the rest of your marketing and sales process much easier to create.

Your market position

The modern business world is very crowded. There's a lot more noise out there than just a few years ago, and making your target customers aware of you is more challenging than ever. To get noticed, you need to make yourself special in the eyes of your personas.

Documenting what makes you unique will make getting noticed much easier. It will also make defining your marketing plan easier. Chapter 10 has information on defining your market position.

Your marketing plan

There are many different ways to market your business, from in-person networking to pay-per-click advertising to influencer marketing and so on. As a solopreneur, you need to focus on only a few, or you'll become overwhelmed.

Think about how you can promote your business to easily reach and engage your target audience. Understanding your personas helps you decide which marketing channels to focus on and allows you to start with a plan that gives you the best chance of success. Chapters 11 and 12 provide guidance on documenting all this in your marketing plan.

Your sales plan

There are many different ways to sell a product, from high-touch in-person meetings with customers, to no-touch encounters where the customer merely submits a form on your website, and everything in between. Which sales approach you use depends on your product.

Once you decide on your touch level, you'll need to define a process for converting your leads into sales, which we cover in Chapter 13. Your sales plan will document all this.

Your plan to delight your customers

Once you get a customer, what will you do? Well, obviously, you should deliver your product or service. But it isn't that simple. You need to communicate with your customer to set expectations, perhaps even before you've given them what they've bought. And you want to continue communicating with them and nurture the relationship to increase the odds that they'll buy more from you and/or recommend you to others.

Beyond that it's just awesome to make people happy. You can set yourself apart from competitors with a plan to delight your customers that defines how you'll interact with them, address complaints, and keep satisfaction high.

This component of the Solopreneur Action Plan outlines the process you'll use to do all this: the onboarding experience (see Chapter 14).

Your daily operations

This part of the Solopreneur Action Plan details the day-to-day processes and workflows of your business. This includes everything from managing supply chains and production (if relevant) to handling customer service and the tools or platforms you'll rely on to streamline operations. See chapters in Part 4.

Your technology

Here, you list the software, digital tools, and IT infrastructure your business will need. This can include everything from customer relationship management software to automation tools that save time and boost productivity. See Chapter 16.

Your growth/expansion

Even if your initial focus is just getting off the ground, it helps to map out how you'd grow your business once it's up and running.

This can include plans for outsourcing, expanding products or services, or targeting new markets. See the chapters in Part 5.

Writing Your Solopreneur Action Plan

The Solopreneur Action Plan is a working document that you should keep improving. Unlike a business plan, the sole purpose of the Solopreneur Action Plan is to keep you on track to build a business that serves your career and life goals.

FIND ONLINE

As you work through this book, you can create your own Solopreneur Action Plan. Although it isn't required, it's not a ton of extra work, and it gives you a framework for thinking about your business and a road map for creating and growing it. We've made it even easier for you by providing a template you can use. Download your own copy at www.dummies.com/go/solopreneurbusinessfd.

We recommend documenting your business plans and decisions in a Solopreneur Action Plan as you make those plans and decisions for these reasons:

>> **Clarity of thought:** You'll be thinking about many different things as you envision and build your company. Putting them down on paper helps you think through your plans and weigh your options.

>> **Organization:** Writing down your goals and strategies provides a clear road map for your business. The Solopreneur Action Plan helps you stay focused and prevents the stress and confusion that can arise from juggling multiple tasks in your head.

>> **Reliability over memory:** If you're like most people, your memory isn't perfect. Documenting your plan helps you ensure you don't overlook or forget important details. Having a written record makes it easier for you to revisit and refine your processes in Phase 3 of the Solopreneur Success Cycle.

>> **Accountability and discipline:** The Solopreneur Action Plan helps you to turn your ideas into actionable steps. It makes it much easier to stay on track and measure your progress.

>> **Ease of revision:** You'll eventually revisit and revise your plan. This will be much easier if it's written down in an organized document.

Here are some pointers to keep in mind as you work on your Solo-preneur Action Plan:

>> **Write your plan in the order the components are presented earlier in this chapter.** This makes sense as each section builds on the work done in the previous section.

>> **Keep it simple to start.** Try not to overthink it. You probably won't present your plan to any venture capitalists, so there's no need to get flowery. The point of this document is to act as a guide and a reference for you. All you need to do is write down what you plan to do and then refer to it regularly as you get your business up and running.

>> **Plan to refine your plan.** As you work through the Solopreneur Success Cycle, you'll make changes to your business. Those changes should be documented in your Solopreneur Action Plan.

REMEMBER

Your plan isn't set in stone. Part of the Solopreneur Success Cycle involves reviewing and updating the Solopreneur Action Plan. It doesn't need to be perfect the first time through, so don't worry about getting every little detail right.

>> **Choose a medium for your plan.** You have a number of options for recording your thinking and planning. You can use a conventional notebook, a three-ring binder, Microsoft Word or Google Docs, or some other option that works for you. You may change your mind about a previous decision and want to update your plan. Having the ability to replace or rearrange pages can result in a cleaner final product.

Regardless of which medium you decide to use, the most important thing is to document each step as you go through the Solopreneur Success Cycle. This book prompts you with suggestions about when to document your decisions in your Solopreneur Action Plan.

2

Starting Your Solopreneur Career

Define your personal and professional goals to make sure your business serves your life.

Brainstorm workable business ideas that fit your skills and interests.

Choose your business type and model, and decide on the products or services you'll offer.

Research your competitors to spot opportunities and position your business to stand out.

Identify your target customer so you can tailor your messaging, marketing, and sales to their needs.

Assess your business idea's risks, costs, and profit potential to confirm it's worth starting.

» Getting to the heart of your *why*

» Envisioning your future and setting SMART goals to create it

» Adding your goals to a Change Chart (and the Solopreneur Action Plan)

» Steeling yourself to overcome challenges

» Tracking your progress and staying accountable

Chapter **4**

Defining Your Goals and Success

G oal setting may not be everybody's cup of tea, but it's necessary not only for running a successful business, but for starting a business you actually like running as well. This chapter helps you get to the root of why you want to start your own business and how to set goals you can stick with. When you know your why and put goals in place, you can plot the path to your new reality. Exciting times! Of course, sometimes things don't go smoothly, so this chapter also includes ideas for navigating those rocky times, as well as tips for keeping your eye on the prize.

REMEMBER

This chapter gets you out of the gate — it's Step 0: Defining your goals and success of the Getting started phase of the Solopreneur Success Cycle. (Chapter 2 lays out the full cycle.)

WARNING

Don't skip the goal-setting step. It's the engine that will propel your business forward. Without it, your days can feel scattered, your priorities unclear, and your motivation may wane. You risk pouring energy into the wrong things, missing growth opportunities, and losing sight of why you started in the first place. Setting clear goals gives you direction, momentum, and purpose, making it far more likely you'll build a business that not only succeeds but actually feels right for your life.

Finding Your Why

Why do you want to be a solopreneur? The answers you give others may be obvious: "Oh, I want to be my own boss," or "I want a more flexible lifestyle." But those are very surface-level responses. You need to dig deep and figure out the real *why* behind your business because that will be your North Star for all your decisions.

Your *why* may change over time, and that's okay! It's part of your evolution as a business owner.

REMEMBER

Knowing the real reasons behind your journey

You may be wondering why it's so important to dig deep for the real reason you want to start your business. Can't you just make a blanket statement and move on to building your company of one? The answer is *no*, and here's why.

Being a solopreneur is tough. Wonderful, but tough. Without a strong grasp of why you're starting your business in the first place, and the story behind it, you may find yourself directionless.

Your *why* helps you make key decisions about how you want to build your business, from creating your schedule, to determining your company's voice and personality.

Your *why* helps you focus and provide meaning to everything you're doing. It gives purpose to all your to-dos, from the ordinary to the extraordinary.

Digging deeper

Having trouble getting to the root of your *why*? Play the toddler game! Anyone who has been around a toddler for more than 10 minutes knows one of their favorite responses to any statement is *why*? So, play the toddler game with yourself and see how specific you can get.

Here's an example:

>> I want a flexible lifestyle. WHY?

>> So that I control my schedule. WHY?

>> I don't want to miss my kid's soccer games and school events. WHY?

>> It's important to me that I'm present in my child's life and that they see they're my priority and know I'm there for them.

See how that's different from simply saying, "I want a flexible lifestyle"?

TIP

Print your *why* on a sheet of paper and put it somewhere you'll see it daily. Look at it every morning when you begin working to stay motivated. Also add it to the "Reasons and goals" section of your Solopreneur Action Plan!

Defining Your Goals to Create the Future You Want

When you have a good understanding of the *why* that's powering your business, it's time to define your goals that support the purpose behind it all. These goals help you find fulfillment in what you do and help you stay motivated because you have intention behind what you're doing.

At the end of the day, you put goals in place to set yourself up to become the future you and create and run your future business. As the saying goes, you want to begin with the end in mind. So, in this section, we begin with high-level questions to get you started thinking about what you want. Then we dig into more details to help you set goals to get you where you want to go. We end the section with a reality check to see if the future you're creating for yourself is indeed the future you want.

Identifying your financial target

After interacting with thousands of solopreneurs, we've found the vast majority choose solopreneurship (company of one) over entrepreneurship (adding employees) because of the lifestyle, not necessarily because of the money. However, you're running a business, and you have to make a living, so you need to visualize what your financial future looks like.

TIP

Instead of asking what you would do if you made X amount of money, flip it around and ask yourself how much income is necessary to live comfortably and maintain your desired lifestyle. Lead with the end in mind, not the number you want to earn.

Financial goals are personal and vary from business to business, but they're often the easiest goals to nail down because you can define them with numbers. Whether you're taking out loans, using credit, funding your business with savings or other means, a variety of factors contribute to your financial goals, but here are some things to keep in mind:

>> How much do you need to make each month to cover known expenses?

>> How much more will you need to make each month above those expenses to live your desired lifestyle?

>> How much do you want to put into savings/retirement?

>> How will you survive the ebbs and flows of your business?

>> Do you want to earn enough to explore investments outside of your business for additional income streams?

>> How much do you want to reinvest into your business?

TIP

Having a firm understanding of your current financial situation is essential for creating achievable financial goals for yourself, so don't start planning your future goals until you know where you stand now.

Designing your dream life

As a solopreneur, you have the potential to work around the clock . . . but who wants to do that? You get to choose how you spend your time now, so how do you envision balancing your work and your personal life?

Will you stick to traditional working hours, or will you work early in the morning and late at night so you can enjoy the day pursuing hobbies or spending time with friends and family? Are weekends off-limits for work? Keep these things in mind as you set your goals.

In addition to the hours worked, you get to create the lifestyle you want to live. Want to work four days per week? Great! Want to work from the beach in Australia? Amazing! But this doesn't just happen overnight or without some effort. You need to put a plan in place and set lifestyle goals for yourself. As you create these goals, consider the following questions:

>> What does your ideal lifestyle look like?

>> What restrictions or obligations are preventing you from having your ideal lifestyle? If you can remove them, how?

>> What are your core values and priorities?

>> What kind of creative freedom do you want in your work?

>> Do you prefer structured tasks or the freedom to experiment and explore new ideas?

>> What brings you joy?

TIP

Ask yourself what a day in the life of your future self looks like. Regularly visualize your ideal lifestyle so it feels attainable. The more you think you can reach the goals you've set, the more likely they are to happen.

Whether you prioritize family time, self-care, travel — you name it — this is your chance to put your values in the spotlight and create a business that allows you to give them some time and attention.

REMEMBER

Building a successful business and having a business you like running aren't necessarily the same thing. Set goals for yourself so you can accomplish both.

Clarifying your impact and contribution objectives

Many of your goals revolve around you (you are a solopreneur after all), but you also get to decide what kind of impact you want to have on your customers or clients (and the world, for that matter). So, what does that look like? Here are a few questions to consider:

>> Do you just want to serve your customers/clients and provide solutions to their problems, or does contributing to a larger purpose matter to you?

>> Do you want to focus on having a greater impact now, never, or as a future goal?

>> Do you want to support nonprofits?

>> Is your business mission-driven? If so, how?

>> How will knowing the answers to these questions impact the way you run your business and craft your messaging?

A lot to think about, right? Having answers to these questions can be a great motivator. Plus, identifying your impact goals can separate you from your competition and help with your market positioning. (Chapter 10 does a deep dive on market positioning.)

Considering what else matters to you

Remember when you were a kid and people asked what you wanted to be when you grew up? You probably had a ready answer. But not everybody becomes a firefighter, a doctor, or a princess, and your dream job evolves over time.

Does your new business feel like a dream job at all? You may not love every aspect of it, and that's okay, but you should revisit that childlike feeling you had when you dreamed about your future self and see how you can intertwine those hopes and desires with the business you're developing.

Take a look at the goals you've already developed and ask yourself, *What's missing?*

Consider how you want to feel in your work. Do you want to feel creative, helpful, energized, challenged, calm? Many solopreneurs overlook emotional and creative fulfillment as a goal, but they can be just as important as financial or lifestyle goals. Ask yourself:

>> What kind of work excites and motivates me?

>> Do I want autonomy in choosing the types of projects I take on?

>> Do I want to innovate, educate, entertain, or support?

These "intangibles" may not show up in your bank account, but they're often the reasons solopreneurs stick with their business long term. Building a business that aligns with how you want to feel and express yourself is part of what makes it truly yours.

Making Your Goals SMART

In the world of goal setting, the concept of creating SMART goals is king. The acronym SMART stands for **S**pecific, **M**easurable, **A**ttainable, **R**elevant, and **T**ime-Bound.

This framework is incredibly helpful for setting clear goals for yourself. For example, you can say:

> I want more clients.

Or, you can turn that into a SMART goal and say:

> I will get five new clients this month by reaching out to ten current clients for referrals as well as booking three guest spots on targeted podcasts.

See the difference? Pairing action steps with your goals makes it more likely you'll achieve them.

With your SMART goal in place, it's tempting to want to hit the ground running. And while it's wonderful to be aspirational, you also have to be realistic.

Ask yourself:

>> What are your current strengths and challenges?

>> What knowledge do you need to make your goals a reality?

>> What can you work on right now, and what needs to wait?

Having a firm grasp on where you stand can be tremendously helpful not only in creating your SMART goals, but also in setting expectations for yourself. It can soften the impact of setbacks and make your wins even sweeter.

REMEMBER

This is Step 0 of Phase 1 of the Solopreneur Success Cycle, which we introduce in Chapter 2. Now is the time to dream big and put a plan together. If you don't feel great about what the future looks like in this phase, you probably won't be excited about it down the road either.

Plotting the Path to Your New Reality: The Change Chart

You have a lot of goals to think about, right? And one of them should be how you're going to document all your goals. It's a lot to keep track of if you just rely on your memory.

Create a Change Chart in a format that makes the most sense to you. A *Change Chart* helps you see what needs to change to reach your goals. It connects where you are now with where you want to be and shows what steps to take to get there. Spreadsheet? Great. Poster on your wall? Awesome. Sticky notes? Do your thing. We all track things differently, so create yours in a way that works for you.

If you've made it this far in the chapter, you already have your goals/answers to everything in the following list, and it's just a matter of putting it all together and documenting it. In the chart, be sure to include the following information:

>> Where you're starting (or where you started if you already have a business)

>> The goals you have in place

>> Your desired outcome

>> Anticipated setbacks and how you plan to handle them

>> How you'll achieve and measure your goals

Put your Change Chart in your Solopreneur Action Plan (introduced in Chapter 3) to keep everything together.

REMEMBER

Preparing Mentally to Attain Your Goals (No Matter What)

Setting your goals is just the first step toward achieving them. It's a big step! But now you have to tackle the hard work of getting stuff done, and things can get in the way of that. This section outlines potential roadblocks and goal-setting pitfalls — and how to overcome them — as well as the all-important activity of celebrating your wins.

Overcoming roadblocks

While we'd like to tell you that solopreneurship is all rainbows and unicorns, the reality is, you'll run into challenges. They just come with the territory of running your own business. Knowing that roadblocks will pop up, you must prepare for them.

You know how salespeople shouldn't take *no* for an answer? Well, you shouldn't let a bump in the road derail you from achieving your goals. That's all many roadblocks are: bumps, not chasms opened up by earthquakes.

Make yourself resilient by identifying how you'll handle challenges, stress, sleepless nights, and the worst — *imposter syndrome,* that nagging feeling that you're not as competent or capable as others think you are, despite clear signs of your success. Building this resilience might mean reaching out to fellow solopreneurs in your community, setting boundaries around work hours, or developing stress-reduction habits. (See Chapter 23 for more ideas on staying strong when things get tough.)

TIP

Roadblocks are often the best motivators, so, instead of seeing them as obstacles, look at them as opportunities for growth and change. They may take you one step back, but they can also propel you two steps forward if you choose to harness the positive energy you get from overcoming them.

Here's what learning from your mistakes can look like:

A solo marketing consultant named Megan once missed an important client deadline after overestimating how much she could handle on her own. The experience lowered her confidence, and she was nervous that it had damaged the client relationship. But rather than dwelling on the mistake, she treated it as a wake-up call.

In response, she began setting more realistic timelines, improved her ability to prioritize, and adopted project management tools to stay organized. She also started building in buffer time to account for unexpected issues. Her client appreciated the accountability and transparency, and chose to renew the contract, and as a result, she became significantly better at managing her workload and expectations. All clients moving forward benefited from that initial mistake.

It all goes back to your *why* and your goals. Having a clear under-standing of the reasons you're creating your business will help you keep your eye on the prize when the going gets tough!

Avoiding common goal-setting pitfalls

Our hope is that none of the points in the following list applies to you. If you follow our advice in the earlier parts of the chapter, you're now prepared to tackle each pitfall head-on. But here's where people (not you, of course) often get stuck with goal setting:

>> **Not making your goals SMART.** Vague goals lead to confusion and lack of direction. Use the SMART framework to clarify your path and measure success.

>> **Having too many goals at one time.** Prioritize a few that matter most right now. If you're juggling too much, pause or drop what's less urgent.

>> **Not preparing for obstacles.** Think ahead about what might go wrong and how you'll respond. If you get derailed, regroup and adjust your plan.

>> **Setting only big goals and not smaller milestones.** Break larger goals into smaller steps to stay motivated and track progress. If you've stalled, create a mini goal to regain momentum.

>> **Neglecting to track your progress.** Regular check-ins keep you accountable and focused. Start now and remember that even a simple checklist helps.

>> **Being unwilling to adapt and evolve your goals.** Be open to adjusting as your circumstances or priorities change. Reassessing isn't quitting, it's smart goalkeeping.

Tracking your wins

This is the fun part. While you'll have setbacks as a solopre-neur, you'll also have incredible victories, big and small. But because you no longer get performance bonuses or promotions, it's on you to celebrate and track your achievements. How will you do this?

It's important to prioritize these celebrations because your wins will help you move forward with your goals and build confidence. Whether you've finished a project you've been working on or landed a huge client, a win is a win, and a pat on the back, at the very least, is warranted.

These celebrations can be anything. Try a solo dance break, treat yourself to a fancy coffee, or jot the moment down in a gratitude journal. When you hit bigger milestones, consider taking an afternoon off, booking a mini getaway, or buying yourself a small reward. You can also keep a "wall of wins" to visually track your progress. However you choose to celebrate, make it a habit, because every win deserves recognition.

Jot your wins down so you can reflect on them over time, and even find patterns that led to success. It's helpful to review your achievements monthly or quarterly. Flip to Chapter 23 for more about tracking wins.

Keeping Yourself on Track: Accountability Hacks

Being your own boss definitely has its perks, but one of the things people aren't prepared for when they venture out on their own is setting schedules and deadlines to keep them on track with their goals. We explore setting boundaries, creating routines, and improving your productivity (among other issues) in Chapter 23. But we touch on this topic here because we want you to think about ways to stay on track starting now — in the Defining your goals and success step — and through all phases and steps of the Solopreneur Success Cycle.

In a regular work environment, schedules and routines are structured for you by your boss, teammates, clients, and so on. As a solopreneur, you're responsible for establishing your own routines and setting deadlines for yourself, and it may not come naturally to you. Working alone can make it easier to procrastinate and let things slide (something always comes up!). But now it's up to you to overcome distractions and figure out how to stay on track. The following sections can help.

Holding yourself accountable

We wish we were able to reveal a magic trick to help you meet your deadlines, but honestly, it comes down to a lot of trial and error based on how you work and how independent you've been in the past.

Many people find self-accountability to be one of the hardest things about flying solo in business, so you need to be real with yourself and identify and eliminate distractions.

For example, consider checking email and texts only at set times of the day. Limit your social media usage with an app that shuts it down. If you're a social person, allocate time for interacting with others to look forward to, so you can keep your head down during the rest of the workday. It isn't easy, but once you figure out what works for you, stick with it.

To help you stay on track, use these simple daily accountability prompts:

>> What were my top one-three priorities today?

>> Did I complete them? If not, why?

>> What distracted me, and how can I avoid it in the future?

>> When did I feel most productive today?

>> What's one thing I can do better tomorrow?

You can jot this down at the end of each workday in a journal or digital doc, whatever works for your style. Building this habit of honest reflection can make a huge difference over time.

Committing to an accountability buddy or group

As much as you believe you can hold yourself accountable, the reality is, that's a lot easier said than done. People are often more focused and productive when they have somebody to check in with. The idea of *commitment bias* in psychology means that when we commit to something or someone, we're more likely to stick with our promises. The human mind can be pretty sneaky!

With an accountability buddy or group, you also have people to bounce ideas off. When you're holding yourself accountable, you may go down a path with very little feedback, which can be detrimental to your business.

REMEMBER

Your accountability group is also your support system. Celebrating milestones is more fun when you can share them with people who have been with you along the way!

Goal setting can seem burdensome and tedious for some people, but it can also be an exciting adventure to create the plan that allows you to achieve the business of your dreams.

Chapter 5

Envisioning Your Solo Business

Take a moment to think about where you are in the process of envisioning your business. Have you decided which skill to bring to your business and which industry to focus on? If not, don't worry. At this point, the most crucial thing is to ensure your goals (see Chapter 4) are served by the vision you create. After you define your goals for your one-person business, it's time to explore what type of business you can start.

It may seem counterintuitive to decide what business to be in after defining your goals. However, solopreneurship is different. You aren't doing this to scale at all costs. If you were, you wouldn't give up employees, the most powerful of all scaling tools. You're doing this because the business needs to serve some aspect of your life. And that means you need to design the business around your goals.

For example, if you never want to work weekends, don't start a business where the clients might have a lot of emergencies. If you want to be at your kids' games, don't start a business that requires a lot of in-person meetings unless they're local.

You may have a firm idea of the kind of business you want to start. If so, skip this chapter . . . or don't. As you read what we have to say, you may come up with something more interesting or sharpen your original idea into the perfect business for you. But it's okay if you don't know what kind of business to start. After working through this chapter, you should have some good ideas that make sense to you.

REMEMBER

This is Step 1: Envisioning your business of Phase 1: Getting started of the Solopreneur Success Cycle, introduced in Chapter 2. As you read through this chapter, keep in mind that this is *not* the time to plan the details of your business; that step comes next, and we cover it in Chapter 6. So, instead of focusing on the details now, let your imagination run free and see what business ideas you can come up with.

Using Ikigai to Create Business Ideas

You may have heard of the ancient Japanese concept of *ikigai* (ee-kee-guy), which roughly translates to "reason for being." Ikigai is often presented visually in a Venn diagram, as shown in Figure 5-1.

FIGURE 5-1: The visual representation of ikigai.

Note the four main aspects of the Ikigai Venn Diagram:

>> What you're good at

>> What you love

>> What the world needs

>> What you can be paid for

The idea is, if your work incorporates all four aspects, you will have a fulfilling career. You can use this concept to think about a business that makes sense for you.

TECHNICAL STUFF

In truth, ancient Japan wasn't all that into Venn diagrams. The Venn Diagram of Purpose was actually created in 2011 by Spanish author Andrés Zuzunaga and then given the name Ikigai Venn Diagram by British blogger Marc Winn in 2014. That said, it's still useful even if it's not based on ancient Japanese wisdom.

When you use the Venn diagram to brainstorm, it's helpful to first define some business ideas that encompass both your skills (what you can do) and passions (what you love). From there, you can determine whether the world needs your skills and passions and will pay for them. This chapter leads you through examining both combinations.

You may know precisely what your business will do. If so, that's great! But thanks to the internet and social media, the world has become very noisy with millions of people clamoring for attention. Getting noticed these days is extremely difficult. Throughout this book, we strongly encourage you to *niche down,* that is, focus your business on solving a specific problem for a specific group of people. This exercise provides the first steps in defining your niche in a way that serves your goals.

It's more likely that you have a rough idea of what kind of business you want to start but haven't fleshed it out. If so, this process can help you immensely. (And if you don't have a clue yet, you definitely need to work through the rest of this chapter.)

Listing what you're good at: Ikigai 1

To start, make a list of all the things you're good at. Don't worry if you think a particular talent applies to a business or not. Just make a list of your skills. If you're good at juggling, write it down.

One real-world example comes from a LifeStarr member named Sarah Sypniewski. She's good at writing, editing, and acting, and she has done lots of each in her life.

Skills

Writing

Editing

Acting

Noting what you love: Ikigai 2

Now, make a list of all the things you love. Again, don't worry about whether you think something you're passionate about relates to a business; just make the list. If you love dogs, write *dogs* on the list. Sarah likes acting in indie films, but she especially loves helping people tell their personal stories.

Passions

Acting in independent films

Helping people tell their stories

Combining what you're good at with what you love

Now look at your two lists. Sarah's look something like this:

Skills	Passions
Writing	Acting in independent films
Editing	Helping people tell their stories
Acting	

If your skill is writing, building a business by simply calling yourself a writer will be challenging. No one will notice you. But if you focus your business on writing about indie films, you may find more opportunities.

Create some ideas by combining items from each column. If none of them sound doable or interesting, you may need to add more skills and/or passions to the list. Try to find one or two that excite you. Sarah combined her writing and editing skills with her passion for helping people tell their stories and created the Legacy Authors Society. She helps people write their memoirs, coaching them through the process and potentially serving as a ghostwriter.

Skills	Passions	Business ideas
Writing	Acting in independent films	Writing about indie films
Editing	Helping people tell their stories	Helping people write their memoirs
Acting		

Be sure to think outside the box. Does something intrigue you, light a fire in your belly, or just sound awesome? If so, be sure to put it on your list and explore the business possibilities. Try to be realistic, but don't let fear keep you from giving an idea a fair shake.

Sometimes, your best option is hidden well below the surface, and you need to be open to ideas beyond the obvious. For example, Joep (pronounced *yoop*) Vermolen was a solopreneur music composer. With his master's degree in music composition, it was an obvious business for him, but he wasn't happy.

Joep had some friends who made comedy videos, and he found himself drawn to them and the process of creating comedy. Despite his lack of acting experience and his deep fear of being in front of the camera, he developed his skills and went on to star in the Netflix comedy series *Toon*. He's still a solopreneur, but now he works in acting instead of music composition.

Discovering what the world needs: Ikigai 3

The last thing you want to do is start a business that no one needs. But how do you know for sure that the world needs your idea? You may have an idea that's unquestionably in demand. If you're a graphic designer or a financial planner, you don't have to dig too deeply into whether the world needs your services. But if you're planning to do something unique, you may need to establish whether a willing customer base exists before you commit to the business.

For example, solopreneur Nathan Faleide created `Boundri.com`, a business that makes custom map-themed items. He had a background in family farming and had the idea to create rugs with aerial images of family farms for kids to play on. He knew he would love this product for his kids, but its marketability certainly wasn't a sure thing. He tested his idea via social media and found that, yes, lots of family farmers wanted a carpet of their farm for their kids, too. Now, he's expanded into other map-themed products for kids, such as rugs that show a construction site as well as rugs displaying famous racetracks.

Determining what you can be paid for: Ikigai 4

Obviously, you don't want to sell something that people won't pay for or won't pay enough for to cover your costs or justify your effort. If you come up with an idea for something the world needs, you still must determine whether people will pay enough for it to support your business.

WARNING

Sadly, the world needs lots of things for which people aren't willing to pay the price. Just because you've established that people want what you do doesn't mean they'll pay for what you do. Sometimes, they can't afford it; sometimes, they just don't see the value.

So, how do you determine if there's a market for your unique idea? You start by talking to people you think may want your product or service. Be sure to explain that you need their *honest* opinion and that saying nice things to avoid hurting your feelings will be *extremely* unhelpful.

Your business idea can determine how to find people to talk with. Ideally, they're in your network, which comes in handy later, when you want to sell to them. If not, go to where they are. This may mean finding groups (online or in person) with interests related to your idea. Check out Facebook or LinkedIn groups, local organizations, and conferences.

As you go through this exercise and explain your business and its product or service, you'll get the following results:

>> **Some people love the idea.** They want to know when you're up and running. This is excellent news. You don't need everyone to love your idea, just some people.

>> **People aren't excited about your product/service.** This isn't great, but you need to find out why people aren't interested. Then, press them on what related products or services they may need or be excited about. Maybe you can get some insight into a superior idea.

>> **You can't find people to talk to.** This is a very bad sign. If you can't find anyone to talk to, how will you find someone to sell to?

>> **People like your idea but say they don't need it.** This may indicate they're not interested but are trying not to hurt your feelings.

TIP

As you're talking to people about your idea, ask the interested ones what they would pay for your product or service. If the number they throw out sounds reasonable, great! If it's iffy, then you may need to reconsider. You probably haven't created a profit and loss estimate for your business idea yet, but if you expect to have significant production costs, you need to consider how they line up with what folks say they're willing to pay. If you're providing a service, make sure the hourly rate generates enough income to justify the business.

TIP

If you aren't convinced you can make money with your business idea, go to Chapter 9 and produce a *pro forma* profit and loss statement.

Picking a Partial Ikigai

People say that finding your ikigai does all kinds of wonderful things, and it probably does . . . most of the time. However, not everyone focuses on getting all four aspects of ikigai perfect to create a business that serves their life and goals.

While it's crucial to start a business that offers something you're skilled at and that people will pay you for, it's possible to build a business based on a product or service the world doesn't need. In 1975, a very successful product called *Pet Rock* (a rock in a box that had air holes for no good reason) was launched. Recently, they're starting to become popular again.

It probably won't come as a shock to you that the world doesn't, and never did, truly need Pet Rocks. However, people bought loads of them. The point? If you hit on the right idea at the right time, you can build a successful business based on something the world will pay for but doesn't need.

Many solopreneurs run businesses they aren't passionate about. They don't hate what they're doing, but their satisfaction comes from the freedom they've created to live life on their terms. Although some people need to be truly passionate about their profession, you shouldn't treat passion for your work as a requirement if you don't feel you need it.

In fact, ikigai misses a crucial concept: how your work serves your life goals. You may be able to imagine a business that covers all aspects of ikigai but would force you to give up one or more of your life goals. This should be a nonstarter. You don't want to be the person who works hard to create a business you don't like running. To avoid this fate, ask yourself the following questions:

>> Focus first on your *why*. Does your business idea serve that?

>> Does it have a reasonable chance of meeting your financial needs?

>> Will it give you the flexibility you need for your desired lifestyle?

At this point, you cannot know for sure if the business you envision will be precisely what you need. In fact, it will probably change as you build and improve it. But you've reduced the risk of wasting time on a business concept that can't succeed or serve your needs.

REMEMBER

Once you've envisioned a business idea, be sure to add it to the product/service details section of your Solopreneur Action Plan (see Chapter 3).

Chapter **6**

Defining Your Solo Business

E nvisioning a solo business is a fun ride for any daydreaming solopreneur. But you can get lost in that daydream indefinitely if you don't start putting together a plan and thinking concretely about your business. This chapter is your road map to actually defining your business, including what to call yourself, which business model to use, and how to describe to others what exactly it is that you do.

REMEMBER

At this point, you're still in Phase 1: Getting started of the Solopreneur Success Cycle. But this chapter covers Step 2: Planning your business . . . progress!

What Are You?

As a solopreneur, naming your business isn't something you should take lightly. No pressure, but it's your first impression with your customers and clients.

To be clear, this isn't where you think about what to call your business (that comes later). At this point, you're focusing on what you want to call yourself: tinker, tailor, soldier, spy? Kidding! We know you're a solopreneur, but when somebody asks what you do for a living, saying you're a solopreneur doesn't tell them much and may not be the best way to describe what your business offers. You need to be more specific.

If you haven't thought about this, look at the following list and see if any of the titles resonate with you and what you do. These are common terms people use to describe one-person businesses, but hey, you're the boss — call yourself whatever you want!

Accountant	Analyst	Bookkeeper	Coach
Consultant	Content creator	Contractor	Designer
Developer	Founder	Freelancer	Handyperson
Influencer	Inventor	Marketer	Photographer
Principal	Solo-entrepreneur	Solopreneur	Specialist
Strategist	Virtual assistant	Writer	Use your imagination!

TIP

Choose a name that's memorable and easy to spell. Ignore jargon, no matter how straightforward you think it is.

The previous table provides a list of titles solopreneurs commonly use, but what you choose to call yourself should match your brand and personality. For example, a virtual assistant who focuses on decluttering inboxes may choose to call herself a Chaos Coordinator instead of an assistant. So catchy and clever!

Have fun with it, but make sure you come up with something that appeals to potential customers and alludes to what you do. Ask yourself the following questions:

>> Who is your target audience (see Chapter 8)?

>> What are your core values (see Chapter 4)?

>> Have you considered the search terms people will use to find you online?

>> What do your competitors call themselves, and should you do the same or stand out (see Chapter 7)?

If you're going back and forth between being clever and creative, or simple and informative, go with the latter. You can have both, but being straightforward helps you avoid confusion about what it is that you do.

Once you land on a title, test it with your friends and family and ask for their honest opinions. Then, as you begin identifying and engaging with your target audience (discussed in detail in Chapter 8), whether that's through social media, online communities, or early networking opportunities, ask a few of those individuals for their honest impressions. Does the title resonate with them?

REMEMBER

Many solopreneurs want to keep everything to themselves until they launch, but this is a mistake. Getting feedback from your target audience through each phase of the development process, including your job title, can help you create a successful business faster.

Defining Your Product or Service

When you envision your business, which is what we discuss in Chapter 5, chances are, you have a product or service in mind. But have you written down the *pain points*, or customer issues, you solve, and how you solve them? If so, well done, ya overachiever! If not, it's time to start defining how you approach your customers' wants and needs.

So, how does your business solve a problem, deliver an experience, or create something that matters to your target audience? We explore ways to answer these questions throughout the rest of this section.

Identifying the pain points you solve

As you define your product or service, you must understand the pain points your customers or clients face. We cannot stress this point enough! In fact, understanding your customers' pain points is one of the most important foundational elements that will impact all areas of your business, including marketing, sales, and operations.

In this phase, brainstorm a list of pain points you believe you can solve. The beauty of this list is that you don't have to be right or wrong about what you put on it. Your ideas just represent your initial hunches. Once you specifically define who your customers are, you'll have a chance to talk to them and test the accuracy of your list.

Nobody actually cares about what you do. They only care that you're solving a problem they're dealing with. So, your product or service *must* keep your target customer's wants and needs front and center. Chapter 8 does a deep dive on how to get to know your customer, along with questions to get to the root of their pain points and desire.

Figuring out what you do to solve these pain points

After you develop a list of pain points, jot down how you'll solve each problem. Avoid vague descriptions and provide concrete information and examples for each solution. Don't just skim the surface. The more work you put in as you develop your business, the easier it will be to actually run your business.

Many businesses only scratch the surface here. By digging deep, you can really outshine your competition. You can use your target audience's pain points to develop products and services specifically for them.

For example, Sarah, a writer, knows that as people get older, many want to tell their life story, but they don't know how. Understanding this pain point, she has narrowed her offerings to focus on a mature client base. Instead of just taking whatever writing project comes her way, she writes memoirs for her aging clients as a service, building her portfolio (and expertise) with each memoir.

Writing your product description

Now it's time to tie all this together.

Once you've defined the pain points you want to solve and the corresponding solutions, you need to come up with two descriptions about your product or service. The first should be lengthy, maybe even a couple of paragraphs. This description should explain in detail what you do, the pain points you solve, and how you solve them. This is great for internal reference and to prove you've been thorough in defining your business.

Your description can and should evolve over time, so don't get hung up on making it perfect. But be sure it properly conveys what your business does so that a random person who stumbles across it would know what you're all about.

The second description should be your *elevator pitch*, a few sentences that describe your business so your audience knows exactly what you do. A perfect elevator pitch leaves people wanting more, which gives you an opportunity to launch into your longer description. Here are a few examples of elevator pitches:

>> Through tools, resources, and community, I help solopreneurs create a business that aligns with their desired lifestyle.

>> I provide a clear social media strategy for busy entrepreneurs who can't find success with this medium.

>> I'm a virtual assistant who helps busy executives manage their email communications and calendar so they can focus on matters that require their time and attention.

If you're thinking, *My business is kind of complicated; I can't create an elevator pitch*, then you have a problem. When you can't clearly and quickly explain what you do and how you help people, establishing trust and credibility is difficult. And that makes it challenging to attract clients and promote your business.

Selecting Your Business Model

Put simply, a *business model* is the method by which you produce, market, and get paid for your product or service. It sounds important, because it is, but it doesn't have to be complicated. What can make it confusing is that the term *business model* has many definitions. Our approach is to simplify the concept so it's most helpful to solopreneurs.

While there are many ways to design business models, you may find that only a few options make sense for *your* business. In the following sections, we discuss three key decisions that can help you define your business model: how you produce your product or service, how you reach your customer, and how you accept payment.

Before getting to those decisions, though, you need to think about the kind of business you want to create, which can help you narrow down your business model options. When you go through the list of options, think about people who are doing something similar to what you're doing. How are they doing it?

Creating a unique business model can give you a competitive advantage (think Uber or Warby Parker), but it can also hurt you if the market doesn't need or want what you're offering.

WARNING

Innovation is cool. But don't do it without careful consideration, especially when you're starting out. It's better to be cautious about getting too creative with your business model. For example, a portrait artist commissioned to paint someone's portrait wouldn't want to use an auction model for payment; that auction would have only one bidder!

Distinguishing types of business models

Business models are defined using the components shown in Table 6-1. The following sections provide more details on each component, which we explain briefly here:

>> **Production model:** Defines how your product or service is created or sourced.

>> **Market model:** Defines how you reach your potential customers.

>> **Payment model:** Defines how you get paid.

Note that when you're defining your business model, you're choosing at least one component from each of the three columns in Table 6-1.

TIP

You can choose more than one component from each section depending on your business. But don't make it too complicated, especially when getting started.

TABLE 6-1 **Business Model Components for Solopreneurs**

Production model	Market model	Payment model
Service provider	Inbound marketing	Per unit sale
Creator / manufacturer	Outbound prospecting	Subscription / membership
Drop shipper	Word of mouth / referrals	Retainer / ongoing services
Broker / referrer	Paid advertising	Hourly / time-based
Community builder / organizer	Platform / marketplace-based	Leasing / rental income
Affiliate promoter	Partnerships / affiliates	Flat fee / project-based
Reseller / retailer	Local / community-based	Performance-based / success fee
Licensee / franchisee	Speaking / teaching / thought leadership	Commission-based / sponsorship
Aggregator / curator	Audience building / personal brand	Equity / ownership stake
		Tips / donations / pay-what-you-want

Production model

How will you source the product or service you're selling? Is it a service that you provide? Are you reselling a physical product made by someone else? Perhaps you're bringing together buyers and sellers.

You have a limited number of ways to create a product or service, including the following options:

>> **Service provider:** You sell your time, expertise, or labor directly to the customer.

>> **Creator / manufacturer:** You make the physical or digital product yourself.

>> **Drop shipper:** You market and sell products that are fulfilled and shipped by a third party.

>> **Broker / referrer:** You connect buyers with sellers or service providers.

>> **Community builder / organizer:** You create and monetize a community.

>> **Affiliate promoter:** You promote other people's products and earn a commission for each sale or lead.

>> **Reseller / retailer:** You buy finished products from others and resell them.

>> **Licensee / franchisee:** You operate under someone else's brand, product, or method with permission.

>> **Aggregator / curator:** You package and organize content, products, or services created by others.

Market model

Your market model defines how you reach your customers. Will you do it yourself, or will there be an intermediary of some kind? Here are the options typically used by solopreneurs:

>> **Inbound marketing:** You attract customers by creating valuable content.

>> **Outbound prospecting:** You actively reach out to potential clients.

>> **Word of mouth / referrals:** You rely on your existing network, past clients, or referral partners to generate leads.

>> **Paid advertising:** You use paid channels to drive traffic.

>> **Platform / marketplace-based:** You acquire customers through platforms that already have traffic.

>> **Partnerships / affiliates:** You collaborate with others who promote your offering.

>> **Local / community-based:** You focus on a geographic community.

>> **Speaking / teaching / thought leadership:** You build your audience through authority.

>> **Audience building / personal brand:** You grow a loyal following and convert them over time.

Payment model

Your payment model simply defines how the customer pays you for your product or service. Options include the following:

>> **Per unit sale:** You sell physical or digital products with a price per item. Maybe paid all at once or over time.

>> **Subscription / membership:** Customers pay regularly for access to content, community, tools, or services.

>> **Retainer:** Clients pay regularly for continued access or ongoing support.

>> **Hourly / time-based:** You get paid by the hour or session.

>> **Leasing / rental income:** You earn money by renting out physical or digital assets.

>> **Flat fee / project-based:** Clients pay a fixed price for a defined outcome.

>> **Performance-based / success fee:** You only get paid if a result is achieved.

>> **Commission-based / sponsorship:** You rely on voluntary payments.

>> **Equity / ownership stake:** You receive ownership or profit participation instead of (or in addition to) cash.

>> **Tips / donations / pay-what-you-want:** You rely on voluntary payments.

Choosing your business model

Most solo business owners typically choose only one option from each business model category (refer to Table 6-1). Keep it simple when you're the only employee. If you plan to do something that's already a well-established business idea and you aren't getting creative to disrupt an industry, then picking a business model will be easy: just do what everyone else does.

If you're starting a business that's unique or one for which people use different business models, then you have decisions to make. That was the case for these real-life solopreneurs we've worked with:

>> Kari is a life coach.

>> Nathan makes custom carpets.

>> Xan (pronounced *san*) makes custom paint-by-number kits.

>> George provides services and training for HubSpot, a customer relations management (CRM) platform.

We use them as examples in the following sections to provide real-world scenarios for how to choose a business model.

Production model considerations

The means of production you choose are based on the business you create. Life Coach Kari and HubSpot George are service providers, and Custom Carpet Nathan is a manufacturer. But Paint-by-Number Xan has a choice. He can buy the machinery and materials to produce his product himself or have it drop-shipped from China.

Xan had to decide between the simplicity of drop shipping and the higher profit margins (but higher start-up costs) of being a manufacturer. He chose the simplicity of drop shipping to start and plans to shift to a manufacturer model once he's established that people want his product.

TIP

If you have a choice, starting simple, cheap, and easy is usually better. You may as well decide your means of production and sourcing now. Make sure you write it down in your Solopreneur Action Plan!

Market model considerations

Solopreneurs often have more options in this category. For example, Life Coach Kari uses referrals as well as an affiliate model. HubSpot George uses a combination of speaking, inbound, and referrals.

Paint-by-Number Xan uses paid advertising. Whereas Custom Carpet Nathan uses a combination of paid advertising and an affiliate model.

How will you reach your customers? Think about the unique qualities of your business idea and which model best fits your needs. Make a choice and document it in your Solopreneur Action Plan.

Payment model considerations

For Customer Carpet Nathan and Paint-by-Number Xan, the choice is simple. They both need to use a per unit sale: Customers pay for it; they send it.

HubSpot George and Life Coach Kari have more options. Kari can use a flat fee in which the client pays a fixed amount for, say, six sessions. George uses a retainer model.

Kari chose the subscription model because she felt she needed multiple coaching sessions to be of help to her clients. George chose a retainer model for his services to ensure that all his time was booked.

Business model examples

Table 6-2 shows a number of typical solopreneur businesses and the production, market, and payment models they typically use.

TABLE 6-2 **Typical Business Models for Various Types of Solopreneurs**

Type	Production model	Market model	Payment model
Affiliate marketer	Affiliate / broker	Content / inbound / SEO	Commission-based
Artist / maker	Creator / manufacturer	Inbound / local / marketplace	Per unit sale, tips, licensing
Blogger / influencer	Creator / aggregator	Inbound / audience building	Ad revenue, sponsorships, affiliate income
Coach	Service provider	Inbound / referrals	Hourly, flat fee, or retainer
Community builder	Community organizer	Inbound / partnerships	Subscription or pay-what-you-want
Consultant	Service provider	Speaking / referrals / inbound	Project-based, retainer, performance-based
Course creator	Creator / manufacturer	Inbound / thought leadership	Subscription, one-time, or performance-based
Drop shipper	Drop shipper	Paid ads / SEO / marketplace	Per unit sale
Freelancer	Service provider	Platforms / referrals / inbound	Hourly or project-based
Newsletter publisher	Aggregator / creator	Audience building / inbound	Subscription, ad revenue, sponsorship
Online creator	Creator / manufacturer	Audience building / inbound	Tips, subscriptions, ad revenue

(continued)

TABLE 6-2 *(continued)*

Type	Production model	Market model	Payment model
Online shop owner	Creator / reseller	Marketplace / ads / inbound	Per unit sale
Photographer	Service provider	Local / inbound / referrals	Hourly, project-based
Podcaster	Creator / aggregator	Audience / referrals	Sponsorships, tips, subscription
Real estate agent	Broker	Referrals / local	Commission-based
Software builder (solo SaaS)	Creator / manufacturer	Inbound / SEO	Subscription or flat fee
Speaker / trainer	Service provider	Thought leadership / referrals	Flat fee, retainer, or licensing
Therapist / counselor	Service provider	Referrals / local / inbound	Hourly or retainer
Virtual assistant	Service provider	Outbound / referrals	Hourly or retainer

Which payment model works for your business? If more than one would work, which do you like best?

TIP

To keep cash flow positive, you need to get as much money up front as you can. In that case, the retainer model or subscription model is better than the pay-as-you-go model.

Recurring revenue is almost always preferable to a one-time payment because you aren't constantly chasing sales to generate revenue. This makes the leasing model and the subscription model superior to the others (and also better than the retainer model, technically). If your business supports one of these payment models, choose it.

REMEMBER

When you've decided on a business model, be sure to add it to your Solopreneur Action Plan.

Chapter **7**

Understanding Your Competition

E very business has competition, it doesn't matter what you do or whom you do it for. If nothing else, people can choose to do nothing over doing business with you, so even inaction or indecision can be competition. If doing nothing is your only competition, you're either creating something amazing that no one else has thought of or developing something nobody wants. The smart money is on the latter (in which case, check out Chapter 6, if you haven't already).

Part of planning your business (Step 2 in Phase 1 of the Solopreneur Success Cycle) is analyzing your competition. In this chapter, we cover why this step is important, which types of competition you need to explore, and how to compare yourself to your competitors.

Knowing Why You Need to Know Your Competition

Competition is a crucial topic for all businesses, but solopreneurs can sometimes have a slightly different perspective on the subject. It's often a huge issue for conventional businesses (ones with employees), summed up in a well-known saying: "If you're not growing, you're dying." And if you're growing, there's a good chance it's because you're taking business away from your competitors.

Some solopreneurs can afford to think of competition differently. This is because they may need such a small piece of the market to feed their business that focusing energy on defining and owning a *niche* (a specialty or area of expertise) that makes sense for them will produce better results than focusing heavily on competitors. Chapters 8 and 10 have more information on defining your customer and your target market, respectively.

However, it's always valuable to understand who your competition is. Even if you don't go head-to-head and steal customers away from your competitors, competition can

>> Allow you to get some insight into how well your type of business performs.

>> Give you ideas for your business you wouldn't have thought of on your own.

>> Inspire ways to *niche down,* that is, focusing your product or service to appeal to a smaller group of potential customers who see it as an excellent option.

>> Potentially allow you to create a cooperative relationship, where you work together or feed each other customers when one of you can serve them more effectively than the other.

>> Help you identify your target customers more clearly.

Speaking of customers, you likely haven't yet done a thorough analysis of who your customers will be (that's Chapter 8), but you probably have an idea. Defining your competition and customers is a little bit of a "chicken and egg" situation, but starting with your competition can help you identify your *target customer* more clearly.

REMEMBER

If your competitors are traditional, employee-based businesses, you may be dealing with a more cutthroat situation than if they're other solopreneurs. This is because the "growing/dying" ethos is probably alive and well with these competitors, and they'll be after your customers. If this is the case, you need to spend some time in this chapter understanding how your product or service stacks up against theirs so you can be competitive. But please remember that you *can* be competitive.

For example, Sara Murray is a solopreneur who focuses on sales consulting and sales training. She competes against other solopreneurs, established training companies like Sandler, and even huge firms that offer sales training as part of their business, like McKinsey & Company. Sara understands this and has figured out how to explain the value of partnering with a smaller firm that can customize and cater to the client's needs as a way to narrow her offering and compete with the larger or more established options. She has successfully worked with teams from small businesses to Fortune 500 corporations thanks to her customized training approach.

Regardless, it's worth it to take the time now to explore whom you will compete with when you get your business up and running. And that's what the rest of this chapter is about.

Defining the Four Types of Competition

There are lots of different kinds of competition, but only three that most solopreneurs should worry about: direct, indirect, and budgetary competition. Oh, and one more, which may be the most relevant of all . . . doing nothing! All these types of competitors are relevant and worthy of your time.

Direct competitors

This is what people usually think of when they think of competition. Your *direct competitors* are the people and companies that do what you do. If you're a software developer who works for the fitness industry making custom apps for iOS and Android, someone else who does the same thing is a direct competitor. Even if it's a company that provides the same service as part of its range of offerings, they are a direct competitor.

Direct competitors are usually the easiest to identify. They do what you do, so imagining yourself as a customer looking for your services usually gives you a good idea of what you're up against.

Indirect competitors

Laura Sorensen is a solopreneur who owns Atelier LKS, a brand design agency. She creates brands for innovative companies and competes with other solopreneurs, as well as agencies that provide graphic design services. But she also competes with the likes of Canva, a DIY graphic design platform.

People can use websites like Canva for logo designs and branding. They don't produce nearly as good a result as Atelier LKS, but they're cheaper. This means that, despite the lower quality of their services, Canva and companies like it are Laura's *indirect competition*. She counters this by "driving measurable results with strategic brand design." For Laura's customers, this tells them she'll use good design and clear strategy, customized to the business and its customer base, to make their brand work better and show results that they can measure (like more sales). This is something Canva can't claim.

Budgetary competitors

Some competition just doesn't look like competition. Imagine that you make custom rings for couples to celebrate special anniversaries. Yes, you compete against other custom ring makers and traditional jewelry stores. But you might also compete with travel agents.

For example, a couple planning their 25th wedding anniversary has some money to spend, and one partner suggests custom rings, but the other suggests a romantic cruise. You now have *budgetary competition*: the travel agent who's battling with you for those limited dollars.

Potential customers who do nothing

Your biggest competitor may be your target customer doing nothing and just ignoring their problem. For some solopreneurs, this is the biggest competitor of all. But don't ignore inaction or indecision because motivating people to solve their problem can be your most powerful selling tool.

Exploring Your Competition

The process of listing your competitors can become an overwhelming task. The goal should be to get the insights you need to understand what you're up against without spending too much time dissecting your competition. Try to find the closest matches to what you do.

TIP

Focus on competitors your customers have a high probability of choosing over you. This keeps your list of competitors shorter. If you make custom jewelry that sells for under $100, you don't need to put Tiffany on your list. Also think about things like geography. If you have a food truck that sells cheesesteaks in Omaha, you don't need to worry about competitors in Philadelphia.

Depending on what you do, you may want to make a comprehensive list of competitors, a list of your top competitors, or a list of examples for each type.

TIP

Even if you don't make a full list of competitors, use specific examples, not general categories, in your competitor list. Sales Coach Sara Murray (from the earlier section "Knowing Why You Need to Know Your Competition") shouldn't list her competition like this:

>> Large sales coaching companies

>> Medium sales coaching companies

>> Solopreneur sales coaching companies

Instead, she should use specific examples like the following:

>> Salesforce (large)

>> Braintrust, Sandler, Velocity Sales Consulting (medium)

>> Jasmine Davis, David H. Wilson (solopreneur)

These are clear examples that Sara can compare herself against instead of dealing with vague categories of competition.

Identifying direct competitors

When identifying direct competitors, you can usually start by thinking about what you do or call yourself: coach, app developer, graphic artist, and so on. For most, though not all, solopreneurs, this may result in a very long list.

For example, Kari Boatner, a life coach we discuss in Chapter 6, could spend the rest of her life putting together a list of all possible direct competitors. To pinpoint her direct competitors, she should instead focus on examples of people and companies that are most competitive within her niche (employee support and guidance for nonprofits).

Brand designer Laura Sorensen tends to concentrate on her local market area. So, she can put together a list of the brand creators in her market area and use those as her direct competitors.

Xan (pronounced *san*) Hong, who produces custom paint-by-number kits from people's photos, gets most of his customers through Google searches. He likely can identify his most meaningful direct competitors relatively quickly by searching online for "custom paint-by-number kits."

Recognizing indirect competitors

To find your indirect competitors, you need a different approach. Instead of focusing on what you do, you need to consider the *pain points* (your customers' problems) you solve. Ask questions about the ways a customer may address these pain points:

>> Are there other products or services they can use?

>> Can they solve the issue on their own?

>> Are there any free products or services they can use?

For example, Sarah Sypniewski helps people tell their life story in a book (she helps them write their memoirs). The pain point she addresses is the difficulty people have when they try to document their story later in life.

One of her indirect competitors is Why Wait Stories, a business owned by Lauren Ferrara that helps people tell their life story through video. This addresses the same pain point as Sarah, getting your story documented before it's too late, but through a different medium.

In addition, people can simply write their memoirs on their own with no help. Or they can find a free course online that guides them through the process. For most customers, these are inferior (though less expensive) options to working with Sarah. But she needs to consider them as indirect competition.

TIP

As you think through your indirect competition, make a list. If it's a long list, choose the ones that most appeal to the people you expect to sell your product or service to.

Spotting budgetary competitors

Budgetary competitors are businesses that may do something completely different but address the same or a similar pain point. Not every business has budgetary competition. If you do, don't ignore it, but don't lose your mind over it either.

Your list of budgetary competitors can get pretty large if you let it. For example, if your business is designing and building custom treehouses, worrying about residential architects as budgetary competition is probably going a bit too far, even though someone may choose to renovate their home instead of building a treehouse.

Budgetary competitors can be tricky to identify. One approach is to search online for things you expect your target customer to search for and see what comes up. Another is to ask AI the kinds of questions someone may ask to find a solution to the pain points you solve. Not all the results will compete with you on budget, but you may find some you didn't think of.

Another way to find budgetary competitors is to expand the definition of your pain point. One way to do this is to ask why the pain point is a pain point.

Consider Sarah from the preceding section; the pain point she solves is that writing a memoir is hard. But why do people want to write a memoir? The answer is usually that they want to leave something behind for their children and grandchildren to remember them by. What else can achieve this? Perhaps the person leaving a legacy could plan a family trip to the old country and spend time with the kids and grandkids in the place where they came from. Instead of spending their money with a writing coach, they spend it with a travel agent.

Identifying why prospects do nothing

Finding the reason that people choose to live with pain or desire instead of dealing with it can be the most challenging type of competition to get your head around.

Comparing Yourself to Your Competitors

The goal is to understand what your competitors do, how they do it, and how their customers perceive them. Try to understand your competitors well enough to compare what they offer with what you plan to offer.

WARNING

Analyzing your competitors can make you feel like you have no way to compete. Perhaps some people are way ahead of you in the marketplace, or you discover big companies operating in your space. If you plan to replace Facebook with your new app idea, you should be very afraid. But in many businesses, niching down allows you to compete, even with the big guys. Plenty of huge companies do digital marketing. But boatloads of solopreneurs are doing the same thing by focusing on, for example, a specific aspect of digital marketing for a specific type of customer and industry, and dealing with a certain pain point in a limited geographic region. See the difference? Keep this in mind and use it as inspiration.

Analyzing your competitors

The process of researching competitors usually involves some or all of the following:

>> Reviewing the competitor's website

>> Searching online for information about the competitor

>> Sleuthing the competitor's social media accounts (as well as people who mention them on social media)

>> Reading online reviews about the competitor

>> Reviewing industry-specific websites

>> Talking with your connections who know the competitor

>> *Mystery shopping* (pretending to be a potential customer) the competitor (But let your conscience be your guide on this one.)

As you research each competitor, analyze them by finding out the following information:

>> What kind of competitor are they (direct, indirect, budgetary)?

>> What is their product/service that competes with yours?

>> How does their pricing compare to yours?

>> What niche do they target?

>> What's the primary way they find customers?

>> What are their strengths compared to you?

>> What are their weaknesses compared to you?

You won't be able to get answers to all these questions for all your competitors. That's okay; just do your best.

FIND ONLINE

We've created a handy Competitor Analysis Sheet that can make this task more manageable. Download your copy at www.dummies.com/go/solopreneurbusinessfd.

Focusing on what makes you different

For a solopreneur, carving out a unique space from the competition isn't always necessary. But niching down is critical, and if you can narrow your focus in a way that reduces the number of competitors you're facing, that can't hurt.

Given that, look at the information you gathered for each competitor and ask yourself the following questions:

>> What makes you different?

>> What can you change to distinguish yourself from them?

Explore your answers and see if anything makes you want to adjust your vision for your business. If so, great. If not, this information will still be valuable as you flesh out your messaging, marketing, and so on.

TIP

This is a good time to set a Google Alert on your competitors so you can keep up with what they're doing. Just go to https://www.google.com/alerts to create email alerts that help you monitor the competition.

REMEMBER

Be sure to add your competitor research, and any changes you decide to make to your business, to your Solopreneur Action Plan, introduced in Chapter 3.

Chapter **8**

Defining Your Customer

No pressure, but defining your customer is one of the most important things you can do when you're getting started because it impacts every aspect of your business. Knowing who your customer is will help you:

>> Develop your product or service to support their wants and *pain points* (the issues they're trying to address).

>> Create your company's messaging and personality.

>> Focus your marketing efforts.

>> Decide where to spend your budget to reach and convert your ideal customer, whether that's in marketing, product development, or operations.

>> Build strong relationships to help increase sales.

>> Understand your competitive advantage.

REMEMBER

This chapter, another part of Step 2: Planning your business of the Getting started phase of the Solopreneur Success Cycle, helps you define and find your target audience, create detailed images of your ideal customers, and develop a plan to ensure you're the final destination on your buyer's journey.

Determining Whom You Can Sell To

When it comes to deciding who your customer is, where should you start? Should you cast a wide net? Reach out to anyone and everyone? The bigger the audience, the better, right?

Wrong.

Ever heard the phrase *riches are in the niches?* Well, that phrase exists for a reason: The more focused you are on a single audience, the more successful you'll be. Suppose you're a photographer who focuses on portraits of dogs in your city. That significantly helps you narrow down the customer base you'll reach out to: pet owners. Because you aren't just a general photographer, you more easily understand the types of publications and forums you should market in, the places your customer hangs out (hello, dog parks), and so on.

Niching down, or concentrating on a specific market or customer, will make your life much easier and give you the focus and time you need to succeed as a solopreneur.

Even if your expertise lies in a crowded market, not all of your competitors will have a deep understanding of your shared customer base. Many businesses assume they can take this phase lightly and just go off a hunch about who their target customer is, but they're wrong. Truly knowing who your audience is allows you to find opportunities and fill gaps where your competition is lacking.

Keep in mind that it's one thing to reach your audience, but it's a whole other thing to actually connect with them. And you can't do that unless you understand all aspects of the customers you're trying to reach, not just the parts of them that pertain to your business.

Go beyond your customers' pain points. Learn how they speak and communicate by listening to how they describe their struggles, in their own words, whether that's through reviews, social posts, or one-on-one conversations. Read between the lines of their needs and desires by paying attention to what they *wish* existed or what they repeatedly complain about.

Know their ambitions, goals, likes, dislikes, troubles, and fears. You can uncover these through one-on-one conversations, surveys, or *social listening*. That's the process of monitoring online conversations, reviews, and social media to understand what people are saying about your industry or areas of interest for your business in order to gain insights and inform business decisions.

REMEMBER

As a solopreneur, you have a unique advantage over large companies: It's easier for you to build personal relationships with your clients and customers. Connecting emotionally with your audience will help separate you from the big guys.

Choosing Your Customer Types

Now the fun begins. This is where you take your general ideas about the clients and customers you want to target and start researching them to make sure your hunch has led you in the right direction.

REMEMBER

Even if your product or service can help anybody and everybody, that doesn't mean it should. Brainstorming the consumers you can serve is a good exercise to help you start whittling down your audience, not to come up with a giant list of all the people you'll go after.

Listing your potential customer types

Before you narrow your focus, start by brainstorming *all* the different people who could benefit from what you offer. These are your potential customer types. A "customer type" refers to a group of people who share common traits, behaviors, or needs that your business can address. Examples might include:

>> Dog owners looking for pet-friendly things to do on a rainy day

>> Retirees seeking new hobbies and social opportunities

>> Busy parents looking for fast and healthy meal options

To build this list, start with a few research methods:

>> Reflect on the kinds of people who've shown interest in similar offerings

>> Search social media groups, forums, and product reviews for pain points and desires related to your target audience

>> Talk to people in your network

>> If you already have some customers or clients, conduct informal interviews or surveys

Once you've compiled your list, look for patterns. Do you notice recurring demographics? Shared challenges? Common goals? These patterns can help you create a few core customer segments. From there, you *niche down* or choose the customer segment(s) to focus on. Before you get there, however, make sure your wide-net list is as inclusive, thoughtful, and research-backed as possible.

Knowing where to find your customers

In order to market, sell, and even adjust your product or service to serve the needs of your customers, you must find out more about your chosen customer types . . . but where do you start?

Online research is a good place to begin, whether you put inquiries about your audience into a search engine, or participate in social media platforms and groups they belong to. For example, if your business targets dog owners, join local Facebook groups for dog lovers to see what they're complaining about, which parks they rave about, what type of lingo they use, and so on. Engaging with the people you're trying to target and observing their real struggles and successes is a great way to better understand them.

If you think your ideal customers read certain publications, scan through those publications to familiarize yourself with what they're writing and reporting on. If your customers consume digital and video content, watch the content to understand what's popular with your customer types. Additionally, check out what your competitors are doing to reach your target customers. Analyze their efforts to figure out what is and isn't working for them so you can get to know your target audience more quickly and effectively.

REMEMBER

The modern world is largely addicted to technology. Use survey apps, analytics tools, and market research technology to reach out to potential customers and find out more about them. And since it looks like AI is here to stay, harness it as a research tool, providing specific prompts to get the clearest description of your target customer. AI can be a great tool for research. It can help you quickly discover trends from customer reviews, summarize industry reports, or create potential customer personas, but it isn't without glitches. Be sure to cross-reference AI-generated insights with your own research and real-world observations to ensure accuracy and relevance.

These research approaches can actually be a fun and eye-opening part of your business planning, so embrace this phase!

TIP

If you have a few dollars to spend, consider A/B testing some pay-per-click (PPC) ads (covered in more depth in Chapters 12 and 17) on social media platforms or search engines where you believe your target audience may see them. A/B testing is a method of comparing two versions of something, like an ad, to see which one performs better based on a specific goal or metric. Most major social media platforms, including Facebook, Instagram, and LinkedIn, as well as Google Ads, include this functionality within their platforms. The point of these ads is to test the messaging that resonates with potential clients or customers. Seeing which variation they click the most will help you understand their preferences and personalities.

Talking to potential customers

When it comes to understanding your potential customers, nothing beats an actual conversation. Reach out to people who you believe fit your ideal customer profile. This could be someone posting in a relevant Facebook group, commenting on a niche subreddit, or engaging with local community meetups.

Whether you meet in person or virtually, consider treating them to coffee. Buy them a drink if you meet in real life or send a digital gift card for a "virtual coffee chat" to show you your appreciation for the time they're giving.

Have a genuine conversation with them and get to know them, but also be sure to vet your business idea with them. You need to know if what you're doing (or what they think you do) will actually help them, as we discuss in Chapter 5. Even if your business will help them, if they don't believe it will, you're in trouble. If your product or service doesn't make sense to them, you need to pivot either your business idea or the customer you're trying to target.

Here are some questions to consider asking during these conversations:

>> What does a typical day look like for you, at home and work?

>> What are your current goals and priorities?

>> What hurdles prevent you from achieving your goals?

>> How do you make purchasing decisions?

>> How do you consume information (social media, TV, podcasts, and so on)?

>> When you're choosing a product or service, what are your top priorities?

>> After hearing about my product/service, what feedback, good and bad, do you have for me?

>> How do you spend your free time?

>> What makes you feel fulfilled?

Notice that these questions expand beyond your product or service so you can get to know your customer types as people, not just potential customers. But you'll also want to dive into their pain points to figure out the problems you can solve, as well as how pressing these problems are or if they aren't as severe as you thought. Follow-up questions may include:

>> What's the biggest challenge you currently face as it relates to (the solutions my business provides)?

>> What have you tried to help solve this problem? Did it work?

>> How do you ideally want this problem solved?

>> How pressing is the issue you're experiencing?

The questions you pose can change depending on your product or service. Pay close attention to the answers you receive so you can ask additional follow-up questions when you need more detail, or when you get an answer that takes you down an unexpected path.

REMEMBER

Be open to feedback and put your ego aside. You may discover that you don't know as much about your presumed target audience as you thought.

Don't rely on your memory to keep track of the details you gather about your customer types. Be sure to jot down a thorough description in the appropriate section of your Solopreneur Action Plan.

Developing and Using Your Customer Persona(s)

While customer *types* identify whom you should target, *personas* help you refine who these people are, what their pain points are, and other details about them. Personas can give you a clear picture in your head of whom you're talking — and ultimately selling — to.

This is helpful because even if you're trying to reach a large number of people, you want all your interactions with them to seem like they're one-on-one. The more personal their experience in any area of your business (marketing, sales, operations, and so on), the more likely your potential client will be to buy from you.

Creating personas

So, what exactly is a *buyer persona*? It's a detailed representation of your target customer based on the data you gathered through the research and interviews we cover in the earlier section "Choosing Your Customer Types." As you look through your customer types, think of all the ways you can get even more specific with who these people are to best craft your personas.

Imagine a solopreneur who acts as a consultant for human resources. Her persona is Glenda, an overworked HR manager in her 40s who needs to implement AI technology to keep her department current. Here are some ways you can get even more detailed with Glenda:

» **Geographical market served:** Local area versus global market

» **Business type:** Start-ups, nonprofits, family-owned businesses, Fortune 500 companies, and the like

» **Business size:** Based on sales, profits, employee numbers, and similar factors

>> **Industry:** Healthcare, finance, e-commerce, and so on

>> **Customer industry:** Companies that serve a specific industry, such as the construction industry, restaurant industry, dentists, and so on

Now imagine Trainer Tim, a personal trainer who helps men over 50 get back in shape. His persona is Larry, a man in his late 50s, college-educated, married, and 25 pounds overweight. Here are some ways he could niche even further:

>> **Life stage:** Newly married, children at home, empty nesters, retirees, and the like

>> **Religion/spiritual beliefs:** Christian, Muslim, New Age, and so on

>> **Job title:** Entry level, middle managers, C-level executives, and so on

>> **Culture or ethnicity:** Black, Hispanic, Asian, and the like

>> **Sexual orientation:** Heterosexual, LGBTQ+, pansexual, asexual, and so on

>> **Special needs:** Physical disability, ADHD, anxiety, and the like

>> **Hobbies or interests:** Skiing, pickleball, stamp collecting, photography, and so on

>> **Special circumstances:** Career change, job loss, divorce, illness, loss of spouse, and other life changes

Imagine that you're a life coach considering a few ways you can position your business, including the following:

>> Life coach who focuses on men over 55

>> Life coach who focuses on men over 55 with ADHD

>> Life coach who focuses on men over 55 with ADHD who work in management

>> Life coach who focuses on men over 55 with ADHD who work in management and who are planning early retirement

Many people fit into the first category, and a lot of coaches work with them as well. Far fewer people fall into the last category, but you can bet any of them that are looking for a coach are going to consider you.

With these ideas in mind, look at how you can take a customer type and turn it into a detailed persona description. If you're a music teacher for kids, for example, you may have an idea of who you're targeting and describe your audience like this:

I target moms with kids interested in music.

That's a solid starting point, but it's too broad to guide your marketing and operational efforts effectively. Instead, take the ideas from the preceding pages and form something like this:

Monica Mom is in her early 30s with two kids, ages 4 and 6. She works remotely part-time and is looking for simple educational activities for her 4-year-old during the day to free up an hour or so to get work done. She doesn't like driving long distances, so activities nearby are preferable. Monica tries to maintain balance between parenting/family time, work, and her personal hobbies. She relies on apps, local magazines, and local mom groups (both in-person and online) to find new activities for her kids.

Big difference, right? Instead of marketing to a general group of people, you're now speaking directly to Monica and where she is, what she cares about, and how your offer can help her.

You may find that you need more than one persona, especially if your product or service serves multiple customer segments. That's totally normal, but the goal isn't to create a separate marketing plan for each one, but to understand your audience well enough that you can tailor your messaging accordingly. Focus in on one-three personas. If you feel like you need more than that, make the first few your primary personas and put a lot of effort toward them; then make others secondary personas. The clearer you are on who you're speaking to, the more effective your messaging will be.

Defining negative personas

As important as it is to define the persona(s) you're trying to reach, it's equally important to define your *negative persona(s)*, or the people you don't want to reach.

Identifying your negative persona(s) can save you time and resources because you're intentionally not going after people who won't buy from you in the end. You can instead focus your attention on people you're more likely to convert from prospect to buyer.

In the previous example, the music teacher may consider identifying Noncommittal Nancy — a mom who lives across town, whose schedule changes regularly, and doesn't consistently keep her kids in any activity — as a negative persona. If you're a music teacher, you want clients to commit signing up for your classes and stay consistent, not only so you can plan financially for your business but also because you want to see progress from the kids you teach, and that comes from meeting with them regularly.

REMEMBER

Negative personas aren't bad people. They're just not right for your business. Identify how you'll approach your negative persona(s) if they want your services. How will you say *thanks, but no thanks?*

Exploring ways to use personas in your business

Persona development is often associated with marketing, but you can do many things with personas, such as the following:

>> **Marketing:** Personas can help you home in on your messaging, choose the right channels to get that messaging across, and create the best content.

>> **Product or service development:** How can you solve more of your persona's problems? Going back to our music teacher example, the teacher should consider hour-long drop-off classes instead of Mommy and Me classes, to allow Monica Mom that hour to get errands and work done.

>> **Sales:** Choosing the right pitch can be greatly influenced by a persona. For Monica Mom, a pitch about saving time due to the class's convenient location as well as freeing up an hour in the day would be just as important as mentioning the details of the class itself.

>> **Customer experience:** Knowing your customer persona can help you connect with your audience and develop empathy for their pain points. As the music teacher, provide such a great experience for Monica's kids that it's a no-brainer for her to drop them off for an hour to take for herself.

Understanding Your Buyer's Journey

Very few people ask someone to marry them on the first date. Typically, people date for a while, get engaged, get married, and then do whatever they can to stay in love throughout their marriage.

Well, that's kind of how you should approach understanding your customers and their *buyer's journey*, which is essentially the process customers go through before, during, and after buying from you.

If you search "buyer's journey" online, you may find lots of jargon about flywheels, funnels, 7 steps, and more ways to break down what it means, but we use a consolidated explanation that's easier to follow for solopreneurs. We also reference the dating/marriage metaphor throughout the following sections to make things more concrete.

Understanding your buyer's journey is important because it can help you market and sell your product or service throughout each phase of the journey and guide your buyers from their introduction to your product/service through the sale. Over the course of the journey, it's your job to build trust and inspire your potential buyers to take action.

The phases of the buyer's journey help explain how you should approach your customers depending on where they are in the buying process. The more you understand your buyer's journey, the more you'll be able to create a positive experience for your customers, which strengthens and sustains your business.

REMEMBER

After you create your buyer's journey, keep it in mind as you approach the sales and marketing sections of this book. We guide you through mapping your marketing content and interactions with your target audience based on the different phases of the buyer's journey.

Awareness

In the awareness phase of the journey, the buyer is trying to understand the problem or need they have. They are beginning to explore their options. This is your chance to get on their radar. In this phase, you're trying to get them to know you.

If we consider this phase in terms of the dating/marriage analogy, this is the moment you lock eyes with a person and notice each other for the first time. Whether it's their laugh, their style, or the way they treat others, you're intrigued, but you don't know each other yet.

To get on your customer's radar during this phase, focus on showing up where your audience already spends time. That might mean sharing relatable stories or tips on social media. The goal here isn't to pitch your product or service, but to spark interest and a connection.

Consideration

At the consideration point in the buyer's journey, the buyer has clearly identified the problem or desire they're trying to solve, and they're comparing solutions and looking for the best approach to solve their issue. This is where you get them to like you!

This is the dating phase of our analogy. The time when you get to know a person, have deep conversations, better understand each other's interests and desires, and ultimately decide if this is a person you want to be with.

In this phase, your goal is to build trust and show potential customers why you're the right choice. You can do this by offering valuable, targeted content that educates and positions you as a solution. This could include, for example, case studies, testimonials, or anything that helps the buyer feel more confident in your offering. The key is to be helpful, not pushy. You're showing up consistently, answering their questions, and building a relationship, just like you would in a developing romance.

Decision

In the decision phase, your buyer has chosen a solution and has decided to make the purchase. They trust you!

Do we hear wedding bells? It's time for the proposal! You've put in the time, you know the person is the right one for you, and you decide to pop the question.

At this point, your job is to make it as easy and reassuring as possible for your buyer to say "yes." Messaging and communication here should focus on building confidence and reducing hesitation. Think strong testimonials, limited-time offers, or even a short thank-you video. Your goal is to seal the deal by showing that not only are you the right choice, but that choosing you is simple and risk-free.

Delight/retention

The delight/retention phase is often overlooked, but it's extremely important to focus on whether you want repeat business or referrals. You need to make sure your buyer is satisfied with their decision and continues to feel valued.

This is the marriage and the happily ever after. The time that requires lots of TLC to thrive and last.

Just as you and your business evolve over time, so will your customers and their needs and wants. Check in with them regularly. Update your research through the year and see if you can identify any shifts or patterns that may impact your product or service and how you get it out into the world.

Chapter **9**

Tackling Potential Obstacles to Getting Your Business Up and Running

You have a business idea that supports your goals and seems achievable from the perspective of both satisfying a need for a product or service consumers will pay for and fulfilling your need to be passionate about (or at least like) your work. But your business still must be a venture you can start and make money running.

This chapter walks you through the process of thinking your idea through at a high level. The goal is to not waste time creating a business that

>> You can't get up and running

>> Won't make enough money to support you

There are two aspects to this. The first is knowing what can prevent you from starting your business, what we call the *show-stoppers*. Some businesses are easy to get up and running, while others face potential complications. If you're doing something that doesn't require anything other than a computer and a desk, you can probably skip the first part of this chapter, "Identifying Showstoppers." But read through that section if your business requires permits, contractual agreements with third parties, or financing.

Second, you want to be comfortable that your business idea can make enough profit to meet your financial needs. We devote the rest of the chapter to this important issue, and no one should skip these sections.

This chapter is part of Step 2: Planning your business of the Getting started phase in the Solopreneur Success Cycle. This step reviews the plan to make sure it's feasible before you spend a ton of time getting into the planning details that we cover in the subsequent chapters.

Identifying Showstoppers

A *showstopper* is anything that can prevent you from successfully starting your business. This can include many things; the specifics will relate to your particular business. Here are some possibilities:

>> **Distributor contracts:** If you will be relying on third parties to distribute your product, you need to know you can get a contract with favorable terms.

>> **Financing:** If you plan on borrowing money to start your business, you need to be confident that you have a lender willing to make the loan with terms you can live with.

>> **Insurance coverage:** Some high-risk businesses can be difficult or expensive to insure. You need to be comfortable that you can get insurance at a rate that you can afford.

>> **Licensing agreements:** If you need to license something from another person or business to produce your product or service, you need to be comfortable you can do so and at a price that makes sense for you.

» **Permits and licenses:** If your business requires government permits or professional licenses (like a food service permit or contractor's license), you'll need to be sure you can qualify and get approved.

» **Supplier contracts:** If you rely on key suppliers for materials or products, confirm you can secure contracts that guarantee reliable delivery at acceptable prices.

» **Government permits:** Does your business require any government permits to operate? Can those permits be denied for reasons outside your control? If so, this is a showstopper.

» **Zoning:** Some businesses aren't allowed to operate in certain areas. If you plan to operate a home-based business, be sure you won't run afoul of local zoning ordinances. If you will, you can request a variance from the zoning board, but getting one is far from guaranteed.

» **Other necessary regulatory approval:** Some industries require special approvals or inspections before you can operate legally (like health department sign-off or zoning approval), so be sure you can meet these requirements.

TIP

You're looking for anything you need to get your business up and running that isn't totally within your control.

Ferreting out showstoppers

Your business might not have showstoppers. Many solo businesses don't. But if you have any, you want to find out what they are before you start spending time and money creating your business.

TIP

Showstoppers can take many forms, depending on your business. Make a list of all the things you need to get your business set up. Think about legal, contractual, permitting, and business requirements. Try to be thorough and consider everything.

Here's a real-world example. Imagine you plan to open a food truck business in Massachusetts, you'll need certain things you don't currently have. Some of your needs are obvious, like the following:

» **A food truck:** This is a truck outfitted with facilities suitable for your concept.

>> **Financing to buy the food truck:** You need to pay for the food truck using cash, a lease, or bank financing.

>> **A food supplier:** You must have a source for the raw ingredients you will use to prepare your menu items.

>> **A business certificate:** You will need this to do business legally in the Commonwealth of Massachusetts.

>> **A food establishment permit from the local board of health:** You will need this to legally prepare and sell food in the Commonwealth of Massachusetts.

But you'll need other, less obvious things, such as

>> **A commissary kitchen:** This is the place where most food preparation takes place. You can only prepare food for sale in Massachusetts in a licensed kitchen.

>> **A hawker and peddler license:** Because you are mobile while operating your business, you will also need this license to operate legally.

>> **Fire department permits:** Because cooking is involved, the fire department will need to approve your food truck.

>> **Other necessary permits depending on the type of food you sell (for example, seafood, ice cream, and so on):** Certain types of foods have additional requirements.

You need all of these things to open your food truck business. But some of them are in your control and are easy to get. Others rely on factors beyond your control. Those are your potential show-stoppers, and you need to identify them.

Showstopper risk

There are two aspects to showstopper risk:

>> The likelihood that you will fail to obtain the required item

>> The cost of the required item exceeding what you can pay

You need to consider your showstoppers to make sure you can afford to run into one without becoming financially devastated. The process involves these steps:

1. **List all the things that need to happen before you can open your business that involve a third party or that you don't have control over.**

These are the requirements shown in the first column of Figure 9-1.

2. **Estimate the cost of each item on your list.**

3. **Estimate the risk of failure for obtaining each item on your list.**

This can range from very low to high (see Figure 9-1).

4. **Identify any items that need to be obtained before other items.**

These are your *predecessors*. An obvious one is that you need a way to finance your food truck before you can buy it.

Requirement	Expected Cost	Risk of Failure	Predecessors
Food truck financing		Moderate	None
Food truck purchase	$ 60,000	Low	Food truck financing
Commissary kitchen agreement	$ 2,000	High	None
Food supplier agreement	$ -	Low	None
Business certificate	$ 50	Very Low	None
Local food establishment permit	$ 500	Low to Moderate	Business certificate Commissary kitchen agreement
Hawker and peddler license	$ 62	Very Low	Business certificate
Fire department permits	$ 200	Moderate	Food truck purchase Business certificate
Insurance (liability and vehicle)	$ 3,000	Low	Food truck purchase

FIGURE 9-1: A list of potential showstoppers for a food truck business.

If you have trouble figuring any aspect of this process, search the web, or talk to people who may have insight. Don't give up until you get the answers you need.

5. **Sort your requirements by risk from highest to lowest.**

Now your list may look something like what's shown in Figure 9-2.

6. **Place predecessor items ahead of the items that depend on them.**

Place each predecessor item immediately before the earliest item that depends on it.

Requirement	Expected Cost	Risk of Failure	Predecessors
Commissary kitchen agreement	$ 2,000	High	None
Food truck financing		Moderate	None
Fire department permits	$ 200	Moderate	Food truck purchase
Fire department permits	$ 500	Low to Moderate	Business certificate Commissary kitchen agreement
Food truck purchase	$ 60,000	Low	Food truck financing
Food supplier agreement	$ -	Low	None
Business certificate	$ 50	Very Low	None
Hawker and peddler license	$ 62	Very Low	Business certificate
Insurance (liability and vehicle)	$ 3,000	Very Low	Food truck purchase

FIGURE 9-2: A list of potential showstoppers sorted by risk from highest to lowest.

Figure 9-3 shows that you need the food truck before you can get the fire department permits, which is a moderate-risk item. You need to find a way of delaying the food truck purchase for as long as possible. The commissary kitchen agreement is another pricey, higher-risk item because there may be a shortage of space at local facilities. You need to research what's available to ensure that finding kitchen space won't be a problem before you move on to the rest of the list.

Requirement	Expected Cost	Risk of Failure	Predecessors
Commissary kitchen agreement	$ 2,000	High	None
Food truck financing		Moderate	None
Food truck purchase	$ 60,000	Low	Food truck financing
Fire department permits	$ 200	Moderate	Food truck purchase
Business certificate	$ 50	Very Low	None
Local food establishment permit	$ 500	Low to Moderate	Business certificate Commissary kitchen agreement
Food supplier agreement	$ -	Low	None
Hawker and peddler license	$ 62	Very Low	Business certificate
Insurance (liability and vehicle)	$ 3,000	Very Low	Food truck purchase

FIGURE 9-3: A list of potential showstoppers sorted by risk from highest to lowest, with predecessor items inserted before the items that depend on them being completed.

The next step is to create a plan that reduces your risk as much as possible without incurring a lot of expense (see Figure 9-4). This involves taking steps to de-risk the higher-cost items. Talking to the fire department in advance, reserving the food truck with a small deposit, and making arrangements in advance for a commissary kitchen can drastically reduce the financial risk of starting this business. Figure 9-4 shows that you can decrease the overall risk level to low while only spending $3,750. Although no one likes losing that much money, it's a lot better than losing $60,000.

Task	Cost	Running Cost	Overall Risk Level	Notes
Identify a commissary kitchen you can lease.	$ -	$ -	High	
Talk to fire department about requirements for food truck permits.	$ -	$ -	Moderate	
Find a lender who will finance food truck.	$ -	$ -	Moderate	
Find a food truck that meets fire department requirements that can be put under agreement subject to fire department approval.	$ 1,000	$ 1,000	Medium High	Deposit to hold food truck
Get fire department permits.	$ 200	$ 1,200	Medium	
Sign agreement for commissary kitchen.	$ 2,000	$ 3,200	Medium	First month and security deposit
Get business certificate.	$ 50	$ 3,250	Medium	
Get local food establishment permit.	$ 500	$ 3,750	Low	
Sign agreement with food supplier.	$ -	$ 3,750	Low	
Finance food truck.	$ 59,000	$ 62,750	Low	This is the cost of the obligation
Get hawker and peddler license.	$ 62	$ 62,812	Low	
Get insurance.	$ 3,000	$ 65,812	Low	

FIGURE 9-4: A de-risked plan to avoid showstoppers costing a lot of money.

Use this process to think through your showstoppers and make sure you can afford the risk of creating your business. If you can, great! If not, don't give up. Instead, go back to Chapter 6 and rethink your business idea to find a less risky way to start.

Put your de-risked plan in your Solopreneur Action Plan.

REMEMBER

Forecasting Your Ability to Make a Profit

Knowing whether your idea can produce a profit is a very important part of the process of starting a business. Most people don't want to start a business that loses money. While you can never be sure how a business will perform, if you can't get it to make sense on paper in a profit and loss statement, it's a very good bet that you won't get it to work in the real world. A *profit and loss statement (P&L)*, also known as an *income statement*, shows your revenue and expenses, highlighting your profits/losses in a given period.

FIND
ONLINE

We provide a sample profit and loss spreadsheet and template at www.dummies.com/go/solopreneurbusinessfd. Download a copy to have handy when you read this section.

TIP

If accounting and finance aren't your thing, you may want to consider hiring a professional to help you with this part. If you decide to do it yourself, developing some basic skills in Microsoft Excel, Apple Numbers, or Google Sheets will serve you well.

Setting your prices

You can spend time in Chapter 10 deciding specifically where to set your prices (and finding ways to charge more than you think you can). For now, you want to see if your business makes sense at a high level. You need to have a rough idea of what you can charge for your product or services before you decide whether your business can produce enough profit to meet your goals. To do that, follow these steps:

1. **Look at what your competition charges.**

   Whatever your competitors are charging should be in the ballpark of what you can charge.

2. **Factor in what you do that's different, estimate what your product/service is worth, and set a price (or prices if you have multiple offerings).**

   For this step, you must decide if what you do differently makes your product/service more or less valuable.

3. **Determine if the personas you're targeting (see Chapter 8 for an explanation of personas) can pay the price you've estimated, or if they can pay more.**

   If they can't pay your estimated price, you need to either change your price or change your personas. If your personas can pay more, that's great! You find out in Chapter 10 how to position your offering to justify charging a higher price.

4. **Use that higher price in your P&L forecast.**

REMEMBER

It's tempting to use costs to determine price. After all, you deserve a fair profit for your work. Unfortunately, the list of people who care about what it costs to produce your product or service is a short one, limited to basically . . . you. People value a product/service based on what it does for them, and your costs don't figure into their equation. Use your costs to determine your profit, but not your price.

Estimating your revenue

Once you have a reasonable estimate of your pricing, you need to estimate your revenue. If this sounds tricky, that's just because it is. Estimating sales volume for a business that doesn't yet exist is difficult and far from an exact science. It almost always involves guesswork.

TECHNICAL STUFF

Your revenue is equal to your Price for Product 1 x the Number of Units Sold of Product 1 + the Price for Product 2 x the Number of Units Sold of Product 2 and so on. You'll want to estimate the units sold on a monthly basis.

TIP

Set some upper and lower bounds on the number of units sold to narrow down the range of possibilities as follows:

>> **Setting a lower boundary for sales volume:** Some people may have already committed to doing business with you. This can give you a rough idea of your sales volume to start. Try to be conservative in your estimate.

>> **Setting an upper boundary for sales volume:** If you're selling your time (for example, if you're a life coach), your upper limit is based on the number of hours you want to work. If you're selling a physical product, your upper boundary may be limited by the production of the product you plan to sell. If it's a digital product, the upper boundary may be based on your ability to generate leads and close sales.

>> **Optimistic, pessimistic, and realistic scenarios:** Plan your revenue for the first year of operations. Creating worst-case and best-case scenarios is one way to think about sales volume. Then, use something in the middle as a realistic scenario for your sales volume.

Estimating start-up costs

If you have a business idea that may be slowed down by showstoppers, make a list of them if you haven't already (see "Ferreting out showstoppers" earlier in this chapter). You'll also usually need to do some other things to set up your company. Some of these will cost money, so you want to account for them.

Here's an approach to estimating start-up costs that works well:

1. **List everything you can think of that costs money to set up.**

Include tools you want to use for scheduling, marketing, and tracking financials, plus setting up invoicing, getting insurance, and planning your taxes. Just a few things you need to consider!

2. **Look at Chapters 15 and 16 for ideas relevant to many solo businesses to see if you missed anything.**

Don't look at Chapters 15 and 16 first. Make your brain think through *your* business before you look at our lists.

TIP

3. **Write down each item and a ballpark cost for it.**

Estimating operating costs

Operating costs are expenses that recur regularly. They can be payments you make monthly, quarterly, annually, or on some other recurring schedule. As you run your business and collect payments for your product or service, you'll pay your operating costs before you make a profit.

We consider four kinds of costs for this exercise:

>> **Fixed costs:** These are expenses that are the same regardless of your sales.

>> **Variable costs:** These are expenses that vary depending on how much you sell.

>> **Financing costs:** These are the loan payments on money you borrowed to start your business.

>> **Income and self-employment taxes:** If you make a profit, some of that profit will be paid to the government.

Fixed costs

Fixed costs are the same regardless of how much you generate in sales. Examples of fixed costs include things like:

>> Rent

>> Insurance

- » Software tools
- » Subscriptions
- » Business filing fees
- » Other fixed costs specific to your business

Your fixed costs will depend on the type of business you're building. Try to consider every expense you'll routinely pay and plan out your first year of operations.

Variable costs

Variable costs go up as you sell more. Examples are:

- » Raw materials
- » Shipping costs
- » Payment processing fees
- » Outsourcing to contractors
- » Other shifting costs specific to your business

Your variable costs also depend on the type of business you're building. These costs are typically either a unit cost per product sold or a percentage of sales. Some costs have both a fixed and a variable component. For example, some payment processors charge a fixed monthly fee, but then require a percentage of the sale for each transaction. In this case, put the percentage in the variable cost section and the monthly fee in the fixed cost section.

Again, try to consider every expense that will vary depending on your sales and plan out your first year of operations.

Financing costs

If you plan to borrow money from a friend, a bank, or (hopefully not) a credit card, you'll need to factor in the debt service payments (for example, loan payments, interest, service fees, and so on).

TIP

If you need help with calculating the loan payment, just search "loan payment calculator" on the web.

Income and self-employment taxes

Income taxes are complicated, and the amount you pay depends largely on how you set up your business. A tax advisor can help you figure this out, and even figure out how to minimize your payments, so it can make a lot of sense to consult one.

If you can't hire a pro at this point, use an estimate. At the time of writing this book, a tax payment of 35 percent of your profit is a good guess in the United States and Canada. Other countries' income taxes can range from 25 percent to 45 percent. Do your homework on this.

TIP

In the United States, the cost of health insurance may be deductible from your tax liability. A tax professional can advise you on how to do this legally.

Creating a pro forma P&L

Creating a *pro forma* P&L sounds more complicated than it is. *Pro forma* just means "projected," and a P&L (also known as an *income statement*) simply calculates how much money you will make or lose, which is a good thing to know.

The two components of a *pro forma* P&L are an estimate of your revenue and an estimate of your expenses (operating costs). Put them together, subtract your revenue from your expenses for each month, and calculate your estimated taxes and then your profit or loss, and the result is something like what's shown in Figure 9-5.

Note that this example is a nonstandard approach for traditional businesses. But the goal is to help you determine whether you can make enough money fast enough to want to start the business without requiring a financial expert.

Once you've created your pro forma profit and loss statement, you can start to explore the limits of income for your business. Hopefully, your business looks profitable on paper. But there are limits on where it can go. You can only work so many hours; there are only so many customers per month you can find with limited resources.

Take a sober look at your P&L analysis. Make sure you're being realistic. Asking an accountant or business consultant for their opinion may be worth it.

Revenue:		Jan-26	Feb-26	~	Dec-26	Annual
Sales		$ 1,250.00	$ 1,750.00	~	$ 10,250.00	$ 62,000.00
Other Income		-	$ -	~	$ 3.69	$ 26.68
Total Income		**$ 1,250.00**	**$ 1,750.00**	~	**$ 10,253.69**	**$ 62,026.68**

Operating Expenses:

Variable Costs

Raw Materials		$ 93.75	$ 131.25	~	$ 768.75	**$ 4,650.00**
Shipping Costs		$ 50.00	$ 70.00	~	$ 410.00	**$ 2,480.00**
Payment Processing Fees		$ 40.63	$ 56.88	~	$ 333.13	**$ 2,015.00**
Contract Labor		$ -	$ -	~	$ 1,537.50	**$ 4,162.50**

Fixed Costs

Marketing & Advertising		$ 150.00	$ 150.00	~	$ 150.00	**$ 1,800.00**
Software & Subscriptions		$ 39.95	$ 39.95	~	$ 39.95	**$ 479.40**
Insurance		$ 125.00	$ 125.00	~	$ 125.00	**$ 1,500.00**
Business Taxes (licenses, fees, etc.)		$ 250.00	$ -	~	$ -	**$ 250.00**
Office Supplies		$ 22.50	$ 22.50	~	$ 22.50	**$ 270.00**
Telephone & Internet		$ 75.00	$ 75.00	~	$ 75.00	**$ 900.00**
Postage		$ -	$ -	~	$ -	**$ -**
Bank Fees		$ 5.00	$ 5.00	~	$ 5.00	**$ 60.00**
Local Fees and Taxes		$ -	$ -	~	$ -	**$ -**
Travel Expense			$ 500.00			**$ 500.00**
Other Fees		$ 150.00	$ -	~	$ -	**$ 150.00**
Professional Services		$ 500.00	$ -	~	$ -	**$ 500.00**

Financing Costs

Interest Expense		$ 150.00	$ 150.00	~	$ 150.00	**$ 1,800.00**

Total Operating Expenses		**$ 1,651.83**	**$ 825.58**	~	**$ 3,616.83**	**$ 21,016.90**
Net Operating Income		**$ (401.83)**	**$ 924.43**	~	**$ 6,636.86**	**$ 41,009.78**

	Tax Rate					
Federal Tax @	35.00%	$ (140.64)	$ 323.55	~	$ 2,322.90	**$ 14,353.42**
State Tax @	6.25%	$ (25.11)	$ 57.78	~	$ 414.80	**$ 2,563.11**
After Tax Income		**$ (236.07)**	**$ 543.10**	~	**$ 3,899.16**	**$ 24,093.24**

FIGURE 9-5: A sample simple monthly profit and loss statement for a solopreneur business (note March through November are not shown to enhance readability).

Calculating If You Can Survive Financially

Given your P&L analysis, is your business worth doing? It will be hard work so it should be worth your while. If the after tax income seems sufficient, great! But you should think about a few other things, including the following:

>> **Do you have enough savings to start the business?** Add up your start-up costs and see what it will take to get this venture off the ground. Is the amount you need something you can cover on your own? Can you ask a friend or family

member to loan you the money you need? Will a bank help you? Sometimes, you can get a bank loan to start your business. Just know that you'll likely be personally liable for the loan if your business fails.

TIP

The Small Business Administration can help people in the United States find loans. You can find more info at `https://www.sba.gov/funding-programs/loans`. In Canada, the Business Development Bank of Canada (`https://www.bdc.ca/en/financing/small-business-loan`) is the go-to agency for small businesses.

>> **Can you handle unpaid leave?** Depending on the nature of your business, your income may stop if you get sick or face some other unforeseen issue that prevents you from working. If you don't have someone to help you in this situation, you need to put aside money as soon as possible to prepare for an emergency.

>> **Should you start as a side hustle?** If your business looks like a good long-term play, but the costs of quitting your job and going into it full-time aren't reasonable, consider keeping your current job and building up the business in your spare time.

This will be hard because you'll have to add your side hustle hours to your workweek. However, the reduced financial risk allows you to figure out the business without as much stress. Eventually, you'll be able to leave your job and step into a thriving solo business.

Asking the Tough Question: Is Your Idea a Solo Business?

If you've worked through the exercises in this chapter, you've hopefully done a deep dive into your business that allowed you to see it more clearly. Ask yourself, *Can I really run this business alone?*

If your answer is *absolutely*, well, that's awesome! If you're less sure, you need to think through all the things you'll need to do to run the business and then ask yourself:

>> What can you outsource?

>> What must you do yourself?

>> What can be eliminated?

If the business seems too big for one person after outsourcing and eliminating certain tasks, you have two choices: Rethink the business or plan to hire employees (and buy *Small Business For Dummies*, 6th Edition, by Eric Tyson and Jim Schell [Wiley]).

REMEMBER

Be sure to go back and update your *pro forma* P&L with any changes you've made. When you're happy with your P&L and start-up cost analysis, put them in your Solopreneur Action Plan.

3

Building Your Solopreneur Business

Position your business to stand out by defining what makes it special and whom it serves.

Create messaging and a brand identity that speak to your audience's pain points and build emotional connections.

Develop a focused marketing strategy that builds trust, creates desire, and reaches your ideal customer.

Adopt a sales process that feels natural and allows you to close mutually satisfying deals with customers.

Design an onboarding experience that turns customers into your biggest fans.

Choose the right legal and financial structure for your business.

Set up internal systems, tools, and services to save time now and support growth later.

» **Understanding different positioning strategies for your business**

» **Mapping out your positioning strategy**

» **Realizing that competing on price is almost always a bad idea**

» **Charging more for your offering than you imagined**

Chapter **10**

Positioning Your Business and Product in the Market

The chapters in Part 2 guide you through the process of envisioning your business. After working through them, you have a product or service that takes competition into account, and you know who your customer is and have one or two *personas* (that is, your ideal customers) defined.

If you think you're done *niching down* (narrowing your focus), you're mistaken. When you defined your personas in Chapter 8, you made a great start. But it's time to niche your business down even more to uniquely target your personas. You need your potential customers to understand your business in a way that makes it stand out compared to your competition. You achieve this by positioning yourself strategically in the market.

In this chapter, we help you position your business based on what you do, the pain points you solve, and the way you solve them. As you work through the positioning process, keep your competition and your persona(s) top of mind.

The content of this chapter falls under Step 2: Planning your business of the Getting started phase in the Solopreneur Success Cycle.

Making Yourself Special in Your Customer's Eyes

Whether you sell to individuals or businesses, you can focus your offering based on the customers you serve in various ways. While you developed your target personas in Chapter 8, there are usually ways you can niche down even more.

You can position your business in many ways, and although they may overlap a bit, you can roughly put them into three categories:

>> What you do

>> Specific *pain points* (customer problems) you solve

>> How you do what you do

You can position your business according to some or all of these categories.

REMEMBER

The more focused you get, the easier it will be to attract customers.

Positioning your business based on what you do

Positioning your business based on what you do will depend on your specific business, skills, and interests. Consider highlighting the following aspects of what you do:

>> **Special skills and expertise:** Unique technical skills, certifications and credentials, specialized knowledge

>> **Specialization:** Focus on some subset of what you could offer, for example, be a wedding photographer instead of an event photographer or logo designer instead of graphic designer.

>> **Price and quality:** Budget-friendly/lower quality versus high-priced/premium quality

BE THEIR FAVORITE

Market positioning may sound like big-company stuff, but it's essential for all businesses. What makes you special to your personas has to be very clear, or they won't pay attention to you.

Imagine you run a successful solopreneur craft business selling your creations on eBay. You decide you need to hire an accounting firm and want someone local so you can meet face-to-face with the people handling your books. You search online for "CPAs near me" and find three options:

- The first one's tagline is "CPAs to the World."
- The second is "Helping Small and Medium Businesses Nationwide."
- The third is "Accounting Services for Solopreneurs and Freelancers in the Metro Area."

Which one are you likely to hire? The first one sounds expensive. The second sounds okay. But the third sounds perfect for you!

You've probably heard that limiting your target customers is one of the hardest things for solopreneurs to do, that it's counterintuitive and just seems like a bad idea. But you need to do it. And you'll likely experience a range of emotions as you narrow your target audience because, if you do it right, you'll do things that limit your appeal to the majority of people on Earth.

And that's a good thing.

Now for some examples. Imagine you're a photographer. You can position your business around what you do in several ways, such as these:

>> Portrait photography

>> Event photography

>> Real estate photography

>> Product photography

>> Macro photography

>> Aerial and drone photography

>> High-speed photography

Specializing in one or more of these areas makes you more attractive to clients seeking that specific service. But you can niche down further if you want by focusing on one or two aspects of the category you choose.

For example, Sarah Montani is a professional photographer who specializes in event photography. But she has niched down even further to only two types of events: weddings and bar/bat mitzvahs. Thanks to this focus, she has no trouble finding customers. Also, by focusing her business on just two events, she quickly became very skilled at photographing them, which led to happy customers early in her journey. That meant plenty of referrals.

If you're looking for someone to photograph your wedding and you live in her area, Sarah would likely make your short list (even though a wedding with drones does sound pretty cool).

Or a content creator can choose a particular industry to focus on, preferably one where they have deep knowledge. For example, Heather Murata owns EcoWellness Journeys, an online community focused on the connection between personal well-being and the health of the planet. While she has the skills to create content across a range of topics, this focus gives her a niche that serves her members well.

Positioning based on the pain points you solve

This can be a powerful dimension for positioning your business. When someone knows they have a pain point and comes across someone who specializes in relieving that pain, they take notice.

However, positioning based on pain points must be used with caution. You need to be able to find your personas out in the world. Sometimes, finding people with the pain point you solve is reasonably straightforward. For example, someone who coaches people with chronic neck pain to continue functioning may find online forums for people suffering from this physical issue. Further niching may not be needed (but is still probably helpful).

For most businesses, it's probably better to start with what you do and/or how you do it. Once you know you can find those people or businesses, you can niche down even further on a pain point and really get noticed.

For example, consider a fitness trainer who targets men between 40 and 55, but really focuses on those who want more energy. They're basically saying *no* to the six-pack crew and the big-muscle folks. But the 40- to 55-year-old man who wants to feel more energetic is instantly drawn to their offer. (Remember, knowing who your persona is *not* is as important as knowing who your persona is. See Chapter 8 for more about negative personas.)

Positioning based on how you do it

Sometimes, how you deliver your product or service matters just as much, if not more than, what you deliver. For solopreneurs, this can be your secret sauce. The way you work can build trust, make customers feel understood, and turn a one-time buyer into a long-term fan.

Here are a few ways you can stand out by focusing on how you do what you do:

>> **Your unique process or method:** Proprietary systems (for example, a trademarked coaching framework), cutting-edge technology, proven traditional methods (for example, classic carpentry techniques).

>> **Custom versus standard:** Custom or bespoke services versus off-the-shelf products. Do you tailor every project to each client, or do you offer a streamlined, consistent package?

>> **Delivery:** Online versus in-person, on-demand versus scheduled, one-on-one versus group offerings, do-it-yourself versus done-for-you.

>> **Customer experience and engagement:** Personal attention versus self-service/automated, personalized versus standardized.

>> **Speed:** You can uniquely position yourself by delivering your product or service faster than the competition. Just know that you'll have to have some way to do it faster than the competition besides giving up sleeping.

>> **Convenience:** If you can make buying from you or consuming your offering easier than your competitors, you can definitely stand out.

>> **Client involvement:** How much the client is involved in your process can be a differentiator. In some businesses, offering lots of involvement can be a plus for some people. In others, offering no involvement may be seen as a plus.

>> **Payment term:** If you offer more attractive payment terms than your competitors, this can be a way to stand out.

>> **Guarantees:** Offering a money-back guarantee can build trust and help you stand out.

An example of this is Zaid Ammari, a solopreneur consultant in pay-per-click (PPC) advertising. As a solopreneur, Zaid, an expert in PPC, can provide personalized attention. Larger agencies typically have the work done by less experienced employees. This results in better and faster results for Zaid's customers. He has fewer customers, but because he has lower overhead, he can position himself this way and still make money.

Deciding on Your Market Position

When choosing where to focus your business based on what you do, you have two major considerations:

>> What do you have credibility in?

>> What do you like doing?

In this section, we help you explore the answers to these questions.

Focusing on who you are

If you decide to make custom golf clubs for left-handed women under 5 feet tall, it would be helpful if you are either a left-handed woman under 5 feet tall or already have a lot of experience making custom golf clubs. That credibility, combined with a number of testimonials from happy left-handed female golfers under 5 feet tall, will position your business well (regardless of your height and dominant hand).

But just because you say you specialize in something (with the implication that you're good at it), it doesn't mean people will believe you. You need some way of proving it, either with years of industry experience or *social proof* (credibility through endorsements, testimonials, reviews, and the like) from trustworthy people. If you have the skill without any credibility yet, consider working for free for a few people in return for testimonials.

Homing in on what you like to do

If you focus your business on doing something you don't really like doing or working with people you don't like working with, you won't enjoy running your business, and that's usually not a good idea. This is why we include the ikigai exercise in Chapter 5, to help you drill down to the thing you love to do that you can build a business around.

Some people, however, put up with doing something they don't love (or don't even like) because it serves their goals effectively. Dave (not his real name) works with high-income clients in his coaching business. They aren't his favorite clients, but they can pay him enough money that working 30 hours per week gives him the flexibility to do what he wants with the rest of his time. So, it's worthwhile to him.

That said, if you can create a business that meets your goals *and* that you enjoy running, you will most certainly be happier.

Niching down to address demand

As you niche down, you're reducing the number of people interested in what you sell while becoming more attractive to the ones who are. By doing this, you may reduce the market for your product too much, and then you won't have enough demand to support your business. If this happens, think about ways you can expand your niche as you grow your business and put those ideas in your Solopreneur Action Plan.

TIP

Niching down too much almost *never* happens. Most of the time, solopreneurs don't niche down enough.

The bigger risk is too much demand. A lot of demand will attract a lot of competition, which makes it harder for you to stand out. Try to find a sweet spot between not enough and too much. When in doubt, aim for not enough (meaning you make yourself more attractive to fewer people but with less competition).

Separating yourself from your competition

As you go through this process of positioning, keep an eye on the competition you've identified. Effective positioning should make you stand out from them in some way that's meaningful to your personas.

Businesses often use certain analytical tools to assess how they are positioned compared to the competition. In the next sections, we discuss two that can be used by solopreneurs.

TIP

Graphs are helpful for some people and not helpful for others. If you find them useful, great! If not, no worries; just use the concepts we discuss to flesh out your ideas.

Using a quadrant analysis

One way to compare yourself to the competition is by doing a *quadrant analysis*, which looks at you and your competitors using two dimensions. These factors can be anything you like: quality, price, age; you name it.

Figure 10-1 shows an example of a quadrant analysis of a solopreneur coaching business targeting recent college graduates starting a side business along with their first job.

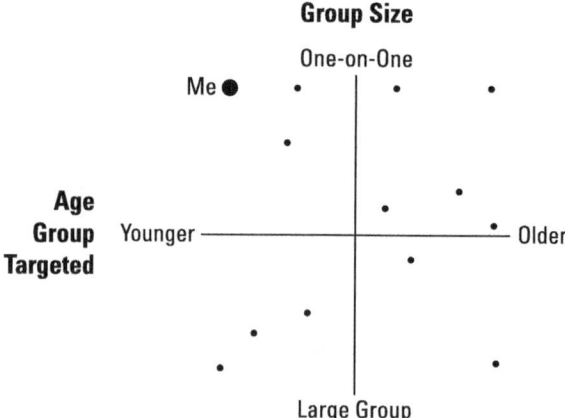

FIGURE 10-1: A quadrant analysis comparing a coaching business to the competition.

This coach had a list of competitors that were entrepreneurs and solopreneurs. One of the aspects of his persona is that they are recent college grads and therefore young. The quadrant analysis showed that no one was providing one-on-one coaching to the youngest cohort. This gave him an opportunity to stand out to that persona.

Exploring the blue ocean strategy

Using a quadrant analysis can be limiting because it's based on only two dimensions. Authors and business professors Chan Kim and Renée Mauborgne developed something called the *blue ocean strategy*. Although this strategy is geared toward large companies, it can be a helpful way for solopreneurs to identify ways of positioning their business.

Blue oceans are distinguished from red oceans in that the fish in red oceans are competing with/eating each other, and that makes the water red. (Yeah, we know, gross.) In blue oceans, there are no other fish, so the water is blue. You want to find a blue ocean for your business, so when your persona sees you, there's no one else to consider.

Figure 10-2 shows a blue ocean strategy canvas for the coaching business we describe in the previous section, and as you can see, it captures more detail. The basic idea is to go high where the competition goes low and low where the competition goes high. This means you've carved out a unique niche for yourself and positioned your business in a way that makes you the logical choice for your persona.

Testing your market position idea

Once you have an idea for how to niche down and position your business, you should give it a reality check. Go out and ask people about your newly positioned offering and your pricing (go to the next section for more information about setting a competitive price for your product/service). See how they feel about your idea. You don't need everyone to love it, but some people should.

Start by reaching out to people who match your personas, perhaps some that you spoke to in an earlier phase of your research. They can give you the best feedback. Talk to them directly and/or send them a survey.

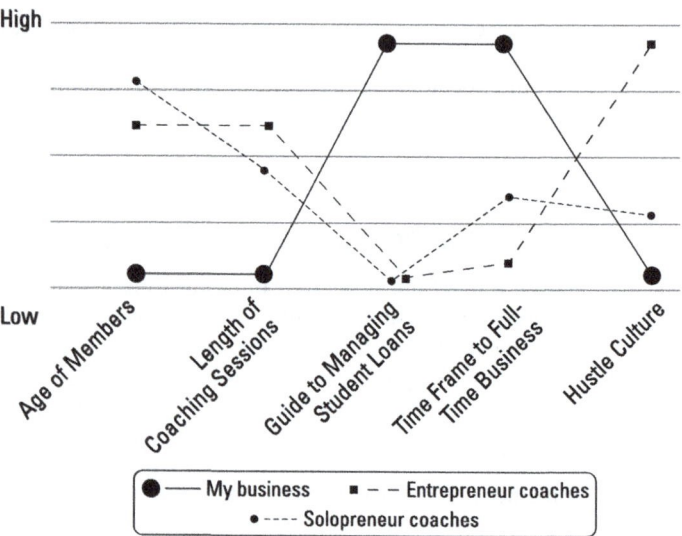

High

Low

Age of Members · Length of Coaching Sessions · Guide to Managing Student Loans · Time Frame to Full-Time Business · Hustle Culture

●——— My business   ■ – – Entrepreneur coaches
●---- Solopreneur coaches

FIGURE 10-2: A strategy canvas for a coaching business targeting new graduates who want to start a side-hustle business.

TIP

Locate in-person and/or online groups (think subreddits) related to what you plan to do and engage with their members. Find out if your ideas are intriguing to some of them.

Setting Your Prices to Be Competitive

Even if people like your product/service, they still need to be willing to pay your price. Chapter 9 helps you determine how to price your offering. Now that you've (hopefully) done some research on your target personas and you've spoken to some folks, you can assess whether your pricing plan seems acceptable.

If it does, that's good news. But if people feel your product/service is too cheap, listen to them and raise your prices. What if people say it's too expensive? Should you lower your prices?

Not yet.

WARNING

Attempting to win business by having a lower price than your competitors can be very tempting. However, this is often a bad idea for these reasons:

>> If you don't have some competitive advantage to produce your offering at a lower price than others, you'll lose money.

>> If your product/service is cheaper than similar offerings, yours may be perceived as lower quality.

At this point, you've made yourself special. Now it's time to make yourself even more special so that price is never the issue.

This chapter focuses on how you can make people feel that you're the perfect solution for them. Entrepreneur Alex Hormozi has taken this process to the next level. Here's a summary of his method:

1. **Identify the customer's dream outcome.**

You're helping people solve pain points. What does their dream outcome look like? For the side-hustle coach (in the "Separating yourself from your competition" section), it's something like *a successful side hustle they enjoy running that works with their new job and provides additional income*. What's your customer's dream outcome? Write it down.

2. **List potential problems.**

Write down all the reasons customers may feel your product/service won't work for them. Find as many as possible. For the side-hustle coach's customers, potential problems may include limited start-up capital, balancing time between a new job and a side hustle, lack of business experience, and uncertainty about viable side-hustle ideas.

3. **Develop solutions.**

For each of the problems, develop a solution. Give each solution a catchy name that conveys its value.

4. **Craft a compelling offer.**

Package up all your solutions into an offer (or offers) in a way that the customer's concerns are alleviated just by looking at them.

5. **Set a premium price.**

Price your offer based on the value it provides to your customer, ensuring it's profitable.

6. **Enhance demand.**

   Create scarcity by limiting the number of customers you serve in a given time period, creating waiting lists, or limiting supply some other way. Scarcity enhances demand, and demand enhances the price.

7. **Guarantee results.**

   Offer a strong guarantee to reduce buyer hesitation and demonstrate confidence in your product or service.

REMEMBER

Whether people will pay your current price or not, you always want to take the opportunity to help them decide to pay you more. This process involves some deep thinking, which is why most people don't do it. But it can make all the difference by increasing your attractiveness to your personas and allowing you to charge more than you would otherwise.

Setting Your Market Position in Stone (for Now)

When you've been through all the exercises and processes in this chapter, make a final (at least for now) decision on how you'll position your product or service. Then be sure to document the following information in your Solopreneur Action Plan:

>> All the categories you're using to niche down and how you're positioning your product/service in those categories

>> Your personas' dream outcome

>> Your personas' potential problems with your offering

>> Your solutions to your personas' problems

>> Your compelling offer package

>> Your new (higher) price

>> Your plan for creating scarcity

>> Your guarantee to your customers

Remember that using the Solopreneur Success Cycle means you can revisit your positioning in the future. So don't get too hung up on it. You now have a much better plan than most solopreneurs do when they're getting started.

Refining Your Product (or Service) to Match Your Market Position

In going through the positioning process, you may have made some changes that require you to update your product or service. Look over your work and take the following steps as necessary (and document any changes in your Solopreneur Action Plan):

>> Update your product (or service) description to match your new, improved offering.

>> Run a check against your goals to make sure you haven't made any changes that will harm your ability to achieve them.

>> Make sure this is still a solo business.

Chapter **11**

Creating Your Messaging and Brand

Peple often associate branding with a clever slogan or creative logo, but there's so much more to it than those obvious elements. Creating your messaging and branding is a pivotal task in building and running your business (and in the Solopreneur Success Cycle, it falls under Phase 1, Step 2: Planning your business).

Messaging and branding are about creating a story that resonates with your audience and then communicating that narrative to your potential customers. In this chapter, we focus on the importance of crafting your message, understanding your audience's story, and defining your brand.

We were once advising a solopreneur on the connection between brand, messaging, and story, and typed the prompt into ChatGPT to help clarify our explanation. We were shocked at how well it summarized our message. Here are the analogies it generated:

>> Your brand is your identity.
>> Your messaging is your voice.
>> Your story is your heartbeat.

Not bad for a robot, right? By aligning all three of these ingredients, you can better connect with your audience and stand out in a crowded market.

Defining Your Brand

A brand is more than just how things look. It's your identity and the perception people have of what you do. If we're getting deep about it, it's the way your business makes your audience feel.

Unfortunately, creating a brand is a step that many solopreneurs skip because it can take time that many people don't feel like they have. However, strong branding is one of the most important aspects of success. The components of a brand include

>> The personality and tone of your business

>> Visual design elements, such as your logo, colors, and typography (the style and appearance of your written material)

>> Your business name

>> Product design (when applicable)

Keep the pain points you've identified in mind as you create each of these components.

Creating a tone and personality for your business

As a solopreneur, you are your brand. Like it or not, people aren't just buying what you're selling. In a way, they're also buying you: the value you provide, the solutions you offer, what you bring to the table, and your personality.

As you think through what this looks like, think of the vibe you're trying to give off to your audience. Are you relatable? Authoritative? Funny? Serious? Because you're a solopreneur, your business's brand and your personal brand are synonymous, so align your business branding with who you are. Don't try to be somebody you're not, but shape your brand's personality around your own.

Think deeply through your values and whom you want to connect with, and let those be your North Star as you develop the tone and personality of your brand.

Developing visual design elements

In today's digital world, solopreneurs have easy access to a variety of templates, stock photography, and visual tools online. These can be huge time-savers, which is why it's tempting to lean on them heavily. While using these resources to build your brand can be beneficial, we recommend doing so sparingly and intentionally. You don't want it to be obvious you're using the same popular visuals as everyone else (this is increasingly common with repetitive website templates).

The visual elements of your business — like photography, fonts, color palettes, graphics, iconography, and even textures — should feel unique and authentic to your brand. But don't confuse "unique" with "complex." Simplicity is powerful. A clean, authentic look often connects better than something overly polished or cluttered. Let your visual branding be guided by:

>> **Your audience:** What would resonate with them? What makes them feel seen or understood?

>> **Your company's personality:** Is it bold and edgy? Calm and grounded? Quirky and fun?

>> **Your unique selling proposition:** What sets you apart, and how can your visuals reflect that?

Let those be your guiding lights and explore the visuals that best represent each component.

TIP

Your visuals don't need to be perfect. DIY photography or video shot on your phone can be incredibly effective — especially if it feels real and relatable. Consider including brand photography of yourself, not just your product or service. A few high-quality, natural shots of you in your work environment or interacting with your product can go a long way in building trust and connection. If a professional shoot isn't in the budget, enlist a friend with a good eye and good lighting. You may feel vulnerable or self-conscious at first, but that's normal.

Naming your business

What an exciting part of your solopreneur journey! You may feel a lot of pressure in this phase of your start-up, but remember, your name isn't necessarily set in stone.

Here are several tips to keep in mind as you think of the perfect name for your business:

>> **Evoke emotion.** If a name arouses emotion in your audience, run with it. Being able to make your audience feel something is a superpower that you'll want to harness.

>> **Keep it simple.** A lot of people prefer to take the creative route when naming their business, but be careful. You want to make things as easy as possible for your audience, so choose a name that's associated with what you do and/or who you are.

>> **Include keywords (sparingly).** The world of search engine optimization (SEO), where businesses use certain words or phrases in an attempt to improve their online visibility, is such a weird place and is constantly changing. We generally don't recommend relying on keywords as a top strategy for solopreneurs. However, if you include keywords in your name, you'll have a better chance at showing up in search results when somebody types in the services you provide.

>> **Make it memorable.** You also want your name to be memorable and easy to pronounce and spell (potential customers won't remember it if they can't say or spell it). Again, the easier you make it for your audience to keep you top of mind, the better.

>> **Avoid trends.** Trends come and go, and just because they may mean something to your audience during your launch, it doesn't mean they always will. Think of a name that can grow with your business and ride any waves you may have to weather.

TIP

Create a short list of names, and before you do anything else, make sure no other business has claimed them and you don't have to consider any legal issues (like trademarks). But don't worry too much about this. For example, LifeStar is a company that supplies medical emergency transport helicopters. A company that adds an r to *star* and helps solopreneurs isn't at risk of being confused with a medical transport business, so it wasn't a problem for LifeStarr.

Once your potential names are in the clear, start testing them with people in your audience. Get a gut check from friends and family. You may think you have a winner, but until you run it by others, you won't know if that's true or not.

136   PART 3 **Building Your Solopreneur Business**

REMEMBER

Your business name is so much more than just a label for your company and what you put on your business card. It's also how you strategically communicate your value to your audience and position yourself in the market.

Tying product design into branding (when applicable)

When it comes to developing a solid brand, consistency is key. If you can tie your product design into the rest of your branding efforts, you're one step ahead of many of your competitors. For example, if your brand uses a minimalist aesthetic with neutral tones, consider using similar visuals in your product packaging. A wellness brand focused on sustainability might use biodegradable materials that match its visual identity online. The more you can reinforce your brand throughout all areas of your business, the more recognizable you'll be, and the more cohesive your audience's experience will be. Your brand is what ties all areas of your business together, so make it strong!

Getting help with your branding

If branding isn't your strong suit, all of this may seem overwhelming. But, as we often say, flying solo in business doesn't mean you're alone . . . so ask for help! Here are a few ideas:

>> **Partner up.** Agencies that specialize in marketing and branding can be expensive. Consider working with another

solopreneur who focuses on branding and messaging. If your services are complementary, consider a trade. Many solopreneurs start off operating on a shoestring budget, but they can still make a big splash by teaming up with the right partners.

>> **Do it on your own, but don't reinvent the wheel.** Design platforms like Canva can be very helpful for people with minimal experience who want to give branding and design a go.

>> **Ask for feedback.** Once you feel like your brand is in a good place, ask others about their first impressions and what kind of emotions you've evoked. Ask yourself if you're getting the response you're hoping for, and if not, rethink your approach.

REMEMBER

When it comes to branding and messaging, you have a lot to think about. Crafting a brand doesn't need to be overwhelming; in fact, this should be an enjoyable phase of your solo journey. How cool is it that you get to create an entire identity for a business? Don't stress over it, but do be intentional. You'll be glad you took the time to come up with the right story for your business.

Talking About Your Customer, Not You

Aside from directly insulting its customers, one of the biggest mistakes a business can make is focusing too much on itself instead of addressing the needs and interests of its audience.

You may have a great story that led you to your amazing product or service, and you can't wait to share it with the world. But here's the thing, and this is something many solopreneurs struggle with: Nobody cares about what you do; they only care that you solve a problem they have (in other words, their *pain point*).

TIP

This may sound repetitive — and even somewhat harsh — but until it truly sinks in, it's always worth repeating: At the end of the day, the only thing your customers are asking themselves is "What's in it for me?" If the answer to that question isn't immediately clear to them, they're probably going to move on to a company that *can* solve their pain point (or at least claims that they can).

People are incredibly busy and are constantly flooded with messaging from outside influences. They want to be able to easily make decisions with limited stress and without being overwhelmed, and as a business owner, you need to help them do that.

Think about it this way: Nobody likes being on a date with a person who only talks about themself (yes, we're using the same dating analogy we use in Chapter 8). You must show genuine interest in the person you're with — or in this case, the audience you're trying to attract to your business.

Focusing On Your Customer's Pain Points

Fully grasping and understanding your audience's pain points will get you nowhere if you can't, through your branding and messaging, show that audience you actually understand their pain. And, more important, that you can ease that pain.

You may be tempted to talk about all your products and services, boast about your accolades, and declare why you're the best of the best. Who doesn't want to point out what they've achieved? But until you address their pain points, people just won't care about any of that.

You need to clearly demonstrate that you understand your potential customers' struggles so they believe that what you're offering is the best solution for them.

Addressing their problems can elicit various emotions from your audience, and that's a good thing. You want to make them feel something when they interact with your business. You may even trigger some discomfort, but that's also beneficial, because you can quickly communicate how to make it go away.

TIP

Write down all the pain points you address, and next to each one, explain how you solve it — and be specific. Having this information readily available will help you craft your messaging and a story that will resonate with your audience and stand out among your competition.

Writing Your Customer's Story

There's a time and place for your story, and telling it can help build your credibility and authority, but it's not at the beginning of your engagement with your audience. As mentioned, when people first come across your business, they need to feel like the hero, because they really only care about themselves.

You must integrate your offering and its value into *your customer's* narrative, not your own. You essentially want to guide your audience from where they are now to where you will take them.

Donald Miller, a bestselling author and business consultant known for his StoryBrand framework, has a concept that explains this process well. In a nutshell, you have:

>> A character (your customer)

>> Who has a problem (pain point)

>> And meets a guide (you/your business)

>> Who gives them a plan (clear next steps)

>> And calls them to action (to take the desired step)

>> Which helps them avoid failure (what happens if they don't solve their problem)

>> And ends in success (the positive outcome)

Do you see how much more impactful that is than gabbing about your products and their features?

TIP

Give this approach a shot. Try a few different stories and see which one resonates with your audience the most. Then write it in your Solopreneur Action Plan.

You can spend all your energy on branding and messaging, but as a solopreneur, you don't have a lot of time. Get the narrative to a place where it speaks to your audience and allows you to build connections. In the beginning, dedicate a solid week or so to really thinking through your customer's story and make sure you feel good about the messaging and branding that goes along with it.

TIP

Once you've put your message out there, revisit your branding efforts quarterly to make sure everything still resonates with your audience and your values, and change things up when necessary.

Chapter **12**

Building an Effective Marketing Strategy

After speaking with thousands of solopreneurs, one thing is clear to us: marketing, especially lead generation, is a common challenge on the path to solo success. *Lead generation* is a part of marketing focused on capturing potential client or customer interest, often by collecting contact info or prompting engagement. Marketing as a whole includes this, but also covers strategy, messaging, research, and so on, to deliver and communicate value.

You may feel overwhelmed by the countless marketing strategies and tactics you can choose to implement in your business. If you can't get your idea (which may be the best business idea in the world) in front of the right people and explain it in a way that resonates with them, you're in trouble. So, in this chapter we whittle everything down to basic concepts that are easy to understand and make marketing feel more approachable and exciting.

REMEMBER

These concepts fall under Phase 1, Step 2: Planning your business of the Solopreneur Success Cycle (see Chapter 2).

Unlocking the Secret of Marketing

When people talk about marketing, it's common to dive right into which tactics and mediums to use to get your message out there. As tempting as it is to get the ball rolling, you must start with strategy first. Tactics and tools come and go, but a good marketing strategy can pivot with new platforms and technologies.

Much of our thinking around this topic is heavily inspired by the ideas of storyteller and marketing expert Jay Acunzo, whose work has shaped how we approach trust, resonance, and emotional connection in marketing. With that in mind, we believe solopreneurs should follow five essential steps to market effectively:

1. **Build trust.** Show up consistently and authentically to establish credibility with your target audience.

2. **Create resonance.** Speak directly to your audience's experiences, pain points, values, and aspirations so they feel seen and understood.

3. **Establish desire.** Show what's possible with your product or service in a way that connects emotionally with your audience.

4. **Inspire action.** Make it clear, easy, and compelling for your audience to take the next step and convert to a client or customer.

5. **Repeat the process.** Your marketing efforts will always be evolving and improving. Keep learning, refining, and reaching new people.

REMEMBER

These steps only work if you get in front of the right audience, which is why you must clearly understand who they are. We go into this in great detail in Chapter 8.

Step 1: Build trust

Easier said than done, right? Here's the thing, though: If a potential customer doesn't trust you, it's going to be really hard to get them to buy from you.

You can build trust in the following ways:

>> **Be valuable — consistently.** Continue to show up for your customers/clients and provide the help they need to solve their *pain points* (the problems they want your product/ service to resolve).

>> **Be your own business (and person).** Instead of following trends, focus on what you do best and share your expertise with your customers. This helps you show you're authentic and not just following what others are doing.

>> **Be human.** In a world where people commonly interact with AI, showing your human side and expressing your emotions can go a long way. Be relatable and vulnerable. People are more likely to trust you if they see you as a person and not a faceless business.

Step 2: Create resonance

Even if somebody trusts you, that doesn't mean they feel deeply connected to you. If you really want to build lasting relationships with your audience, you need to establish a real emotional connection with them. Aim for the "this is exactly what I've been feeling" reaction. If a person feels you truly understand them, rather than just see them as a number on a spreadsheet, they'll be much more likely to buy from you.

Actually, you should prioritize creating *resonance* over *reach* (yet another phrase inspired by Acunzo). Think quality over quantity.

You'll be amazed how far one-on-one conversations (and speaking your customer's language) can take you and your business. Don't hide behind your computer screen sending out emails and social media posts. Get out there and talk to your audience. Show them you're a real human they can relate to.

REMEMBER

Many solopreneurs don't need a ton of clients to have a successful business. If you're one of those people, connecting with others should come before any other marketing campaigns or tactics.

Step 3: Establish desire

Isn't that the goal of every business? To make your audience want what you're selling?

But how do you do that?

Purchasing something can often be more of an emotional decision than a practical one. Everyone has experienced this, even if they didn't realize or understand it at the time. Well-known, respected marketer Nancy Harhut, who specializes in applying behavioral science to marketing strategy, uses psychological triggers for her clients that can influence purchasing and increase desire. Some of these include

>> **The principle of scarcity:** People want things more when they think those things are in limited supply. Make potential customers think time is running out to acquire your goods and services.

>> **Loss aversion:** Ever heard of FOMO (fear of missing out)? Framing your offer in a way that shows customers what they'll miss out on as opposed to what they'll gain can be very effective.

>> **The authority principle:** People trust experts. So, be the expert and show your customers that you are.

>> **Commitment and consistency:** Encourage micro commitments leading up to the big purchase. People will be more engaged if they've already bought into the idea in one way or another.

Ask yourself how you can apply some of these triggers to your messaging to create more of an impact.

Step 4: Inspire action

You'd think that after the first three steps a potential customer would be ready to buy what you're selling, but the reality is, once all that's said and done, you still have to make the ask — and make it clear what that ask is. In other words, give your customer a clear *call to action* spelling out what you want them to do, like making a purchase, signing up for a free trial, booking a call, or downloading a resource.

REMEMBER

Make the desired action as easy for your customer to take as possible. Any barriers (like a complicated checkout process) that get in the way can result in a lost sale.

It's not uncommon for people to need several nudges and reminders to make a purchase, so be sure to reach them in different ways, like email, social media, or your website. These are called *touchpoints*, and having multiple ones helps keep your business top of mind.

Step 5: Repeat Steps 1 through 4

By following these steps, you'll be able to create a marketing process that's much less salesy, and much more trustworthy and relationship-building. For solopreneurs with limited time, a sound strategy mixed with an emotional connection can lead to excellent results!

As you think through these strategic guidelines and principles, consider your buyer's journey (see Chapter 8), which includes the following stages:

>> Awareness

>> Consideration

>> Decision

>> Delight/Retention

You'll want to implement marketing efforts across these four areas. To do that, you'll align specific content to each phase, which is known as *content mapping*.

Become a good storyteller. Mastering this craft creates emotional responses, builds trust, and makes you more memorable. We discuss storytelling when we talk about branding in Chapter 11, but keep your customer's story in mind with all your marketing efforts. It's a great way to stand out among your competition.

Acknowledging Lead Generation Is Different for Solopreneurs

Before we dive into marketing tactics that solopreneurs should be aware of, we wanted to highlight the importance of continuous lead generation and why solopreneurs need to approach it differently than other companies, because lead generation really is the lifeblood of any one-person business.

Even when your list of clients is full, you should never stop generating leads. Too often, solopreneurs get a handful of clients and then only focus on client work, only to be left high and dry when those clients decide to leave . . . because clients *will* come and go.

To avoid the feast or famine cycle, and the scramble that comes along with it, you must keep lead generation front and center of your business. Plus, the more leads you have coming in, the more selective you can be with your clients, which is always a nice luxury.

Solopreneurs don't have big teams devoted to large marketing campaigns. Big business lead generation tactics don't often apply to one-person businesses. What we've found is that solopreneurs are most successful with personalized relationship-driven marketing. Networking is absolutely key and a few approaches that have been most successful for individuals include:

>> **Informing your current network about what you do:** Make sure they're clearly aware of what you offer so that they can help spread the word for you.

>> **Getting involved with niche communities:** Whether online or in person, become active and helpful in these communities to establish yourself as an authority in your space. The more trustworthy and reliable you are in these groups, the more likely you'll be to become their go-to expert.

>> **Being active in your local community:** This doesn't have to be work-related. Being seen as a helpful presence in your area naturally attracts clients who want to work with someone they know, like, and trust.

>> **Partnering up:** Find other complementary businesses and collaborate with them to help you reach new audiences who are aligned with what you offer . . . plus, you can share the workload with the other business!

For solopreneurs, lead gen is less about casting a wide net, and more about making meaningful connections over time. That doesn't mean you need to limit all of your marketing efforts to just networking, so we list other marketing tactics to consider to supplement these efforts — keep reading!

Understanding Marketing Tactics — and Which to Use (or Not)

As you build out your marketing strategy, keep the following points that are relevant for many solopreneurs in mind:

>> **Your time (and potentially your budget) is limited.** Prioritize high-impact tactics (like networking with people in your target audience and repurposing content) that are low cost and don't take a lot of time.

>> **You are your business.** You've spent time thinking through your personal brand (see Chapter 11), so don't forget to showcase it in your marketing efforts.

>> **Get really good at a few marketing channels.** These *channels* are the platforms or methods you use to reach your audience, like Instagram, email newsletters, or podcasting. Get good at a couple of channels, then streamline your efforts to expand to more (if desired).

>> **You should automate and delegate wherever you can.** If you aren't a marketing consultant, think of ways to take some of these tasks off your plate so you can focus on the aspects of your business that rely on your attention and expertise.

TIP

As great as automation and outsourcing can be for your business, it's usually more effective to first get really clear on your approach and processes on your own. Then, once you know what's working, you can explore marketing automation tools or bring in external support. You can find a list of these tools at www.dummies.com/go/solopreneurbusinessfd.

Review the marketing tactics in the tables that follow. We've organized them into categories, from those we strongly recommend you use, to ones we suggest you avoid. For the first two tables, we include how the tactic works as it relates to the buyer's journey (see Chapter 8).

This information is meant to get your creative juices flowing and help you put a plan in place. In Chapter 17, we dive into how to execute these tactics and best practices to follow.

Table 12-1 shows the marketing tactics we recommend you strongly consider. These are tactics often used by solopreneurs.

TABLE 12-1 Marketing Tactics for Solopreneurs
to Strongly Consider

Tactic	How It Works	Buyer's Journey Uses
Networking	Building relationships with other people and businesses in an effort to increase referrals, collaborations, leads, and sales	Helpful at every phase of the buyer's journey; it builds awareness as you get in front of new people, fosters trust during consideration, and helps close deals when people are ready to buy
Content marketing	Using content, like videos or written articles, to attract, convert, and keep clients or customers	Helpful at every phase; use it to attract new people, educate them in the consideration phase, and reinforce trust when they're ready to buy
Social proof	Using trust-building tools like testimonials, case studies, and reviews to build credibility with potential clients or customers	Decision phase; reinforces credibility and confidence when someone is close to buying
Email marketing	Connecting, building trust, and converting potential customers using email	Nurtures relationships from the first interaction to conversion, while delivering value, building trust, and inspiring action throughout
Educational webinars and virtual events	Showing expertise and value in an effort to generate leads through engaging virtual presentations	Great during consideration to offer helpful insights that position you as a trusted expert and authority
Organic social media marketing	Building brand awareness by sharing valuable content and information on social media platforms without paid promotion	Increases visibility in the awareness phase and builds trust throughout the journey when posting consistently and authentically
Referral marketing	Using customer recommendations to attract new clients (done for free or using incentives for current clients)	Key in the decision phase; gives buyers trusted recommendations from people they know
Warm calling	Engaging potential customers who have already expressed interest in your product or service or whom you have an existing relationship with	Most effective at the Decision stage, as you reach out to interested leads with a personal touch that can lead to a sale

Table 12-2 shows the marketing tactics solopreneurs sometimes use that we urge you to consider.

TABLE 12-2 Marketing Tactics for Solopreneurs to Consider

Tactic	How It Works	Buyer's Journey Uses
Public relations	Boosting credibility and visibility through media coverage and managing your brand's public image	Impactful in reaching new audiences early in the journey, while also reinforcing trust as people evaluate and consider your business
Search engine optimization (SEO)	Optimizing content, keywords, and technical elements to get found online and at the top of search engine results	Helps people discover you when they're searching online; guides them from initial awareness to deeper consideration as they research to find a solution
Local SEO*	Using local keywords, directories, and listings (such as Google Business Profiles) to boost ranking in your geographical area in search engine results	Works the same as SEO but focuses on your location, making it easier for nearby potential customers to find and consider you
Podcasting	Recording and distributing audio content via podcast platforms in an effort to educate and entertain your audience in a flexible and engaging format	Raises awareness and keeps your brand top of mind as potential customers consider their options
Podcast guesting	Showcasing your expertise and insights on other people's podcasts to increase your audience, awareness, and conversions without having to produce episodes yourself	Expands your reach and helps drive both awareness and intent, especially when the podcast audience is aligned with your values and solutions
Influencer marketing	Collaborating with brands or individuals who have a large following to promote your business to their audience (The business often pays or does trades with the influencer to get exposure)	Builds awareness and interest, and influences buying decisions since the influencer is often already trusted by its followers

*Local SEO is applicable only for businesses who target people within their geographic area.

(continued)

TABLE 12-2 *(continued)*

Tactic	How It Works	Buyer's Journey Uses
Event marketing	Hosting in-person or virtual events to engage and educate your audience while building rapport (Events don't have to be large to make an impact)	Builds trust in the awareness phase and deepens connections throughout the journey
Paid advertising and pay-per-click (PPC) adverting	Paid advertising gets your business in front of a virtual audience (through banner ads, for example) or print audience (through magazine ads, for example). For solopreneurs, PPC can be relatively affordable because you pay only when a person clicks on your ad (hence the name).	Boost visibility and awareness, while also delivering targeted messages that guide prospects through the journey
Affiliate marketing	A strategy where you either promote another company's product or service and earn a commission for each sale generated through your efforts or offer your own products or services for others to promote and pay them a commission for each successful sale they sent your way	Trusted affiliates introduce your offering to their audiences and their promotion helps drive conversions by providing social proof
Direct mail	Sending physical promotional materials via regular mail	Grabs attention and can spark curiosity, provide value, or influence action, depending on how it's used

Not every tactic listed in Table 12-2 is right for every solopreneur or every stage of business. Start with what aligns best with your goals, audience, and resources. Tactics like networking or organic social media are often lower-cost ways to build awareness while you refine your message. As your business grows, you can add more strategies that support and grow what's already working.

WARNING

Finally, Table 12-3 shows the marketing tactics we recommend you use with caution or avoid altogether.

TABLE 12-3 Marketing Tactics for Solopreneurs to Avoid or Use Cautiously

Tactic	How It Works	Cons
Cold calling	Reaching out to people who haven't shown interest in your product or service	Cold calling *can* be effective, but it takes a lot of time that solopreneurs may not have. Used incorrectly, it can come off as spammy. Use cautiously.
Buying followers	Paying for fake or inactive accounts to artificially inflate your social media following to appear more popular than you are	Follower count is a vanity metric; if followers don't convert, it doesn't matter how many followers you have. Many sites penalize you for doing this. Avoid it.
List purchasing	Buying lists of potential leads rather than growing a contact list organically	These lists often contain outdated or inaccurate contact information. This tactic can lead to spam complaints and legal issues. Avoid it.
Spamming (intentionally or not)	Using unsolicited or invasive messaging to get your audience's attention	Spamming damages your brand reputation and leads to lower trust and fewer leads and customers. Avoid it.
Clickbait marketing	Using attention-grabbing headlines to get people to click and then not delivering on what was promised in the messaging	Misleading tactics may get attention but often lead to disappointment, high bounce rates, and fewer real leads and customers. Avoid it.
Following trends for no reason	Jumping on popular marketing tactics or trends on social platforms just because others are doing it, without regard for your own strategy or brand	If trends don't resonate with your audience, you're just wasting your time. If certain trends work with your audience, give it a shot, but use cautiously.

Tailoring Your Marketing Tactics to Your Needs

As we note in the preceding section, you can choose from a variety of marketing tactics, but don't worry — you don't need to pursue all of them. In fact, we highly recommend that you don't. Keep your goals and your audience in mind as you think through your options. You should be realistic about how much time and effort you can put into your marketing efforts. Start small and choose just a couple of tactics. You can always add to your initial tactics, but you don't want to burn out from the get-go.

Marketing can get expensive, but it doesn't have to be! Organic social media and email marketing, for example, can be totally free (other than the time you spend on them). Alternatively, influencer marketing and paid advertising can get pricey depending on the channels (Instagram, YouTube, Google), and popularity of the influencer you select. But, they can also be effective more quickly.

Setting a monthly marketing budget can help you decide which marketing tactics to use in the beginning. As your business and marketing dollars grow, the types of marketing you decide to implement may change as well. So, just because you can't afford an influencer at the beginning, that doesn't mean you'll never be able to!

TIP

Keep your own strengths and weaknesses in mind. The purpose of the Solopreneur Success Cycle is to create not only a successful business, but one you enjoy running. So which marketing tactics light you up? Which would you enjoy doing? Which do you have previous experience in or an idea of how to manage? If you're a good writer, perhaps focus on tactics involving that skill. Do you like recording video? Consider starting there.

REMEMBER

You don't need to reinvent the wheel. See what's working for your competitors, and what isn't, and fill in the gaps.

Knowing the Importance of Your Website

We can't talk about marketing without mentioning your website, which can be the hub that all your marketing drives to. Many solopreneurs survive off word of mouth and often look at their website simply as a digital business card, but this is a mistake.

Regardless of how someone finds out about you, one of the first things they'll do is research your business online. If they come across a dated website (or worse, can't find you because you have no website at all), it decreases your credibility and doesn't give a great first impression.

Too often, solopreneurs focus on working for their clients and customers and neglect their own business's needs. Keeping your website up-to-date and appealing for your audience may not be at the top of your priority list, but that needs to change. You should view your website as a dynamic tool that works hard for your business, not a static landing page. It should support the goals you've set for yourself. Use it to

>> **Show your unique value proposition and brand personality.** Let the visitor know who you are and what you offer for them immediately through storytelling, clear messaging, and visuals.

>> **Establish trust and show authority and credibility.** Prove you're the go-to expert by featuring testimonials, certifications, credentials, press mentions, and so on.

>> **Generate leads.** Provide clear and prominent calls to action along with lead capture forms (to collect contact info, like email addresses), throughout your website.

On top of that, make sure your site is:

>> **Optimized for search.** Get the basics down (see implementation in Chapter 17) as you build your site.

>> **Functional.** This depends on the kind of business you run, but can include insuring payment functionality is set up, post-purchase product delivery is ready, calendar booking tools are available, and so on.

>> **Secure and compliant.** Do your research on current HTTPS, cookie notices, and privacy policies, which all assist with keeping your website, and its visitors, safe.

>> **Set up with analytics tracking.** You can find tutorials on YouTube and across the web for how to implement analytics on your website so that you can learn from the activity on it. For a list of analytics tools we recommend implementing, visit www.dummies.com/go/solopreneurbusinessfd.

TIP

As you plan your website, look at how other people with similar businesses have done it to help you generate ideas.

Chapter **13**

Defining Your Sales Process

Your sales process should be just that . . . a process. Without a process that matches your offering and your target customers, you end up with a sales effort that's both time-consuming and ineffective, an unsustainable combination, especially for solopreneurs.

This doesn't mean your sales process has to be complicated. As a solopreneur, you need it to be as simple as possible, just not any simpler. If you haven't done the following activities, you need to complete them before working through this chapter. These are key steps in building your sales process:

>> Identifying your *persona*, or ideal customer (Chapter 8)

>> Understanding their problem (Chapter 8)

>> Developing a lead-generation strategy (Chapter 12)

>> Setting your prices (Chapter 10)

>> Defining the buyer's journey (Chapter 8)

>> Positioning your business (Chapter 10)

>> Crafting a compelling offer to maximize value (Chapter 10)

All these activities inform your sales process and prepare you for the next five steps:

>> Deciding how much *touch* (contact with customers) to put in your sales process

>> Creating your sales pitch

>> Determining how you'll qualify sales leads

>> Creating your contracts

>> Developing how you'll document sales

This chapter continues guiding you through the process of planning your business (it falls under Phase 1, Step 2 of the Solopreneur Success Cycle). We can't emphasize strongly enough that selling is one of the most crucial aspects of any business, although it's one that solopreneurs tend to shy away from. Selling your product/services doesn't have to be sleazy or scary, which is why we start this chapter with a short section debunking some common myths about selling. You may never love it, but you'll find that you can do it. We then walk you through the five steps to building your sales process.

REMEMBER

Marketing is about *attracting* potential customers. Sales is about *converting* them into a customer. Marketing says, "Hey, look at me!" Sales says, "So, let's sign you up today?"

Overcoming Your Fear of Selling

For many solopreneurs, selling their offering (whether it's a product or a service) makes the list of least desirable activities. But you have to sell your offering, or your business won't last very long. Here are some commonly held but incorrect beliefs about selling, along with the truth, which we hope will make you feel good about sales:

>> **Being able to sell is an innate talent.** Many solopreneurs believe they're not natural salespeople, assuming that selling is talent you're born with rather than a skill you can develop. Selling *is* a skill and anyone can figure out how to do it. Many highly effective salespeople are not effortlessly outgoing.

>> **Selling is sleazy.** The thought of selling your offering may conjure images of pushy used car salesmen. But when you genuinely help your customers solve a problem, sales become an act of service, not manipulation.

>> **Rejection is a sign of failure.** But being rejected is actually a good thing because it tells you precisely what the customer needs to hear before they buy. Instead of fearing rejection, use it as a guide to adjust your pitch.

>> **"Asking" for money is awkward.** This is especially true if you doubt the value of your offering. When a customer (and you) truly believes your product or service can solve their problem, they'll want to exchange their money for that product or service. And that's a fair trade.

The idea is not to sell to people but to help them buy. If you're talking to people who have a *pain point* (a problem that needs a solution) and they see that you can solve that pain point, they'll want to buy from you. The rest of this chapter focuses on helping you to design your sales process. Chapter 18 digs more deeply into the actual process of selling.

Determining How Much Touch Is in Your Sales Process

We don't like it when salespeople touch us! But don't worry, that's not what we're talking about here. In this case, *touch* refers to how much interaction you have with a potential customer. If you have a number of face-to-face meetings with a customer before closing the sale, that's a *high-touch sale.* If a customer orders something from your website and the item is shipped from the manufacturer, that's a *no-touch sale.* A *low-touch sale*, where you may communicate with the customer via email or have just a single voice or video call, falls in between these two.

The amount of touch you put in your sale has a significant impact on your sales process. And your price point and profit margin have a lot to do with how much touch you can afford to incorporate. More revenue and profit allow for more touch. Less revenue and profit allow for less touch.

Another factor is the number of deals you close. If you close only 1 in 20 sales opportunities, spending a lot of time on each one won't give you much time to actually produce your product or service.

High-touch selling

High-touch sales involve a great deal of work before you close the deal. You'll do things like

>> **Contract negotiations:** This may involve legal fees and lots of time.

>> **Customization of your product/service:** You may need to determine how you will adapt your offering to each customer's needs as part of the sales process.

>> **Customized demonstrations:** You may need to tailor your presentation for each prospect.

>> **Customer onboarding:** You may spend a good deal of effort getting customers up and running.

>> **Free consultations:** You may need to prove yourself by engaging in work for the client before you have a deal.

>> **Meetings:** These may involve in-person contact with individual prospects and/or virtual contact with groups of potential customers.

>> **Proposals:** Your sales process may require putting together extensive documentation.

High-touch sales need to be profitable because you'll be doing a lot of work to close them, and the hours you invest need to pay off.

This kind of selling is appropriate for

Coaching and consulting	High-end freelance services
Boutique agency owners	Private trainers and therapists
High-end personal services	Business advisors
Custom product–based businesses	Other high-end products and services

TIP

If you think that high-touch selling is right for your offering but are concerned about how much time it will take, you can find ways to reduce your effort in the future. High-touch sales in the early days can help you discover valuable information about your customers. Later, you can do things like

>> Creating an automated lead qualification form on your website to identify prosects that are a poot fit before you engage.

>> Creating standardized packages that meet your best customers' needs.

>> Outsource parts of your sales process to a contractor.

Low-touch selling

In a low-touch sales process, you're still interacting with customers but spending much less time per customer. This may mean communicating via email or another kind of messaging, or making a single voice or video call. Low-touch selling often involves these kinds of activities:

>> **Automation:** Using computerized invoicing and payment systems

>> **Messaging:** Answering questions via *chatbot* (an interactive computer program that imitates a human), email, or *support tickets* (requests customers submit, which are tracked in a helpdesk system, allowing you to respond efficiently)

>> **No negotiating:** Setting fixed prices and transparent terms

>> **Online purchasing:** Enabling direct online purchases with minimal human interaction

>> **Package deals:** Offering preset service packages to avoid custom quotes

>> **Promotions:** Offering discounts, limited-time promotions, or free trials

This reduction in time spent closing deals is usually appropriate for lower–price–point businesses like these:

Online course creators	Content services like creating blog posts
Group coaching programs	
E-commerce (sometimes, for example, live chat to close the deal)	Local service providers like a dog waste remover or plumber
Membership-based communities	

No-touch selling

No-touch selling, when you don't spend any time directly interacting with customers, is obviously the most adaptable approach to selling.

In no-touch selling, your sales process may involve

>> **Automated emails:** Prewritten email campaigns can educate and convert buyers.

>> **Automated order fulfillment:** The product is delivered without human intervention.

>> **Customer reviews:** Hearing from satisfied customers convinces buyers to trust your offering.

>> **Instant payment processing:** This speeds up transactions.

>> **One-click upsells:** You can increase revenue by encouraging additional purchases at checkout.

>> **Product comparisons:** Contrasting your offering with your competition helps buyers make informed decisions independently.

>> **Retargeted ads:** These ads target people who visited your website but didn't buy, reminding them about your product.

>> **Self-service answers:** FAQs, *knowledge bases* (a digital collection of information about your offering), or community forums allow customers to find answers without human interaction.

>> **Self-service checkout:** Customers can complete their purchase without any interaction with you.

>> **Promotions:** Offering discounts, limited-time promotions, or free trials.

This approach to selling is usually best for either very standard products or low-priced products like these:

E-commerce (usually)	Digital products
Automated courses	Mobile and web apps
Self-published eBooks	Similar products

Putting the finishing touch in your sales process

You're still in the planning phase, so you're likely going to be making adjustments as you run and improve your business (the focus of Parts 4 and 5 of this book). Use Table 13-1 to assess your business. Circle the word that best describes your product for each row.

TABLE 13-1 Sales Process Touch-Level Comparison

Your Product's	High-Touch	Low-Touch	No-Touch
Price point	High	Medium	Low
Customization	Lots	Some	None
Complexity	Very	Some	None
% of deals closed	High	Medium	Low

You usually need to favor the highest touch level indicated by this analysis. But keep in mind that this is a continuum. You want to use the lowest touch level that will close the sales opportunities you want. For example, a website copywriter may look like this:

Price point	Low touch +	Likely $500 to $1,500
Customization	High-touch	Must be able match brand's voice
Complexity	Low-touch	Customer provides the concepts
% of deals closed	High-touch	Once the customer is sold once, additional deals are simple

The copywriter needs to use a high-touch approach with each new customer to learn their brand voice and convince them that they can effectively represent it in their writing. But this only needs to be done once, and then additional work from the customer will be low or possibly even no-touch.

TIP

Starting with a higher touch approach is often better because high-touch sales give you a chance to understand how prospects respond to your offer. This can be valuable for improving your offer while reducing your touch level in the future.

Creating Your Sales Messaging

One of the most crucial aspects of sales is the ability to explain what you do for your customer clearly and concisely. While this sounds like a direct quote from Captain Obvious, in truth, very few people do this well. You, however, will be one of the select few.

Writing a value statement

Denny Ward is a solopreneur and founder of Velocity Sales Consulting. He coaches businesses (including other solopreneurs) on sales. He is one solopreneur who isn't afraid of selling. Denny has created a process for designing your value statement, which can aid solopreneurs in the sales process.

A *value statement* is a short statement that explains whom you help and how you help them. Ideally, this statement is brief enough that you can easily say it to someone in 30 to 60 seconds. It can give you immediate confidence in your ability to describe what you do in a compelling way, leaving your prospect open to finding out more about your product or service, and possibly becoming a new customer! Hopefully, it will also prevent you from feeling *imposter syndrome*, a belief that your achievements aren't legitimately earned or deserved.

A value statement is an extension of your elevator pitch with the goal of helping others quickly identify whether you are a good fit for their needs. It contains the following pieces of information:

>> A clear description of what you do

>> An explanation of why people come to you

>> A description of the problems you solve

>> A question asking if any of the problems you solve resonate with the prospect

Here is LifeStarr's value statement:

> LifeStarr is a hub for solopreneurs who are building one-person businesses to serve their lives and goals. We help them build businesses that run more smoothly, sell better, and free up time for the life they truly want.

People come to LifeStarr when they're tired of so-called "gurus" selling them on the latest fad or hack to start or grow their business. They're good at what they do, but they know there has to be a smarter way to work. Solopreneurs typically come to us when they want to start or improve their solo business, for one or more of the following reasons:

>> They don't know how to start their business.

>> They can't get attention for their business.

>> Their selling skills are poor, and they don't close the leads they get.

>> They can't do all the work that needs to be done.

>> They want to grow their revenue but not their hours.

Some are just starting to leave corporate life and don't know where to begin. Others are already deep in it and wondering why this still feels so hard. Either way, they're done going solo alone.

What about you? Does this sound familiar?

A value statement gives you a concise way to explain your business. You can use it at many points during the sales process, particularly when you first engage a lead. We cover this in Chapter 11, where we help you define your messaging.

Producing sales tools

You need ways to convey what you do and who you do it for, and your value statement can help with this. Depending on your touch level, the tools you use can vary. They may include the following:

>> **Sales page:** A web page designed to turn the visitor into a buyer (no-touch).

>> **Landing page:** A web page designed to engage the visitor in the sales process (high- and low-touch).

>> **Launch sequence:** A planned series of marketing actions, like emails, social posts, and webinars, designed to build anticipation and drive sales for a new product, service, or offer (all touch levels).

>> **AI sales chat:** Interacting with a chatbot on your website allows a lead to ask questions (no-touch).

>> **Interactive demos:** For some offerings (like apps), allowing the prospect to experience the product can be useful for closing sales (high-, low-, and no-touch).

>> **Live sales chat:** Having a chat on your website allows a lead to ask you questions (low-touch).

>> **Sales deck:** This is a PowerPoint-type presentation that you use to walk the prospect through your offering, either in person or virtually (high-touch).

>> **Video pitch:** This is similar to a sales deck content-wise but it's on video, so the prospect has no opportunity for real-time questions (low- and no-touch).

REMEMBER

The kind of sales tools you create must be very specific to your business, but beyond that, they should be impactful for your prospect. Selling isn't about pushing a product; it's about helping people solve problems. Follow these easy steps (and use your value statement for inspiration) to create sales tools that turn potential buyers into happy customers:

1. **Make the customer the hero and yourself the guide.**

   Your customer is the star of the story. Your job? Help them succeed! Instead of bragging about your product or yourself, focus on how it solves their biggest challenges.

2. **Get engagement, not just agreement, by starting real conversations.**

   Listen, ask questions, and make your prospect feel understood. If you aren't speaking to them in person, rely on your persona definition to speak to the pain that they're feeling, if they're a good prospect.

3. **Start with your customer's challenges, which shows that you understand what they're going through.**

   Help customers open up by asking the right questions, such as

   - "Is [pain point] making things harder for you?"
   - "How has [pain point] affected your business?"

4. **Connect on an emotional level.**

   People buy with their emotions first, and then justify the purchase with logic. Help them imagine success by asking

   - "How would it feel if [pain point] disappeared?"
   - "What's the biggest frustration this product/service would solve?"

5. **Follow up with logic by bringing in the facts.**

   After your prospect's emotions are engaged, help them justify the sale with some numbers.

   - "Solving [pain point] can boost efficiency by [such-and-such] percent."
   - "Companies that fix [pain point] see [specific statistic] improvement."

6. **Paint a picture of the future by helping your prospect see the possibilities.**

   Ask questions that help them see your offering in a positive light, such as

   - "What would change for you if this problem was gone?"
   - "How would your daily life improve?"

7. **Test their readiness by checking their interest.**

   Instead of a hard closing pitch, ask follow-up questions.

   - "Does this sound like the right solution for you?"
   - "Would this make your life easier?"

8. **Make the next step super clear and easy to follow.**

   Your approach will depend on whether it's a high- or low-touch sale.

   - High-touch: "I'll send over a contract to get the sale started."
   - Low-touch or online: "Just fill out this form to take the next step."

REMEMBER

Selling is about guiding, not pushing. Focus on the customer's needs, build real engagement, and make the buying process simple and clear.

Qualifying Sales Leads

If you completed the steps in the preceding section, you're probably convinced that spending time on a sales opportunity that has no chance of closing isn't on your short list of things you want to be doing, particularly if you have a high-touch sale. And you aren't wrong. The process of *qualifying sales leads* enables you to identify the leads that are likely to result in a sale so you can focus on them and avoid the ones that are probably a waste of your time.

Depending on your touch level, the importance and nature of lead qualifying can go from make-or-break to not very important. Not surprisingly, higher-touch sales processes tend to come with higher-touch qualifying processes. Figure 13-1 gives you an idea of the kinds of approaches you may consider for your lead-qualifying process.

Qualification Criteria	High-Touch Sales	Low-Touch Sales	No-Touch Sales
Budget	Ask them during calls/meetings	Lead fills out an application form or selects a pricing tier	Self-selection at checkout
Need and Fit	Personalized consultations, discovery calls	Short survey or form, perhaps AI-assisted chatbots	Customer self-assesses via product descriptions and FAQs, perhaps AI-assisted chatbots
Decision-Making Authority	Directly confirmed through conversations	Indirectly inferred from form responses	Not checked
Urgency and Readiness	Ask during sales calls, follow-up emails	Tracked through engagement (email opens, clicks)	Tracked through engagement (email opens, clicks), abandoned carts
Past Behavior and Interest	Evaluate in meetings as well as note from past meetings	Tracked interactions (downloads, webinar attendance, time on website)	Fully automated tracking (site visits, clicks, sign-ups)
Purchasing Process Complexity	Custom proposals, contracts	Pre-set pricing with some negotiation	Instant checkout, subscription sign-ups

FIGURE 13-1: Ways of qualifying leads for different levels of touch.

Professional salespeople realize that the worst thing you can do is waste time selling to leads who will never buy. Some people don't need what you sell, some can't afford your product/service, and some don't have the authority to make the purchase.

Why these people spend time being sold to when they cannot buy from you is one of the universe's great mysteries. But know that these leads exist, waiting to suck your valuable time into the void. Qualifying your leads as early in the process as possible is the best way to avoid wasting your time.

Particularly if you have a sales process that involves some touch, you need to decide how to qualify your leads as they come in. Please, please create a lead-qualifying process. You should probably err on the side of caution, with more effort put into qualifying early on. This will do two things:

>> Prevent you from wasting a lot of time when you're just getting started.

>> Help you to figure out what works best with regard to qualifying leads so you can simplify the process later.

Decide what you'll do to qualify your leads and when you'll do it, and add your lead-qualifying process to your Solopreneur Action Plan.

Recording the Sale: Contracts and Statements of Work

Every business needs to have a contract with their customers, without exception. Sometimes, you don't have to write the contract; it's covered by existing law. For example, when you buy a hot dog from a street vendor, you don't need a contract promising that it's up to standards set by the board of health; there are laws covering that. You can only hope they're being followed.

However, in many cases, you need to create a contract that details the relationship between you and the customer. Sometimes, your contract will be on your website, and you will provide a link to it so the customer can review it if they want. In a high-touch sale, it may be dozens of pages in multiple documents that need to be negotiated.

The most complex sales a solopreneur is likely to see will involve two documents: a *contract* or *master services agreement (MSA)* and a *statement of work (SOW).* The contract/MSA covers the overall and legal aspects of your relationship with your customer. The SOW details the work that you will do. While not all solopreneurs need a contract and statement of work, too many who do neglect to create and use these documents.

TIP

If you have a no-touch sale, your contract can be in the form of a terms of service (TOS) page on your website. You should include a checkbox on the order form with a link to the TOS page that indicates the customer agrees to the terms and require them to check the box to complete the sale. This keeps the sale no-touch.

Understanding contracts

A contract should create what's known in legal terms as a *meeting of the minds.* This means that both parties understand and agree to the terms contained in the contract. This is important because no one can claim that the deal differs from what is stated in the contract.

A good contract covers several topics, highlighted in the following list, but note that not all of them may apply to all businesses:

>> **Parties involved:** This spells out the full name, address, and business type (corporation, LLC) of both the business and the customer.

>> **Scope of agreement:** This is a general description of the service/product being provided. If it's complex, the details will be covered in the SOW and the SOW should be referenced here.

>> **Payment terms:** The contract should include the amount and method of payment, due dates, late fees, and refund policies.

>> **Obligations of each party:** The document should explain the responsibilities of the business and the customer. If their obligations are involved and detailed, they will be in the SOW.

>> **Timelines and deadlines:** These are the key dates for deliverables, completion of the work, and milestones. If they're simple, put them in the contract. If they're more complex, use an SOW and refer to it in the contract.

- » **Dispute resolution:** This explains how conflicts will be handled (through mediation, arbitration, or legal action). Do not leave this out!

- » **Liability and indemnification:** A statement of liability clarifies who is responsible for damages, risks, or legal claims. Indemnification means that under certain circumstances, one party agrees to compensate the other for losses or legal claims. It may include legal fees and damages.

- » **Intellectual property rights:** This states who owns the work being created. (This is especially important for writers, artists, designers, software developers, and solopreneurs in other creative industries.)

- » **Confidentiality and nondisclosure:** In this statement, the parties agree to protect sensitive information.

- » **Assignability clause:** This explains whether the contract can be assigned to another party and, if so, under what conditions. An assignability clause prevents both parties from winding up doing business with someone other than the contracted party.

- » **Termination clause:** This is an explanation of how the agreement can be ended and under what conditions.

- » **Force majeure clause:** This spells out what happens if unforeseen catastrophic events (storms, earthquakes, fires, and the like) prevent performance of the contract.

- » **Jurisdiction and governing law:** This part of the contract details which state/country's laws apply.

- » **Amendment and modification terms:** This is an explanation of how changes to the contract will be handled.

WARNING

Contracts are complex, so it's never a bad idea to either hire a lawyer (which lowers your risk but can be expensive; see the next section) or find a contract form that seems ready to adapt to your business (which is cheaper but riskier). Some people have used AI to create contracts, but this is very risky without a review by an attorney.

Deciding if you need a lawyer

For some solopreneurs, a simple contract template or basic TOS document will work fine. But if your sales process involves custom agreements, negotiations, or long, detailed contracts, hiring a business lawyer is a smart move.

Call a lawyer in these circumstances:

>> If your contract will be negotiated by the customer

>> If it's possible that legal disputes may arise

And keep the following tips in mind:

>> **Specialists over generalists:** A contract lawyer, especially one who understands your business area, is better than a general attorney in most cases.

>> **Fixed fees versus hourly rates:** Fixed fees work best if you're hiring someone to draw up standard contracts, while hourly rates are usually better if you need an attorney to negotiate terms.

WARNING

Always look for a lawyer who's a dealmaker. A good lawyer helps you close deals, not overcomplicate them. Check references to determine if the lawyer you're considering is focused on making deals or writing bulletproof contracts that never get signed.

Understanding statements of work

As a solopreneur, you will have a lot of jobs. But one job you don't want is arguing with unhappy customers who don't want to pay for your product/service. That's where a statement of work (SOW) comes in.

An SOW is the road map for a project, clearly laying out what will be done, when the work is due, who does it, how much it costs, and what happens if something changes. It helps you and your customer stay on the same page, setting expectations up front so you aren't hit with surprises down the road.

To determine whether you need an SOW, answer these questions about your product or service:

>> Is my product/service customized or bespoke?

>> Does the project involve multiple phases?

>> Does the client need to do things for me (provide information, review specifications, test the product, and so on)?

>> Does the client expect specific deadlines or deliverables that need to be documented?

>> Do I require deposits or milestone-based payments?

>> Will my work possibly require revisions?

If you answered *yes* to any of these questions, we recommend that you strongly consider using an SOW in your sales process.

Creating your SOW

Depending on your business, your SOW may be a standard form that never changes or a highly negotiated document. Regardless, a solid SOW will typically include these sections:

>> **Scope of work:** This covers everything you're doing to deliver the product or service, which means it also defines all the things you're *not* doing, thereby preventing the customer from expecting things they're not getting.

>> **Deliverables:** This is a description of the final product or service you're providing.

>> **Key individuals:** You'll identify each person involved in the process, what they do, and their contact info. One of these will very likely be you.

>> **Responsibilities:** Often, you will require information and approval from the customer in a timely fashion. These are explained in your SOW.

>> **Timelines:** This covers deadlines for each phase of the project and timelines allowed for reviews and approvals.

>> **Pricing and payment terms:** Your SOW should state how much, when, and how you get paid.

>> **Revisions:** This indicates how many rounds of tweaks the client gets before extra charges kick in and how much the extra charges will be.

>> **Assumptions and limitations:** This part explains what you're counting on from the customer so you can do your job.

>> **Usage rights:** Clearly define who owns the final deliverables and how they may be used. This is especially important for creative services (design, video, influencer content), where ownership or reuse rights may vary.

If your product or service is complex, requires some effort by the buyer before you can deliver it, or is bespoke or highly customized, an SOW is an essential addition to your sales process.

 Download a Solopreneur Statement of Work template at www.dummies.com/go/solopreneurbusinessfd.

FIND ONLINE

Knowing the importance of SOWs

If your business needs an SOW and you don't use one, you may experience a lot of pain, including things like

>> **Confusion:** Different expectations from you and your customer will lead to headaches.

>> **Delays:** Projects will stall when roles aren't defined.

>> **Extra work:** You may have to make more revisions, and waste more time, possibly without receiving additional payment.

>> **Legal disputes:** Get ready for arguments if you don't have clear statements about deliverables and timelines.

>> **No finish line:** Without clear criteria, "done" is never done.

>> **Scope creep:** Clients will keep adding tasks without paying anything extra.

This list should convince you that the effort you put into creating an SOW is worthwhile.

Documenting Your Sales Process

Before you set the world on fire selling your offering, make sure you have the pieces in place to document the sale. Here's a checklist:

>> Determine what kind of contract you need.

- Implicit contract (covered by existing law)
- Terms of service (on your website)
- Standard (fixed) contract
- Negotiable contract

>> Decide if you need an SOW.

>> Decide how you will create the contract (for example, hire a lawyer, borrow and adapt a template, or use AI).

>> Create your contract form (if you need one).

>> Create your SOW (if you need one).

REMEMBER

List your sales process and the documents you'll need in that process in your Solopreneur Action Plan.

Chapter **14**

Crafting a Delightful Onboarding Experience

Have you ever purchased a product or service and then . . . crickets? It's an unsettling feeling, right? One that often leads to instant buyer's remorse. As a solopreneur, you're juggling a million things at once, and you may be tempted, like many other solopreneurs, to put the majority of your time and effort toward lead generation and sales. But trust us when we say that you need to pay just as much attention to onboarding and connecting with your new clients.

Your onboarding process doesn't need to be fancy or complicated, but it should be intentional and engaging. You need to let your buyer know they've made the right decision by continuing to guide and nurture your relationship after they've made a purchase.

If you handle onboarding well, you not only increase the odds of getting a repeat customer, but you also open the door for referrals. If you don't handle it well, you risk unhappy customers, disengagement, potential refund requests, and negative remarks being spread about your business moving forward. Don't let this happen to you.

In this chapter, we discuss how you can create an onboarding experience that delights your customers and helps you grow an amazing referral-worthy business.

REMEMBER

You're still in the planning phase of the Solopreneur Success Cycle, Step 2: Planning your business, which is part of the first phase. You're still getting started but you're getting close to actually implementing your plan! You just need to get through a few finishing touches.

Knowing the Benefits of Creating an Onboarding Process

Before we dive into how to build an effective onboarding process, we want to explain why it's so important. Successful onboarding can benefit you in the following ways:

>> **Saves you time:** You may have to invest significant time as you build out the onboarding process, but you can save hours in the long run knowing you aren't reinventing the wheel every time you get a new client or customer.

>> **Establishes expectations:** Not only do you get to inform your customer about what they'll receive from you, but you also establish the expectations you have of them. Setting boundaries and responsibilities early on leads to a more productive and enjoyable working relationship in the long run.

>> **Builds trust:** Having an onboarding process in place exemplifies professionalism and shows that you've put time and effort into caring about your customer's experience.

>> **Starts the process of delighting your customers early on:** It's never too early to wow the people who have purchased from you. The earlier you do it, the better they'll feel and the more fondly they'll think about your business.

>> **Increases retention and upselling potential:** A well-thought-out onboarding process encourages client buy-in and makes them feel like they're active participants in your client–service provider relationship as opposed to just someone you once sold something to. If they feel valued and appreciated from the beginning, they'll be more likely to stick around and buy from you again in the future.

» **Builds a foundation for referrals:** We've talked to countless solopreneurs who've told us that referrals and word of mouth are some of the most desirable ways to bring new clients in, although it isn't always easy to establish a referral process. Creating happy customers from the outset is the first step toward building a successful referral network.

TIP

You're trying to create lasting relationships, but you don't want to spend all your time on onboarding. As you create the onboarding sequence, think about how you can streamline processes and save time with automated programs. For example, you can automate your welcome emails, send personalized video introductions, or use scheduling tools that let clients easily book calls.

WARNING

Automate only if the process doesn't lose its personal touch or human connection. Use automation to enhance the relationship-building experience, not take away from it.

As you create your onboarding experience, track it in your Solopreneur Action Plan (see Chapter 3), updating your plan whenever you make changes to the sequence.

Providing a Warm Welcome

Onboarding is your chance to give your new customers the "warm fuzzies." Let them know immediately that they made the right decision when they bought your product or service. Their purchase isn't the end of your connection with these people — it's the beginning — so start off your new relationship by delivering an outstanding first impression.

TIP

When customers immediately feel acknowledged and welcomed, and not like just another number in your contact list, they'll be more likely to stick with you. Solopreneurs often rely on word of mouth and referrals from their customers, so if you want to generate those more seamlessly, getting the welcome right is key.

Some effective "welcome aboard" gestures include the following:

» **Send a personalized message or video.** Make your new customer feel seen and congratulate them on taking the first steps toward solving their *pain points* (the issues that brought them to you). Let them know how to contact you if they ever need assistance.

>> **Give them a next steps guide.** Set clear expectations and provide a road map of what they'll experience in the next few weeks. If applicable, this is a good place to inform them of what you may need from them to kick things off (new client questionnaire, background info, and so on).

>> **Link to resources.** Include a link to helpful resources that can answer questions, offer additional support, or dive deeper into topics they might be curious about.

>> **Send a welcome basket filled with little goodies from your business.** Think branded pens, notepads, a handwritten note, or a small self-care item to make clients feel valued.

>> **Reinforce their choice.** Share success stories or testimonials from other customers.

>> **Give them a peek behind the curtain.** Let them know what you'll be doing behind the scenes until your next interaction. Give them confidence that you're there for them every step of the way. Make them feel like you're partners.

Preventing Buyer's Remorse: Week 1

Buyer's remorse (the guilt or regret a person feels before receiving the benefits of something they just bought) isn't inevitable, but it can happen and typically occurs right after a purchase. Your efforts to prevent buyer's remorse should begin during the welcome phase and stay top of mind as you move your new customer through the onboarding process.

This week, your goal is to make the new client feel confident, seen, and supported. Here's what that can look like:

>> **Offer a quick-start tutorial or checklist.** Help them take immediate, meaningful action. This builds momentum and reduces uncertainty.

>> **Host a live Q&A.** A brief session where they can ask questions or hear more about how to get the most out of your offering can ease doubts and increase engagement.

>> **Send a "here's what others wish they'd known" list.** This feels exclusive and supportive. Share a few power-user tips or avoidable mistakes that past clients learned the hard way.

As Maya Angelou once said, "People will forget what you said, people will forget what you did, but people will never forget how you made them feel." Remember this as you welcome people to your business.

If someone *does* express regret or even asks for a refund, don't panic. Sometimes the product simply isn't the right fit, and that's okay. Handle the situation professionally so that you can still leave the door open for a future relationship or referral.

Delivering Your Product or Service: Weeks 2 to 4

After you welcome a new customer to your company and give them the proverbial pat on the back, it's time to *get your product or service into their hands,* literally or digitally. Whether you ship a physical item, deliver a digital product through email, or kick off a service through a calendar invite, make sure the delivery is prompt, clear, and easy to access. You never want a new customer to feel confused about how or when they'll receive what they paid for.

When delivery is complete, your job isn't done. You need to be your customer's guide to getting the most out of what they purchased. Here are a few ideas:

>> Make getting started with your product easy by providing clear instructions, tutorials, and guided walk-throughs.

>> If your product requires assembly, check in with your client to see how setup is going and ask if they need help.

>> If you run an online platform, provide video tutorials showing your client how to navigate the system.

>> If you're a coach or consultant, stick to the meetings and deliverables you promised, and consider sharing light-touch resources like checklists, templates, or recommended reading that support your core service.

Build on this list in a way that makes sense for your business. Encourage small wins throughout delivery to keep clients engaged and motivated. Break your offering into simple steps and celebrate progress, like finishing a module, reaching a milestone, or completing setup. Use tools like progress trackers to highlight success and build momentum.

REMEMBER

Depending on the type of business you've created, implement a process to not only deliver your product or service but also make sure your customer is using it correctly and enjoying it.

Bringing Success to Your Customer: Weeks 5 to 13

Your clients will feel successful when they see the problems you promised to solve start to vanish. How do you make that happen? This process may be easier for solopreneurs with service-based businesses, because they're typically engaging with their clients for longer periods. Here are some ideas to get your wheels turning:

>> **Help your customers see their progress.** Offer incentives for reaching milestones, give them a journal to track their journey, and so on. How you make their success apparent will depend on your business, but let your customers see their victories, big or small.

>> **Foster ongoing support.** Offer weekly check-ins or host live Q&A sessions. These touchpoints give your customers consistent opportunities to learn, ask questions, and gain momentum with your guidance.

>> **Be accessible and responsive.** Don't leave your customers in the dark. Make it easy for them to get help by replying to inquiries promptly and offering tools like an online chatbot to troubleshoot issues when you're not available.

If you own a product-based business, you can still help customers experience success in various ways, including these:

>> **Providing follow-up guidance:** Send customers recommendations and tips on how to get the most out of your product,

as well as ways to track their progress. For example, provide a printable checklist that helps them mark off milestones as they go.

>> **Encouraging community interaction:** Create a moderated online community such as a private Facebook group, where customers can share successes, ask questions, and support each other. This not only builds connection but also fosters ongoing engagement with your product.

At the end of the day, you want it to be easy for people to work with you, and you want them to feel like they've finally found the solutions to their problems. Think through your persona(s) and their pain points, and put yourself in your customers' shoes. What would make *you* feel the most successful? When you come up with the answer, work to help your customer achieve that feeling.

Transforming Customers into Fans: Weeks 14 to 15

The real goal of providing a stellar onboarding experience — turning a customer into a fan — begins in weeks 14 and 15. Someone may become a fan simply because you have a fabulous product or service, but you can't sit back and just wait for that to happen. Consider these ways to turn a customer into a fan:

>> **Build a personal connection from the start.** Don't just make customers feel like a number. Make them feel seen and heard by using their name, referencing past interactions, and showing genuine interest in their goals. While it's important for this phase, begin doing this in the first week, as small, thoughtful gestures early go a long way in creating emotional connection.

>> **Under-promise and over-deliver.** We know, we're far from the first people to say this, but it's popular advice for a reason. Deliver exactly what your clients expect based on what they paid for, then exceed those expectations with thoughtful extras or exceptional service. That surprise element is what turns satisfied clients into loyal ones.

>> **Make your customers feel like you're solving their pain points together.** Collaborate openly, welcome their input, and celebrate each milestone as a shared success. A win for them is a win for you.

>> **Be there for them.** Don't leave your customers hanging and feeling lost. You've been with them for a few months at this point so don't let them feel forgotten. Check in periodically with helpful tips, encouragement, or even a simple "How's it going?" to show them that you still care about their success.

If some of the points in this section feel familiar, that's intentional. Certain ideas bear repeating because they're foundational to your success.

When running a solo business, it's easy to overlook the basics in the pursuit of doing everything at once. By reinforcing key strategies and mindsets throughout this chapter, the goal is to make them second nature because it's often the simple, consistent actions that provide the biggest results.

Converting Fans to Evangelists: 16 Weeks and Beyond

You'll work hard to turn customers into fans of your business, so that should be enough, right? Not quite. In a perfect world, your fans will become superfans, or — as many experts in the business and marketing world like to call them — *evangelists*. These are clients who not only love you and your business but enthusiastically promote it and sing its praises to others. (the best kind of marketing you can get!)

The key here, which is different from, say, organized referral programs where people get a finder's fee or other incentives, is that these brand evangelists aren't paid or rewarded. They just love what you do so much that they want to spread the word.

Identify who these people are and really take care of them: Send them a handwritten thank-you note, surprise them with early access to a new product, or feature them in your newsletter. Acknowledge their efforts so they feel your gratitude. Your appreciation will motivate them to spread the word about your product or service even farther.

WHITE GLOVE SERVICES

Even if you're a team of one, thoughtful touches for your highest-level clients can go a long way in building loyalty, trust, and long-term value. So if your business offers a premium service tier or high-ticket product, consider offering *white glove* onboarding experiences to match, such as these:

- **Providing personalized onboarding calls:** Replace generic welcome emails with a one-on-one onboarding call to help them get set up and answer early questions. Frame it as their personal strategy session.

- **Handpicking high-touch welcome gifts:** Choose one or two meaningful, high-quality or personalized items tailored to the client's personality or goals. Do your homework and figure out what they would really appreciate.

- **Granting priority access and rapid response:** Let your premium clients know they're at the top of your list. Offer a guaranteed response time and consider setting aside specific blocks on your calendar for them to book first.

- **Offering invite-only perks:** Create small-group virtual masterminds, bonus resources, or exclusive behind-the-scenes content just for your top-tier clients. These extras can deepen the relationship and create a sense of belonging.

It's such a breath of fresh air when clients and customers become your referral engine and essentially do your marketing for you through word of mouth. The support and time savings that can come from your evangelists sharing their love for your product or service can truly be game changers for your business.

Chapter **15**

Setting Up Your Business

I n this chapter you enter the final step of Phase 1 of the Solopreneur Success Cycle, Step 3: Setting up your business. By this stage, you've hopefully done oodles of planning, and now it's time to execute your plans. This is exciting!

Okay, we know you didn't decide to work for yourself because you get excited about all the administrative tasks we discuss in this chapter, and there are many: from incorporating your business, to getting a business bank account and credit card, to buying insurance, doing some tax planning, creating a payment process, and finally safeguarding your ideas. But getting all these things in order sets you up for long-term success to do that thing you really love and create the life you want to live.

And we promise we've made all these tasks as painless as possible.

Creating Your Business

You've got a plan for your business. Now it's time to create the company.

Understanding corporate structure

Corporate structure?! Why do you need a *corporate* structure? By comparison, setting up a sole proprietorship is easy. But so is microwaving old fish in a metal bowl. Easy doesn't always mean good. And sole proprietorships aren't usually good because your liability is unlimited; if something goes wrong, your house, your car, and maybe your dog are all at risk from the aggrieved party. That's why you need a corporate structure. It limits your liability to the assets of the company.

While every country is different, most of them offer some incorporation option that works for solopreneurs. We can't cover all countries in this chapter, so we look at the options available in the United States as an example. In the United States, the following three options usually make sense for solopreneurs:

>> **Single-member limited liability company:** A *limited liability company*, or *LLC*, is a form of incorporation that protects your personal assets from business debts and claims while maintaining simplicity with respect to filing requirements. A single-member LLC is typically taxed like a sole proprietorship, meaning that profits and losses flow to your personal tax return.

>> **S corporation:** An *S corp* also protects your personal assets and allows profits and some losses to pass through as well. If you designate yourself as an employee and pay yourself a reasonable salary, you can potentially save on income taxes. But be aware that S corps require more rigorous record-keeping compared to LLCs.

>> **An LLC with an S corp election:** This option reduces the reporting and documentation requirements while potentially maintaining the tax benefits. Speak to a tax advisor to find out if this makes sense for you.

If you're outside the United States, your country likely offers a business structure that limits your personal liability.

Setting up your corporation

Deciding on and then creating the corporate structure for your business is best left to professionals. The two types you want to have in your corner are a tax planner and a tax attorney. They can help you decide which corporate structure makes the most sense for you and then assist with the legal aspects of setting up the corporate entity.

Finding a professional tax planner

Taxes aren't just about filing paperwork; they're about keeping more of your hard-earned money while staying on the right side of the IRS or other taxing authorities. A great tax planner helps you maximize your deductions while staying out of trouble.

TIP

Use your network to find one. Other solopreneurs, small business owners, and professional groups can offer suggestions from experience. Look for pros with solid credentials. Certified public accountants (CPAs) and enrolled agents (EAs) have specialized training in tax law and planning. Online reviews and affiliations with industry associations like the National Association of Tax Professionals (often shortened to NATP) can also help you find tax pros.

Choosing a corporate structure

Deciding on a corporate structure isn't easy. Your choice (see the earlier section, "Understanding corporate structure," for an overview of your options) may be impacted by your personal circumstances and which state or province you live in. Your tax attorney and a tax planner will help you to make the best decision for your business.

Incorporating on your own

Having a professional tax planner (or maybe a tax attorney) in your corner is a very good idea. But many solopreneurs view the expense of hiring a professional as a reason not to incorporate and simply choose to operate as sole proprietors. Because of the unlimited liability, that's the worst of all worlds.

If you can't afford a tax planner, in the United States you can use business formation services. Typically, these companies will also help you manage your reporting requirements. While you may not incorporate in the most optimal way, you'll be light years ahead of the people who don't incorporate at all. These services can help you with your corporate filing requirements as well. They are very cost-effective for this, even if you don't use them to set up your business.

Download a current list of business formation services at www. dummies.com/go/solopreneurbusinessfd.

FIND ONLINE

You want to incorporate before setting up the rest of your business because you'll need your business entity to open bank accounts, get a business credit card, sign contracts on behalf of the company, and so on. So, get your corporate structure set up now.

Getting a tax ID number

Most countries require that you register your business with a taxing authority. In the United States, you get something called an *employer identification number* (EIN), which is like a social security number for businesses. Some states and provinces may require tax registration as well.

EINs are typically straightforward to apply for, but you can consult your tax attorney (if you have one) or search government websites (for example, https://www.irs.gov/ or the site for your state's department of revenue) for info.

Tackling the Showstoppers

If you have any *showstoppers* (anything that can prevent you from starting your business) in your business setup, refer to the de-risked showstopper plan we recommend you create in Chapter 9 (and if you haven't made such a plan, maybe now is the time). Once everything is in place, you should start working through the tasks on it. If one of your potential showstoppers becomes an actual one, you'll have risked as little as possible finding that out.

If a showstopper does stop the show, don't just quit. Think about ways you can move forward without the thing you lack. If you're starting a food truck business and you can't finance the food truck, perhaps you can open a food preparation service and use Uber Eats or DoorDash to deliver. As your business and credit grow, the bank may have different feelings about loaning you money for a truck.

The important thing is to think creatively in the face of adversity. Some of the best businesses are born from creative problem-solving.

TIP

You may need to check off some of the items later in this chapter before you tackle certain showstoppers. For example, you may need a business credit card and a checking account before you apply for any financing.

Opening Bank Accounts

You have a huge number of options for opening your bank accounts with only one hard-and-fast rule: Open business accounts tied to your corporate entity, not personal accounts in your own name. You never want to mix your personal finances with your business finances. Doing this can create tax headaches, complicate your bookkeeping, and put your personal assets at risk if a legal issue arises.

After that, your banking options are almost limitless. You can choose between the following types of financial institutions:

>> Traditional brick-and-mortar banks

- **Local banks:** These are community-focused banks. They offer personalized service, but they may offer fewer digital tools.

- **Regional banks:** These banks serve multiple states. They offer more resources than local banks but may still be somewhat personalized.

- **National banks:** These are large banks. They have a widespread network of branches, extensive services, and business perks, but often charge higher fees.

>> Online-only banks and *fintech* or *challenger* banks (digital and online banking and financial technology platforms)

- **Virtual/online-only banks:** The banks have no physical branches. Their fees are low, and they have digital-first features, but you can forget about in-person support.

- **Fintech and challenger banks:** These banks are tech-driven, often offering innovative features like easier and cheaper automation, integration with accounting tools, as well as no-fee banking.

>> Niche and specialized banking options

- **Credit unions:** These banks are member-owned. They have lower fees and personal service but may lack business-specific tools.

- **Neobanks for solopreneurs and freelancers:** These are online-only challenger or fintech banks that cater specifically to one-person businesses.

- **Business-focused banks/banking services:** These banks/services tailor their offerings to entrepreneurs and small businesses. They may have built-in invoicing, payment processing, or tax tools.

WARNING

In the United States, be sure the bank is FDIC-insured or you may lose your money if the bank fails.

One thing to keep in mind is that if your business handles cash, you'll want to have access to a local bank branch so you can deposit it.

You should open a business checking and a savings or money market account. Some banks can also supply you with a credit card, which can make for added convenience in managing your finances.

Download a list of current banks by type here www.dummies.com/go/solopreneurbusinessfd.

FIND ONLINE

Applying for a Business Credit Card

You should get a business credit card, with the understanding that most credit card companies require you to agree to be personally liable for outstanding balances. Still, it's a good idea to keep your business purchases separate from your personal finances.

The card you choose depends on what you'll be using it to buy and what kind of credit limit you need. Table 15-1 outlines considerations and some options for business credit cards.

TABLE 15-1 Business Credit Cards for Various Needs

Card Type	Description	Best for . . .
Flat-rate cash-back	Same cash-back percentage (often 1.5–2 percent) on every purchase	Simple, set-it-and-forget-it rewards on widely mixed spending
Tiered/category-bonus cash-back	Higher cash back (3–5 percent) on select categories (ads, office supplies, dining, and so on), lower base rate elsewhere	Businesses that concentrate spending in a few predictable buckets
Flexible-points travel	Earn points you can transfer to multiple airlines/hotels or redeem for cash, travel, or gifts	Solopreneurs who travel and want maximum redemption flexibility
Co-branded airline/hotel	Linked to a single loyalty program; perks like free checked bags, elite-night credits, or companion passes	Brand-loyal travelers who squeeze every perk from one carrier or chain
Low- or no-annual-fee value	Basic rewards and purchase protections with little (or zero) annual cost	Fee-averse owners and first-time business-card users
0% Intro APR/financing	Long interest-free window on new purchases (and sometimes balance transfers)	Funding a big project or smoothing cash-flow dips without a bank loan
Premium-perks and lounge-access	High annual fee but rich extras: lounge entry, travel credits, premium insurance, status upgrades	Road-warrior solos who live in airports and will use the perks
Expense-management platform	Fintech-issued cards bundled with virtual cards, spend rules, real-time dashboards, and accounting sync	Digital-first businesses that value automation over travel perks
Secured/credit-builder	Requires a refundable cash deposit; reports to business credit bureaus to build history	New ventures or owners repairing thin/damaged credit profiles
Fuel and fleet-focused	Extra cents-off-per-gallon or EV-charging rebates plus mileage-tracking tools	Mobile service pros, contractors, or delivery-based businesses that live on the road

Preparing to Get Paid

To have a thriving business, you need to get paid. And to get paid, you have to ask for the money. How you get paid depends on the type of business you're in. If you have a cash-only food truck, you just need a place to stash the cash (and perhaps a cash register to keep track of sales). An app with a monthly fee involves automatically billing the customer's credit card each month. Other products and services likely involve creating an invoice specific to the customer. If you're charging by the hour, you'll need to track your time and invoice the customer based on that. If you charge in phases or at the end, you'll need to get those invoices out in a timely fashion to maximize your bank balance.

Defining your payment terms

Clear payment terms are critical to avoiding disagreements and late payments. You'll enter your payment terms into your invoicing system so they can be displayed on your invoices and you can keep track of late payments.

You need to outline when payment is due (for example, upon receipt, within 15 days, or net 30 days). Make it very clear to your customers what late fees or interest charges for overdue payments look like. You don't have to rub your customers' faces in your payment terms, but don't hide them in the fine print either. It's best to list them on your invoices. Payment terms include

- ▶ **Payment due date:** Standard terms include *net 30* (due within 30 days of billing) or due upon receipt.
- ▶ **Late fees:** Decide whether you will charge a penalty for overdue payments.
- ▶ **Payment methods:** You can choose to accept various forms of payment, including credit cards, PayPal, ACH transfers (electronic payments), and checks.
- ▶ **Up-front deposits:** For larger projects, you may want to require a down payment before work begins.

>> **Milestone payments:** If you require payments as the project progresses, state these terms clearly in your contracts or statements of work, and list what happens to trigger a payment and how much is to be paid.

Creating a refund policy that works

A solid refund policy isn't just about protecting your business; it's about building trust with your customers. When people know exactly what to expect, they feel more confident making a purchase.

Here are some options to help you decide what kind of refunds you'll offer:

>> **Full, partial, or store credit:** Choose the type of refund that makes sense for your business.

>> **Time limited:** A 30-day return window is common, but shorter or longer limits may work for you.

>> **Exceptions:** Digital products, services, or custom work may need a no-refunds or conditional refunds rule to prevent *charge-backs* (refunds provided by a credit card issuer after customer complaints) or misuse.

Keep your policy clear and simple; avoid legal mumbo jumbo!

TIP

Here are a couple real-world examples of reasonable guidelines for both businesses and customers:

>> A coaching program may offer full refunds before the first session but only partial refunds afterward.

>> A digital product can have a no-refunds-after-download rule to prevent abuse.

Your refund policy shouldn't be hidden away, so put it on your website, on invoices, and even in onboarding emails if you send them.

If refund requests start piling up, take a step back. Are you setting the right expectations? A smart refund policy doesn't just protect your business; it can also help you improve it.

Dunning when you don't receive payment

Dunning is the process of following up on overdue payments to make sure customers pay up. This involves a series of reminders that start out friendly and become more assertive if the invoice remains unpaid, including a warning that nonpayment can lead to legal action. A strong dunning strategy helps you keep cash flowing by reducing late payments and minimizing bad debt. And cash flow is critical for any business. You can automate your dunning process using invoicing or accounting software that sends reminders at set intervals. We look at these tools in Chapter 16 and show you a sample dunning process in Chapter 18.

Decide what will happen when payment is overdue (1 day late, 10 days late, 15 days late, and so on). Don't skip this important step. And make it part of your Solopreneur Action Plan.

Signing Up for Business Insurance

Skipping business insurance coverage? Bad idea. One lawsuit, fire, or data breach can sink your business. But don't just buy an everything-and-the-kitchen-sink policy. Talk to a reputable insurance agent to ensure you get only the coverage you need.

Here are some common types of coverage you may or may not need:

>> **Business interruption insurance:** This type of policy replaces lost income if your business is forced to shut down.

>> **Business owner's policy:** This is a bundle of general liability and property insurance, often provided at a discount.

>> **Commercial auto coverage:** This is an insurance policy that covers business-related vehicle use (your personal policy won't).

>> **Cyber liability insurance:** If you store customer data, this helps you weather hacks and breaches.

>> **General liability coverage:** This insurance covers injuries, property damage, and lawsuits. It's critical to have general liability insurance if you meet with clients in person.

- **Home-based business insurance:** If you work from home, don't assume your homeowner's policy covers your business.

- **Product liability insurance:** This protects against defect-related claims and is a must if you sell physical products.

- **Professional liability insurance (also known as *errors and omissions insurance*):** A must-have for consultants and coaches, this coverage protects against claims of bad advice or services.

- **Property insurance:** This shields your equipment and workspace from disasters like fire or theft.

Obtaining Health Insurance

If you live in a country that provides health insurance for you, skip to the next section. Otherwise, you need to have some type of health insurance. If your solo business is a side-hustle, then you may still have coverage through an employer. Or perhaps your spouse has a job that will cover you. In the United States, health-care coverage is complicated and constantly changing. Do your homework, talk to an agent, and find coverage that fits your needs.

Exploring the Benefits of Tax Planning

When you work for a company, in most countries your employer withholds income taxes from your wages. As a solopreneur, you need to do this for yourself. Check with a tax professional (see "Finding a professional tax planner" earlier in this chapter) or do some research and figure out how much to put aside for taxes and when to pay them. Paying penalties and interest is never fun. Chapter 16 explores software options that can help you get your tax obligations right.

A professional tax planner can save you money . . . a lot of money. Many expenses you may not be aware of can be offset against your earnings, including things like renting your home office to your business and hiring your kids. But figuring out what can be deducted or written off isn't easy, and making the wrong decision invites a visit from the tax auditor.

You may not choose to bring on a certified public accountant (CPA) or enrolled agent (EA) immediately upon starting your business because you won't have a lot of revenue yet. But consider hiring a professional as an investment, not as an expense, and do it as soon as it makes sense (or after you pay that uncomfortably high tax bill and say, "Never again").

Protecting Your Intellectual Property

Intellectual property (IP) encompasses the unique things you create that set your business apart. This includes inventions, names, logos, written content, designs, or trade secrets. If it adds value or gives you an edge, it may qualify as IP. Protecting your IP helps you

>> **Keep control of your ideas:** Without legal rights, others can copy or profit from your work.

>> **Protect your reputation:** Trademarks and copyrights give you legal rights if someone tries to impersonate your business or misuse your materials.

>> **Grow your business value:** Registered IP can attract investors, lead to licensing deals, or increase what your business is worth if you sell.

Whether you need to protect any IP depends on your business. The following sections offer a quick breakdown of the key types of IP protection to consider.

Trademarking your brand

Trademarks protect your business name, logo, slogan, or product name, and help you distinguish your brand. If your business name is just your own name (and you're not Taylor Swift or Michael Jordan), you probably don't need any trademarks. This list highlights the various types of available trademarks:

>> **Common-law trademarks:** These trademarks automatically protect a name, logo, or slogan if you use it in commerce, but your trademark rights are limited to the country where you got the trademark.

>> **Registered trademarks:** These trademarks offer stronger protection. The two types of registered trademarks are

- *Word marks,* which protect the trademarked name itself (for example, LifeStarr is a protected word mark in the U.S.)
- *Design marks,* which protect a logo's visual design (and are often easier and cheaper to register)

If you have a unique brand or product, trademarking can add to its value, especially if you plan to sell your business.

Copyrighting your content

Copyrights protect original creative works, written content, videos, graphics, music, online courses, and software. You automatically have a copyright as soon as a work is created and fixed in a tangible form (like a blog post or recorded video). But formal registration with your national copyright agency (for example, the U.S. Copyright Office) strengthens your legal rights and makes enforcement against unauthorized use of your work easier. If you're a creative, it may be worth considering formal registration with a copyright agency for any of your high-value content.

Patenting your invention

Patents protect inventions and unique processes. For most solopreneurs, patents probably aren't relevant. But if you have some unique invention or process, a patent can protect your work. Getting a patent (for example, from the U.S. Patent and Trademark Office) is expensive and time-consuming, and involves doing significant research, filling out detailed applications, paying hefty fees, and often hiring a patent attorney or agent. But patenting your work can add significant value to your business.

Having a patent is no guarantee against someone violating it. There are countless stories of big companies violating a patent and tying up the patent holder in court for years. Sometimes having a trade secret (covered in the next section) is a better option.

Using trade secrets

If you have a unique invention or process, keeping it a *trade secret* is sometimes smarter than filing for a patent, which requires you to make your ideas public. This route is also a lot cheaper. With a trade secret, you simply keep your idea confidential and non-public and use *nondisclosure agreements* to protect your idea from theft when you need to share it with a third party. As with patents, unethical companies can and do steal trade secrets and use their army of lawyers to keep you at bay. Telling people who are asking that certain information is a trade secret can dissuade them from pursuing the information and may even add to your company's allure.

Looking in the IP mirror

Protecting your business is important, but make sure you're not stepping on anyone else's IP rights. Do a quick online search (free) or hire an IP lawyer (not so free) to check.

If someone thinks you're violating their IP rights, they may send you a cease-and-desist letter. This doesn't mean they're right; it just means they think they are. You have three options:

>> Comply and stop using the material.

>> Fight the claim if you believe you're in the right.

>> Ignore the complaint and carry on (this can be risky).

If the issue affects your business, talk to an IP lawyer before making a move.

Finalizing Your Business Setup

The process of setting up your business depends almost exclusively on your specific product or service, so unfortunately, we don't have a lot of general advice. But as you prepare to set up your systems and launch your business, double-check if anything you need is missing. For example, ask yourself these questions:

>> **Do you have all the necessary contracts in place?** Think client agreements, vendor contracts, or terms of service — whatever keeps things legal and running efficiently.

» **Do you need any permits, licenses, or certifications?**
Some industries (like food, health, or legal services) have lots
of hoops to jump through. Make sure you've cleared
all of them.

» **Do you need to do anything else before you start setting
up your systems?**

Working from your Solopreneur Action Plan during this process
will help keep you on track. Still, you will quite likely miss some
things and, in fact, it's probably better that you do — the amount
of time it takes to think through every possible detail can delay
you longer than it's worth. You want to cover the obvious, the
critical, and the showstoppers. If you miss anything, that will
become apparent as you get up and running, and you can address
the issue at that point.

» Creating sanity-saving systems

» Avoiding overwhelm when looking for tools

» Automating the tasks you repeat again and again

» Integrating tools smartly into your business

Chapter **16**

Choosing and Setting Up Your Tools and Services

Running a solo business doesn't mean doing everything manually or all by yourself. The right tools and services can help you save time, reduce stress, and stay focused on what really matters, growing your business.

In this chapter, we discuss the importance of setting up standard business processes and when to automate or outsource. Then, we show you how to choose smart, easy-to-use tools that fit your workflow.

REMEMBER

This chapter is part of the final step of Phase 1 of the Solopreneur Success Cycle: Setting up your business. Once you have the right tools in place, your life will be easier.

Starting with Business Processes

You don't need fancy charts or software, but business processes do have a fancy name: *Standard operating procedures (SOPs)* are your playbook for repeatable tasks. In simpler terms, these are your step-by-step instructions for how to get something done.

SOPs boost consistency, reveal bottlenecks, and make it easier to hand things off. Even when the process involves only two or three steps.

Before you start buying tools or outsourcing tasks, you need to decide what needs to be documented and how. Is this task repeated often? Is it something you might want to delegate in the future? If the answer is yes to either of these, it deserves an SOP. These steps can help you develop your SOP:

1. **Start with the outcome:** What does success look like in one sentence? For example, "Welcome email is sent within 10 minutes of purchase."

2. **Sketch the flow:** What four-six major steps are needed to get there? Write a checklist, not a script.

3. **Draft the roles and tools:** For each step: Who's doing it (you, a VA, automation?)? What tool is involved, if any? Leave blanks where you're unsure. It helps to reveal gaps.

4. **Do a quick dry run:** Try it once, preferably with a dummy scenario. Did anything break or feel awkward? Take notes.

5. **Refine and save:** Clean it up, name it clearly (for example, "Client_Onboarding_v0.1"), and store it somewhere easy to find.

6. **Review the SOP after three real-world uses.**

Go through these steps for all the recurring tasks you've imagined for your business, and then document the answers. The rest of this chapter helps you with Step 3 with drafting the roles and tools.

Your first attempt to document your SOPs won't be perfect, and that's fine. Once you have each process broken down into steps, you can spot what's missing and adjust them over time. Even a simple checklist can save you hours of guesswork and help you delegate tasks for outsourcing (see the next section) when the time comes. By improving your SOPs over time, you'll continuously improve your business.

TIP

You don't have to invest in fancy software. Google Docs, Microsoft Word, or screen recordings work great for documenting your SOPs.

Deciding What to Outsource

Outsourcing is when you hire a contractor to perform certain tasks for you. It's one of the best ways to buy back your time and focus on what really moves your business forward. Whether you need a few hours of admin help or a pro to handle the stuff you dread, the goal isn't to do less work; it's to free you up to do more of the right work. The sooner you make it a habit to delegate low-value tasks, the faster you'll grow your business without burning out.

One of the smartest ways to protect your time and conserve your energy is to outsource the right tasks to the right people at the right time. Ask yourself these four questions:

>> **Is it mission-critical?** If the task directly affects your revenue, brand, or customer results, you may want to keep it in-house for now.

>> **Are you the best person to do it?** If you're slogging through tasks a pro can handle better and faster, that's a clue those tasks are good candidates for outsourcing.

>> **Does it take too much time?** Repetitive or low-value tasks drain time you can use to grow your business.

>> **Would outsourcing save money?** If your time is worth more than what you'd pay someone else, you're losing money by doing outsourceable tasks yourself.

Consider outsourcing include these common tasks:

>> Bookkeeping, accounting, and tax prep

>> Website development

>> Admin and scheduling

>> Legal setup and compliance

Start small by outsourcing one time-consuming task. Then build from there. And remember: Doing it all yourself isn't free. It costs you focus, energy, evenings, and weekends.

FIND ONLINE

Use the free Hire a Pro or No evaluator to figure out what you should delegate next. It's located at https://www.lifestarr. com/should-i-hire-a-pro-or-do-it-myself.

Choosing Tools for Your Business

When it comes to picking business tools, many solopreneurs fall into a common trap: overthinking. You read dozens of "best app" lists, sign up for free trials, and wind up more overwhelmed than when you started. Here's the real secret: The best tool is the one that makes your next step easier, not the one with the most bells and whistles.

TIP

Automated business tools should support how you work, not create more work. If you're juggling sticky notes and mental lists, it's time to upgrade. Good tools will

>> Fit your business size, SOPs, and budget.

>> Reduce effort and errors.

>> Expand their usefulness as you grow.

Automation isn't just for tech pros; it's for anyone tired of doing the same thing over and over. Start by identifying tasks you repeat daily or weekly. Some of the processes you may be able to automate with tools include

>> **Customer relationship management systems (CRM):** Organize contacts, track leads, automate reminders (for follow-ups, renewals, tasks), and save communication history.

>> **Customer support tools:** Generate auto replies for common questions.

>> **Email marketing tools:** Send welcome sequences and follow-ups to clients/customers.

RECOMMENDED TOOLS AND APPS

FIND ONLINE

Technology changes fast. That's why we provide ongoing, updated recommendations on our companion website. We'll keep the list fresh, so you always have access to tools that are relevant, reliable, and worth your time. Download a list of our latest app and tool recommendations at www.dummies.com/go/solopreneur businessfd.

>> **Invoicing tools:** Automatically send invoices and follow-up on late payments.

>> **Social media management tools:** Schedule content in advance.

WARNING

Automation helps you do more with less, but only after you know what works manually. Never automate a broken process. Test it first. Then automate what already works.

Six simple rules for picking smarter tools

Don't try to plan your entire *tech stack* (the collection of tools that help you run your processes) up front. Pick tools that solve immediate problems, are easy to figure out and use, and can grow with your business. When you start looking for tools, keep these simple rules in mind:

>> **Start slowly.** Don't overbuild your tool kit. The fewer tools you use, the easier it is to stay organized.

>> **Automate repetitive tasks first.** Look for tools that handle the tedious tasks automatically, such as sending follow-up emails or payment reminders.

>> **Use all-in-one tools when possible.** If one tool can manage contacts, send emails, and track sales, great. Fewer tools mean fewer problems.

>> **Make sure your tools can work together.** If your tools don't talk to each other, you'll spend too much time copying and pasting. Look for apps or platforms that sync.

>> **Avoid app collecting.** It's tempting to try the latest thing. But more tools usually mean more hassle. Stick with what works until you outgrow it.

>> **Keeps costs low.** Use free trials or start with the lowest-cost version, and don't sign up for annual payment plans until you know if a tool fits your tech stack long-term.

TIP

There's no one-size-fits-all setup. Your tools should fit your business type, the way you deliver your services or products, and how you like to work. If you're unsure where to start, talk to other solopreneurs and find out which tools work for them.

FIND ONLINE

Download a list of recommended tool types for different kinds of solopreneurs at www.dummies.com/go/solopreneurbusinessfd.

Tools every solopreneur should consider

No matter what kind of business you run, you need automated tools to help keep things running smoothly. The tools we cover in the following sections fall into these broad categories:

>> **Productivity:** These include calendars, to-do apps, file storage, password management, time tracking, and more.

>> **Website management:** You'll need an app or software to build and maintain your website and a service to host it.

>> **Marketing:** Many email marketing tools come in a suite of other tools, but you also need to think about content planning, material design, video creation and editing, lead capture, and search engine optimization (SEO).

>> **Sales and fulfillment:** These tools help you close the deal and then deliver your product or service seamlessly.

>> **Financial:** You can use these tools to simplify the way you get paid (and pay others), track expenses, and prep your taxes.

>> **Customer support and engagement:** Tools that interact with customers, track issues, and gather feedback will help you provide great customer support.

Picking productivity tools

Productivity isn't about doing more. It's about getting the *right* things done with less stress and more clarity. You don't need a stack of fancy apps. You just need a few tools that help you focus, stay organized, and protect your time. See Table 16-1 for some ideas.

Don't schedule every minute of your calendar. Leave space for life to happen.

REMEMBER

TABLE 16-1 Time- and Task-Management Tools

Tool	How to use it for maximum effect
Calendar	Use it to block time for focused work and prevent back-to-back commitment overload. A simple tool like Google Calendar is often all you need.
To-do list	A basic task list will do or, if you're juggling bigger projects, a Kanban board (which shows your work in progress). Your tools should support your work, not become extra work.
Note-taking	Use a simple note-taking app or document tool to keep things organized. You can always upgrade to something more structured later.
Time tracker	If you bill by the hour, use a time tracker. Many sync with invoicing tools, which saves time and helps you bill accurately.
Password manager	Store login info and generate strong, unique passwords for every site you log into. No more reused passwords, security risks, or "forgot password" loops.
File organization	Cloud storage tools are your digital file cabinet, where you can store contracts, receipts, and assets; access files from anywhere; and share folders with clients or partners.

Cloud storage also protects you if your computer crashes, and it makes collaboration much easier.

TIP

Artificial intelligence (AI) won't run your business for you, but it can help you run it more efficiently. Think of it as a virtual assistant that doesn't sleep, not as a brain replacement. When used intentionally, as shown in Table 16-2, AI can save you hours of brainstorming, planning, and researching; spark ideas; and improve content quality without taking away your unique voice or judgment.

Start with AI tools that

>> Feel like a natural extension of how you work.

>> Don't require coding or technical know-how (unless you're a techie).

>> Let you stay in control of the output.

TABLE 16-2 Using AI Effectively

Task	How to use AI
Writing and content creation	Draft blog posts, sales pages, emails, and course outlines (but always review, edit, and make it yours).
	Rewrite or summarize long documents.
	Improve grammar and tone to make writing more reader-friendly or persuasive.
Email assistance	Generate polite and professional replies faster.
	Summarize long email threads.
	Draft cold outreach to customers or follow-ups without starting from scratch.
Research and analysis	Get quick summaries of trends, competitors, or tools.
	Ask *What if?* questions to explore new strategies.
	Brainstorm content ideas for your niche.
Thinking partner	Clarify your thoughts by explaining them out loud (or in writing).
	Talk through new offers, messaging, or workflows.
	Spot gaps in logic or planning by testing ideas conversationally.
Admin support	Create SOPs or checklists from scratch or based on rough notes.
	Draft contracts, proposals, or onboarding templates (for review by a pro).
	Help create systems to streamline how you work.

You don't need to use AI for everything, but knowing where it fits into your business can dramatically improve your speed and reduce your mental load.

TIP

Use AI to get out of a rut, not to create your brand voice. The best results come from pairing your judgment with the tool's suggestions, not accepting whatever it spits out.

Creating and hosting your website

Social media is great for creating and maintaining visibility, but your website gives you control, credibility, and the ability to grow on your own terms. Before you promote your business or sell anything online, you need a website. It's where people find out who you are, what you offer, and how to take the next step. You can use these two tools to build and maintain a website:

>> **Website builder:** Helps you design and create your pages.

>> **Hosting and content manager:** Keeps your site online, secure, and running smoothly.

While different products can be used for these two functions, most solopreneurs will be better served using a combined service that provides both. This eliminates the need for constant security updates and requires much less technical skill.

Considering marketing tools

Marketing isn't just about getting more attention; it's about reaching the right people and turning them into paying customers. The right tools — like those that assist with various marketing tasks, shown in Table 16-3 — help you attract, warm up, and convert your leads without wasting time or energy.

TIP

You don't need pro-level software or equipment to make great videos. Focus on decent lighting, clear audio, and content that actually helps your audience.

REMEMBER

SEO takes time. For faster results, focus on email and social media unless local online searching is key to your business.

TABLE 16-3 **Tools for Common Marketing Tasks**

Task	What a tool can offer
Email marketing/list building	Email tools help you build and segment your list; send newsletters, promos, or updates; and nurture leads until they're ready to buy. Several email tools are available as standalone apps or as part of a suite of tools (which can add a lot of power and automation).
Designing	DIY design tools offer ready-made templates for everything from social media posts to brochures. Pick a design and plug in your content.
Video editing	Beginner-friendly tools are more than enough for most solopreneurs to produce clean, branded video content. These tools offer drag-and-drop simplicity, built-in templates, and plenty of export options.

(continued)

TABLE 16-3 *(continued)*

Task	What a tool can offer
Social media management	Social media tools help you to schedule posts in advance, stay active and consistent, and track what's working (and what's not).
Lead capture	*Landing pages* are web pages designed to prompt the user to take a specific action (typically, submitting a form that captures their email address). Lead-capture tools let you offer lead magnets,* collect contact info, and then send leads directly to your CRM or email tool.
Content planning/SEO	SEO can drive traffic to your website over the long term, but for most solopreneurs, it's a tough game to win, unless you serve a local area or a super-specific niche. Use SEO tools to find useful keywords, plan content, and optimize your site.

A lead magnet is a useful piece of content offered to potential customers in exchange for their contact information, usually an email address, but also a phone number and/or mailing address.

Your marketing efforts will mean nothing if you aren't tracking what works with analytics tools. Marketing should be based on results, not guesses. Analytics tools help you measure the numbers shown in Table 16-4.

TABLE 16-4 **What Analytics Tools Measure**

Analytic	What's measured
Traffic	Who visits your site and what they do there
Conversions	Who takes action (like signing up or buying)
Behavior	Which links visitors click, how far they scroll, or where they drop off (often visualized with heatmaps)
Campaigns	How emails, ads, or posts perform

WARNING

Don't fall into the vanity metrics trap, counting things like social media followers and likes. Track things that impact your business, not things that make you feel good.

Selecting sales and fulfillment tools

Converting a lead is only half the game. Once someone says *yes*, your job shifts to delivering your product or service smoothly and professionally. The right tools help you stay organized, get paid faster, and offer a satisfying customer experience. Table 16-5 shows various sales and fulfillment tools that help you do all that and more, without burning out or reinventing the wheel each time.

TABLE 16-5 Helpful Sales and Fulfillment Tools

Tool	What it does
Customer relationship manager	CRM tools can
	Track calls, emails, and notes.
	Sort leads by stage or priority.
	Set reminders for follow-ups.
	Segment your contacts into different groups.
eSignature tool	These tools let you send, sign, and store contracts without printing or scanning, helping you
	Protect your business with clear terms.
	Look professional.
	Reuse templates and set automatic reminders.
Quoting software	Create clean, professional documents clients can review, approve, and even pay, all in one place.
Sales funnel or checkout tool	Use this tool to
	Sell one product or service at a time.
	Provide a distraction-free customer experience.
	Test a new offer before launching a full site.
e-Commerce platform	If you offer multiple products or want shoppers to browse, compare, and buy in one place, these platforms help you
	Manage product listings and images.
	Handle tax, shipping, and payments.
	Run promos with discount codes or coupons.
	Provide customer updates and receipts.

(continued)

TABLE 16-5 *(continued)*

Tool	What it does
Online course and membership platform	Most platforms offer features such as
	Video, download, and content hosting
	Release lessons as student progresses, progress tracking
	Pay for courses in the platform,* membership control

Having a payment system as part of the course platform simplifies customer payments and tracking.

TIP

Here are a few additional points to keep in mind as you evaluate and choose sales and fulfillment tools:

>> Some CRMs are focused just on contacts. Others bundle in email, *sales funnels* (guided paths on your website that move visitors from just browsing to buying), or support tools. Start with one that fits your current needs, not one built for a 50-person sales team. Get what works now, and upgrade when you grow.

>> Whether you charge by the hour, offer packages, or sell digital products, having a reliable platform to generate quotes, invoice customers, and collect payment is key to keeping your cash flow healthy and your business stress-free. See "Choosing Financial Tools" later in this chapter for more about invoicing and payment tools.

>> Online course and membership platforms that are hosted are quicker and easier to launch but charge fees. Self-hosted setups give you more control but take more effort. Most solopreneurs start with a hosted platform and upgrade if they outgrow it.

Saving time with chatbots

Chatbots (computer programs that mimic people) can handle routine tasks for you, like answering FAQs, collecting leads, or directing visitors to the right place, even when you're off the clock.

>> *Rule-based bots* follow a script you write.
>> *AI-powered bots* respond more flexibly, using natural language.

Chatbots are great for

>> Capturing leads outside office hours

>> Guiding people to the right product or page

>> Prequalifying prospects before a sales call

WARNING

Always offer a way to reach a human. A frustrated prospect or customer with no backup option is a lost sale waiting to happen.

Choosing financial tools

A well-oiled financial setup may not be flashy, but it's mission-critical. The right tools help you get paid, stay organized, avoid tax-time chaos, and pay others, even if you outsource your book-keeping. See Table 16-6 for some guidance on financial tools to consider for your business.

TABLE 16-6 **Time-Saving Financial Tools**

Tool	What it can do
Invoicing tool	Send branded invoices.
	Accept payments online.
	Automate reminders for overdue accounts.
	Accept credit cards, PayPal payments, or ACH transfers securely.
Bookkeeping tool	Track income by type.
	Sort expenses by category.
	Log refunds and receipts.*
	Tag tax deductions (like travel or software expenses).
	Store docs for tax time.
Tool to pay others**	Handle outgoing payments to contractors and vendors.
	Automate recurring bills to save time.
	Connect your payment tool to your bank.

*Save every receipt. If you're ever audited, clean records are your best defense.
**Look for invoicing and bookkeeping tools that include features to pay others.

TIP

Some tools, like many online course and membership platforms, have built-in payment tools. This can make life easier for you and your customer. Don't forget to see if your tool can integrate with your CRM.

TIP

Many invoicing tools integrate with your CRM for smoother workflows. And don't stop at sending invoices; track who's paid, receive alerts about overdue balances, and protect your cash flow, because the longer someone goes without paying you, the more likely they are to default on paying.

Supporting and engaging your customers

The customer experience doesn't end with the sale. People expect fast, helpful responses to their inquiries, even from solopreneurs, and the right tools help you stay organized, professional, and efficient. Good customer support builds trust. Great customer support brings people back. Let the tools in Table 16-7 be your customer support team.

TABLE 16-7 **Essential Customer Support Tools**

Task	Possible tools and what they offer
Responding to customers	A shared inbox pulls customer messages (from email, chats, forms, or social media) into one place; nothing gets lost, and you can reply faster.*
Helping customers help themselves	A help center on your website with FAQs and how-to articles saves time and provides your customers with 24/7 answers, eliminating the need for follow-up.
Tracking issues	A help desk or ticketing tools Track and prioritize requests for help. Assign delivery statuses and log updates. Stay organized and appear more polished.
Getting feedback	Feedback tools Spot recurring issues early. Gather suggestions. See what's working (and what's not).

Some tools combine email, forms, chats, and social media messages into a single dashboard. No tab juggling required.

Real-time chatting can feel productive, but it often kills your ability to focus on deeper work. If you're constantly responding to messages, you're not building your business; you're reacting to it. Use real-time chat tools only if it's crucial to respond to customers immediately; otherwise, stick with asynchronous (delayed) communication like email and a support request (ticket) system.

Buying and Setting Up Your Tools

Picking the right tools is important, but how you buy them matters too. A smart purchase can save you hours of work each week. A rushed one can cost you money, time, and sanity.

Avoiding regret

Wasting money is never fun. Most tools offer free trials or starter plans. Use your trial period to solve one real-world task, not just to poke around the dashboard. If it's intuitive, useful, and solves your current problem, it's worth keeping.

If a tool offers a monthly plan, start with that. Upgrade to the annual plan once you're sure it's working for you. Yes, you'll spend a little more if you like it, but you'll save a lot if you don't.

Setting up your tools the right way

Buying the right tool is only half the battle. After you decide on an app or platform, you have to set it up so it actually performs the task you're automating. These steps can help:

1. **Start with your workflow.**

   Before you touch a single setting, map the process you're trying to support. Tools should fit the way you work, not the other way around.

2. **Focus on the essentials.**

   Most tools have tons of features. You don't need them all. Start with the basics that help you run today's business processes. You can always add more later.

TIP

Set up one core tool at a time. Start with the one closest to your customers (like your CRM or payment system) and then build from there. Use templates or a guided system (known as a *wizard*) when available. They'll get you 80 percent of the way there faster.

3. **Integrate programs when it saves time.**

   Use integrations or automation platforms when they clearly reduce manual work, not just because the feature exists.

4. **Test, tweak, and document.**

   Pretend you're the customer. Sign up, buy, or book through your automated system and see if everything works. Fix what's broken, and make note of how it's all connected.

Documenting Your Tool Selection

Be sure to document your tools in your Solopreneur Action Plan. Even basic documentation can save hours down the line (especially when you bring in help) because you'll have all the information about a tool stored in one place. Use this list to ensure you're including the necessary info:

- ➤➤ **Tool name:** HubSpot (for example)

- ➤➤ **Functions supported:** Email, CRM, sales tracking, web development, web hosting, chatbot

- ➤➤ **Reason for choosing:** Functionality, support, and price

- ➤➤ **Price:** $20/month

- ➤➤ **Billing schedule:** Monthly

- ➤➤ **Number of seats:** 1

- ➤➤ **Required integrations with other tools:** Mighty Networks

4

Running and Learning from Your Solo Business

Execute your marketing plan with proven best practices, track your results, and focus on tactics that grow your business.

Master sales conversations, manage your money, and run your solo business like a pro.

Document what's working and what's not, and prioritize your next moves by learning from both wins and setbacks.

Chapter **17**

Executing Your Marketing Plan

I f you've worked your way chronologically through the book to this chapter, you've completed the initial planning phase of your business. That's quite the accomplishment! Before you continue, take a deep breath and applaud yourself. You're now entering the executing/learning part of the Solopreneur Success Cycle. The *doing* phase of the business is officially beginning. Congrats!

As you kick off this new part of your journey, consider your marketing plan *first*. After all, you need to get clients/customers in the door. To that end, this chapter covers best practices for common marketing tactics that you, as a solopreneur, can benefit from implementing.

TIP

Some solopreneur businesses may already have established relationships with customers/clients they can start selling to. If that's you, you may be tempted to skip to the next chapter, which covers sales execution. But we highly encourage you to read this chapter because you'll likely need marketing at some point.

Following Best Practices for Executing Your Marketing Plan

As mentioned in Chapter 12, you have a wealth of marketing tactics to consider using for your business. Part of planning your business is selecting which ones you think will work best for you. It's important to note that these can certainly change over time. You can tackle marketing in tons of ways, but as with other chapters of this book, we look at the tactics in this section through the lens of a solopreneur and provide three best practices or helpful tips you should pay attention to so you get the most return on your investment without spending countless hours and too much energy on marketing. You have other areas of the business to focus on too, you know!

REMEMBER

Knowing who your audience is and the *pain points* (problems in need of solutions) they experience needs to be at the root of your marketing efforts. We cover that in Chapter 8. Although we don't specifically mention audience and pain points as we explain each tactic in this chapter, keep in mind that they need to drive your marketing efforts, no matter which tactics you choose or best practices you follow. Chapter 12 gives examples of how to use these tactics throughout the buyer's journey. Many of them can be used throughout each stage, it just depends on how you use them!

TIP

This book should serve as a starting point for your marketing efforts. While we stand by the best practices in this chapter and believe they're the top things for solopreneurs to keep in mind, we encourage you to do a bit of additional research to get the most comprehensive information to run your marketing successfully.

FIND ONLINE

Several great tools (many of them free!) can help you with your marketing efforts. Find our current list of recommended tools at www.dummies.com/go/solopreneurbusinessfd.

Content marketing

Content marketing refers to a broad strategy where you create and share valuable, relevant content, like videos or blogs, to attract an audience, driving that audience to a desired action, and keeping them for the long-run. It encompasses some of the other tactics in this chapter (we created separate sections for each of those because they warrant their own tips and best practices). The biggest hurdle for solopreneurs with content marketing is time and effort. To make it easier on yourself, follow these tips:

>> **Repurpose content.** This is an excellent shortcut that saves tons of time. Here's an example: Record a video, maybe of you addressing a pain point your audience experiences. You can turn the transcript into a blog post for your website and use AI to take clips to use on social media, and — boom! — you have a ton of content from one original piece.

>> **Keep your buyer's journey and content mapping in mind (see Chapter 8).** You need to create content for each touchpoint, meaning any interaction or moment a prospect/customer has with your business. Address each phase of the buyer's journey so they feel like you're guiding and speaking to them with their current situation in mind.

>> **Rely on others to create content for you.** Who says content has to be your own? Share posts from other social media accounts, repost videos others have created, or encourage happy clients to post videos of themselves using your product or write reviews raving about it.

Networking

Networking is the act of building relationships with other businesses to increase referrals, collaborations, and, ultimately, leads. The real value in networking comes from relationship building, not collecting business cards or LinkedIn connections. Here's how you do that:

>> **Focus on quality over quantity.** If you're in a room of 50 people, it's better to form deep connections with five people than it is to briefly shake hands with everybody in the room. Those five people are more likely to convert to clients over time than the people you just say hello to.

>> **Offer value and don't be salesy.** Focus on fostering relationships and truly trying to help people and listening to them. You can talk shop once the trust is there.

>> **Remember that practice makes progress.** Networking can be scary, but the more often you do it, whether virtually or in person, the easier it gets.

Referral marketing

A *referral engine* is a method you use to encourage (or even incentivize) people (especially customers) to bring you new business. Generating referrals is one of the most useful things you can do as a solopreneur to take some of the marketing pressure off yourself. These pointers can help you build an effective referral engine:

>> **Create a great onboarding and customer experience.** Your best referral tools are happy clients, so put some time and attention into providing a great experience for your customers. Chapter 14 covers onboarding customers.

>> **Leverage your existing contacts and network.** Once per quarter, reach out to your personal connections. Check in and inform them what you're up to (but don't sell to them). They can recommend you the most readily, so keeping them updated is important.

>> **Create processes to build your referral engine.** This means developing repeatable systems that make it easy for people to refer you. These might include providing prewritten referral request emails or post-purchase thank-you messages with a referral prompt or incentive (consider automating these processes). The goal is to make referrals a natural part of how people interact with your business.

Warm calling

Cold calling (reaching out to prospective customers without previous contact or connections) sometimes has a negative connotation, but what about *warm calling* (contacting someone who's already shown interest in your product/service)? Warm calling is all about relationship building instead of the hard sell. For many solopreneurs, this is a much more comfortable place to operate from. Start by collecting numbers through your website (like contact forms or sign-ups), networking events, or from referrals. These contacts have already opened the door, now you just need to follow up and build that relationship all the way to the sale. Ask yourself, would you want to receive the call you're making? If so, pick up the phone. If not, change your approach. Here are tips to make the calls impactful:

- **Have a genuine conversation.** Simply listen to your potential client/customer and respond to them, without being salesy. Make them feel heard.

- **Ask questions.** Focus the conversation on the prospective client/customer and their needs.

- **End with a soft next step.** Make a low-pressure offer (*Can I send you a quick overview from this call?*). Convince them to stick with you, without making a direct pitch until they're ready.

Public relations

The idea is to get media attention for you and your business. You can do this by pitching compelling stories to local reporters or submitting expert commentary to online publications. Public relations isn't just for big companies with big budgets, although may be a better option as you get more experience and clients under your belt. Solopreneurs can really make a splash using some of these techniques:

- **Be authentic.** Don't try to tell other people's stories. Keep in mind, as a solopreneur, *you* are your brand. Having something unique and specific to say makes it easier to get the attention you're looking for.

- **Focus on local and/or niche media.** Getting national attention or feature stories in big publications can be hard. Instead, focus your efforts to local and *niche media* (outlets that focus on specific interests). You'll be more likely to get noticed and spend less time spinning your wheels.

- **Use PR wins in other areas of marketing.** Repurpose any media attention you get as content for social media posts, case studies, and the like.

Search engine optimization

Search engine optimization (SEO), or improving your website's content, structure, and visibility to rank higher on search engines, is really just about understanding your audience's search intent. It's a great tactic to play the long game and build online exposure over time, but you need to be patient to see results. Start with these tips:

>> **Educate yourself on keyword optimization.** Focus on relevant, low-competition keywords and add them to your website pages, content, page titles, meta descriptions, and headers. Use SEO tools to understand customers' search intent and which keywords to go after.

>> **Create high-quality content that focuses on intent.** Make your online content relevant to your audience. Follow Marcus Sheridan's *They Ask, You Answer* approach and answer all the questions your audience may have about your business in your content. Be transparent.

TECHNICAL STUFF

>> **Get relatively familiar with technical SEO.** This isn't as scary as it sounds, but knowing your website's page speed, crawlability, and so on can really help your search rankings. Many free tools can help you do this.

REMEMBER

SEO is a buzzy term you may come across in the marketing world, but it isn't always the most impactful activity for solopreneurs depending on how many clients you need. SEO is a marathon, and your time may be more wisely spent sprinting to make one-on-one connections if you're looking for only a handful of clients. If having a lot of customers is essential, and you expect high search volume for your business, SEO is a good marketing option.

Local SEO

SEO improves your website's visibility in search results by optimizing content and keywords for a broad audience. Local SEO is a subset of SEO that focuses on location-based searches, helping your business appear in local listings and results. Local SEO can be a game changer for businesses serving people within their geographical area, so it's important to put some attention toward it. Here's how to do that:

>> **Optimize your Google Business Profile.** Claim your business on Google Business Profile. Fill in every section of your profile. This may be a potential customer's first impression of your business. Make it a good one!

Even if you don't have a physical storefront, you can still create a Google Business Profile and set your service area by entering a city or postal code under the Location and areas section. That way, you can still appear in search results.

» **Get your business in local directories and listings.** These are online platforms like Google Business Profile and niche-specific directories where businesses can list their contact info, services, and reviews. Being listed can boost your local SEO and make it easier for nearby customers to find you. Do online research to find directories in your industry and area.

» **Encourage online reviews.** Social proof, or evidence that people value your product or service, is one of the most powerful trust-builders for potential customers. Positive reviews in local listings, directories, and on Google can increase your credibility. Make it easy for satisfied customers to leave a review by sending a follow-up email with a friendly prompt and direct link. Showcase these reviews on your website, social media, and elsewhere.

Podcast guesting

Appearing on a podcast is a great way to get your product/service in front of a new audience without a lot of time and effort. But not all podcasts are worth your energy. Here are some suggestions:

» **Use podcast appearances as relationship-building opportunities.** Interviews conducted by podcasters can be excellent referral sources as well as great networking tools.

» **Be a guest on podcasts that serve your business goals.** If your audience isn't aligned with the podcaster's audience, why be on their show? Do your research before reaching out to the podcaster. The more aligned with the podcaster and the shows you're on, the less prep you'll have to do.

» **Make it easy for the host to say yes to you.** Submit a one-page proposal with clear messaging, links to your website, your bio, topics you'd like to cover, and sample questions to make the selection process as easy as possible for them. The more research they have to do to determine if you're a fit, the less likely they'll be to invite you.

Influencer marketing

Influencer marketing is when a brand (in this case, you) partners with an individual with a significant online following. It's not just for big brands, and it's a great way to expand your reach. Follow these tips to get the most out of joining forces with an influencer:

>> **Consider partnering with micro influencers instead of celebrity or macro influencers.** *Micro influencers* have a smaller, but often more engaged, following. Finding someone with a loyal following within your niche can get you in front of the right audience without spending a dime.

>> **Start small.** Managing and tracking these relationships can be time-consuming. See what works for your business before expanding to more influencers.

>> **Focus on long-term relationships.** You can collaborate for one-off engagements, but wouldn't it be nice if you had an ongoing relationship with an influencer so they develop an actual interest in you and your brand? It makes the partnership feel much more authentic.

Event marketing

Event marketing involves hosting in-person or virtual events to engage and educate your audience. These don't have to be large events; they just have to include your target audience and people you want to build relationships with. Let these tips guide you:

>> **Don't sell.** Use events to build relationships and engage with your audience. You can find a time and a place for a soft sell after you nurture these relationships. The goal of being at the event is for new contacts to get to know, like, and trust you.

>> **Let your personal brand shine.** You are your brand, and people may not see the real you if you're hiding behind your website and online content. Let potential clients/customers see who you are and what you represent.

>> **Focus on the follow-up.** Dare we say the main event of the event is the post-event? Make a plan to stay in touch with attendees to nurture real relationships with them.

Pay-per-click advertising

Pay-per-click (PPC) advertising is an online advertising model where advertisers pay a fee each time someone clicks on their ad. It can be cost-effective, provided you have a clear strategy and know how to implement it. Keep the following best practices in mind:

» **Start small.** Scale and increase your budget only when you pinpoint the message and strategy that's working. Getting started in this space can feel like throwing spaghetti at a wall. Until you find what sticks, don't increase your spending.

» **Focus on conversions.** Clicks don't necessarily equate to sales. If your landing pages aren't converting visitors into clients, something is wrong. It may be the ad's message and images, your offer, the landing page, or all of the above. Test each element separately to see which ones aren't working.

» **Consider using look-alike audiences to expand your reach.** For example, on certain platforms, like Facebook, you can upload an email list of past warm leads and clients, and the platform can find similar audiences that you can target.

TIP

Think about outsourcing this tactic. You can certainly teach yourself how to run PPC ad campaigns, but your time is better spent elsewhere.

Direct mail

Direct mail is making a comeback! With the digital advertising world becoming increasingly crowded, sending snail mail to potential clients/customers may help you stand out from your competitors in the digital world. You can collect addresses through lead capture forms on your website, event sign-ups, or client intake forms. Just be sure people opt in to receive communication from you so that you don't spam anybody. Use these tips to be most effective:

» **Make it personal.** How often do you immediately throw away mail that's very clearly been sent to the masses? What a waste! Make recipients feel like they're the only person receiving your marketing piece. Don't waste your time creating bulk mailings that nobody will ever look at.

- **Niche down as small as you can.** Not only will narrowing your target audience save you tons of money on postage, but it can also help you home in on your message and strategy. You can always do a second mailing targeted at a different audience later. A well-chosen list of 50 people can outperform a general list of 500. Be intentional and do your research on the audience before sending anything.

- **Have a clear call to action (CTA).** If you take time to create, print, and send marketing material, don't you want to make it clear what your audience should be doing on their end? Make your CTA specific. Don't just drive people to your website. Give them an offer that will be difficult to turn down and provide clear instructions on how to access it. Have a promo code or unique URL to more easily track results.

Some solopreneurs purchase targeted mailing lists from reputable list brokers but be careful. These lists can be expensive, outdated, or not fully compliant with privacy laws. If you go this route, vet your source carefully and prioritize permission-based, accurate data.

Affiliate marketing

Affiliate marketing is where you either promote another company's products or services and earn a commission for each sale generated through your efforts or vice versa. Note, this is a great tactic as your business matures and more people are aware of you and want to share your brand. Start with these pointers:

- **Affiliate marketing should add value to your product or service, not replace it.** Whether you're promoting someone's offering or vice versa, affiliate marketing should complement your core business. Look for opportunities that benefit your customer experience and allow affiliates to promote your brand in ways that align with your values and offerings.

- **Don't be deceptive.** Don't try to hide the fact that you'll get a commission when a person purchases something from these links. Be transparent, stay authentic, and communicate why you're using affiliate links and how your customers will benefit from them. Likewise, when others promote your brand, encourage them to be up front with their audiences. Honesty builds long-term trust in both directions.

» **Track and optimize.** If you're an affiliate, focus on the programs that are earning income for you. If you're running a program, keep an eye on which affiliates are most effective so you can support and reward them accordingly.

Educational presentations

Hosting online presentations or webinars can be a great way to connect with your audience, but as a solopreneur, your time is limited, so consider the following to streamline your efforts:

» **Think quality over quantity.** Don't stress yourself out by hosting too many of these sessions. Think about how you can make the greatest impact without doing too much prep work or taking too much time out of your busy schedule.

» **Create value and have a clear CTA.** The presentation should genuinely help your audience. If you feel like you've won their trust, provide a valuable offer, like a discount on the first few months of your service, for attendees.

» **Create a simple and repeatable registration process.** Find ways to automate the sign-up procedure so you don't have to reinvent the wheel for every event.

Organic social media marketing

Social media can be a powerful marketing tool or a distraction. Use social media to market your product/service *strategically*, but don't spend too much of your time posting. These tips can help:

» **Don't spread yourself too thin.** Do your research and narrow down your social media activity to the platforms your audience uses regularly.

» **Show up consistently.** Engage with your audience, provide value, and be supportive. Use social media to build meaningful relationships. Instead of just publishing a post and thinking you're done, respond to comments and engage with your followers', and target audience's, content as well.

» **Create a content calendar and schedule posts.** Scheduling content to post automatically throughout a month helps you focus on engaging with users the rest of the time (and on other areas of your business).

Podcasting

Podcasting can work wonders for your business, but it can also be one of those fun things you do that isn't moving the needle. Use these tips to make sure your podcast is providing real value:

>> **Be intentional about how you'll use your podcast in your business.** Are you doing a podcast because you think it's cool or because it genuinely helps you build relationships and increase revenue? Podcasting can be a wonderful marketing tactic *if* you have clear direction on how you'll get a return on your investment. How can you make podcasting work for you instead of becoming another item on your to-do list?

>> **Repurpose podcast content.** Podcasts can be repurposed as blog posts, video clips, social media posts, you name it. They're a great way to get a lot of content without spending hours creating it.

>> **Be selective about your guests.** At the beginning, it's okay to feature guests only who offer value to your audience, but don't add a ton of promotional benefits. Once you gain momentum, you'll want to ensure they also provide value to your business by promoting you to their large audience or putting you in contact with their connections.

Email marketing

Email marketing for solopreneurs isn't always about creating giant campaigns. It's about making your audience feel like you're speaking to them one-on-one. Here are some ways to do that:

>> **Focus on value, not just promotion.** Emails are a great way to build trust. Don't ruin that by constantly talking about your product and yourself. A value-focused email shares helpful tips or insights. A promotional email pushes a sale. Take a value-first approach to make eventual promotions more effective.

>> **Make the emails personal.** Write your messages like you're emailing a friend. You aren't a major corporation, so you shouldn't sound like one.

>> **Put time and effort into the subject line.** Everyone is flooded with emails every day. If your subject line doesn't stand out in the sea of messages in your recipient's inbox, then your email content won't matter because nobody will see it. SubjectLine.com is a great free resource to test the appeal of your subject line.

TIP

These days, the name of the sender is getting more and more important for email opens. If you're just starting out, be consistent by using your brand name or full name as the sender. Repetition will help you build brand awareness and can help to increase those opens.

Social proof

People trust other people, and if a potential buyer sees that others like your product/service, they'll be more likely to purchase what you're selling. But you have to be proactive, using best practices like these:

>> **Ask for customer reviews.** Making the ask can be intimidating, but these days it's common to request customer feedback. People see it as you being proactive in making your business great.

>> **Use social proof in multiple areas.** Use social proof not only on different mediums (Google Reviews, your website home page, social media, and so on) but also at different touchpoints during the buyer's journey.

>> **Choose the right platforms.** If you aren't a local business, Google Reviews may not be an effective marketing tool. If your audience isn't on Facebook, don't go after Facebook reviews. Figure out where your audience goes for reviews and focus your attention there. Be sure to include reviews on your website, in emails, and on your social media channels.

Where and how to begin

You don't have to do all of your own marketing. Outsourcing to professional marketers who specialize in the tactics you want to pursue can save you tons of time that you can put toward other areas of your business. If you want to approach it on your own, choose only a couple tactics as you begin so that you don't spread yourself too thin. Depending on how things are going, you can always add to your efforts. Many solopreneurs find a lot of value with relationship-driven marketing, like networking, especially as they're starting out, so consider starting there.

TIP

A good way to see what's working in your specific field is to check out the marketing tactics your competition is using and the varying degrees of success they're having.

REMEMBER

Put the tactics you plan to start with in your Solopreneur Action Plan and jot down the strategy for each to easily remember your starting point so that you can reference it as you grow and iterate. We recommend planning out 90 days in advance for how you plan to implement each tactic so that there's a plan in place, but not too far out into the future if things change.

FIND ONLINE

For a list of tools to consider using in your marketing efforts, visit www.dummies.com/go/solopreneurbusinessfd.

Making Your Website Work for You

As we mention in Chapter 12, your website should work for you behind the scenes while you're focusing on other things. Some of the ways your website can work for you include these:

>> **Bringing traffic to your website.** SEO may not be a priority for solopreneurs (unless you're local), but it's still wise to follow best practices so that SEO helps drive some traffic to your site, even if it's not your primary marketing focus.

>> **Engaging your audience.** You need to highlight your brand on your website in a way that sparks interest in your audience. You have three seconds (seriously) before a person decides if they want to stay on your site. Let your brand shine to keep them around. Make your messaging about your potential client/customer (not about you).

>> **Converting visitors to leads.** Feature a desired action, like an event signup, on your website that allows you to collect email addresses so you can nurture relationships with leads.

>> **Tracking and collecting data.** Set up analytics on your website so you can figure out who your visitors are and how they interact with your site and content.

Tracking Key Metrics

Tracking the performance of your marketing efforts is critical to saving time and money. After all, if you don't know which efforts are working and which aren't, you won't know where to focus more of your time and money. Beware of tracking vanity metrics, such as social media followers. These numbers may be ego boosters, but if they aren't converting prospects to customers or adding to your bottom line, they're meaningless. Instead, focus on tracking metrics that relate to your business goals, such as:

>> **Conversion rate:** Track the percentage of visitors who complete your desired action (buying your product or service, downloading a guide, and so on).

>> **Customer acquisition cost:** Knowing how much you spend to acquire a new customer helps you figure out if your marketing efforts are profitable.

>> **Engagement rate:** The amount of interaction you get from your content (email open and click rates, social media comments and shares, and the like) shows how engaged your audience is. If your engagement rate is good, you're getting your business in front of the right audience.

REMEMBER

The best marketers run tests on all their marketing efforts. Some strategies and executions fail to launch, and some take off. Apply your key findings to your marketing efforts moving forward. Stay consistent and stay curious. And, of course, don't forget to document your findings in your Solopreneur Action Plan.

Chapter **18**

Executing Your Sales, Finance, and Operations Plans

The idea of selling has a certain "yuck" factor for most solopreneurs. This is often because they believe they're not a natural salesperson or people have to be sleazy to sell. (See Chapter 13, where we encourage you to overcome common fears of selling.) The truth is that

>> Selling is an acquirable skill.

>> Ethical sales focus on solving real problems, not sleazy tactics. (See the nearby sidebar for more on this point.)

>> Objections are people telling you how to sell to them.

>> People want to pay for solutions to their *pain points* (the problems they're looking to fix).

The idea is not to sell to people but to help them buy. If you can solve their pain point, they'll want to buy from you.

AVOIDING THE SLEAZY SIDE OF SELLING

You'll be happy to know that you never, ever, ever have to be sleazy in your sales process. It's easy to avoid sleaze if the following three conditions exist:

- **The customer has a need or problem.** If they have an actual need or problem, the customer will view a solution as a good thing.

- **You can address that need or problem.** If you can help them, you have an obligation to do so.

- **You genuinely want to help them.** If your goal is to help the customer meet their need or solve their problem, you will be willing to send them elsewhere if you don't have the right solution for them. People will sense this and trust you.

If you keep these three conditions in mind, you'll never need to resort to sleazy tactics to sell your product/service.

In this chapter, we continue in the doing/learning phase of the Solopreneur Success Cycle. If you've been through Chapters 13 and 17, you've created your sales messaging and started executing your marketing plan. Hopefully, you'll soon have sales opportunities followed by the need to deliver your product or service and get paid for it. That's what we cover in this chapter.

Following the Solopreneur Sales Blueprint

If sales feel scary, it's because you don't understand the process. Selling isn't about pushing your product/service; it's about guiding prospects through a process that makes buying feel natural. The solopreneur sales blueprint may look familiar because it expands upon what Chapter 12 discusses about the secret to marketing:

>> **Step 1:** Build trust.

>> **Step 2:** Create resonance.

>> **Step 3:** Establish desire.

>> **Step 4:** Inspire action.

>> **Step 5:** Repeat Steps 1–4.

REMEMBER

The steps of this sales process need to be followed in this order. Changing the order is like asking someone to marry you on the first date. You're not likely to get the response you hoped for.

Yet you see people doing this all the time. Someone you don't know reaches out to you and asks if you want to buy their product or service. If you're like most people, you ignore them. They have no credibility; they've established no trust and created no resonance. Because they started at Step 4, their offer gets a fast trip to the deleted folder.

TIP

Some of this content is focused on *higher-touch sales*, where you have lots of contact with potential customers. *Low-touch* and *no-touch sales*, with little to zero customer contact, need to stick to these concepts as well.

The rest of this section walks through each step of the solopreneur sales blueprint.

Step 1: Build trust

Hopefully, you've already established some level of trust with potential customers via your marketing. If your marketing has already built strong trust, this step may be easier, but you should always reinforce trust through your direct interactions. Here, we focus on two ways you can build trust with a prospective customer.

Helping people

We talk about helping people a lot throughout this book. After all, helping is forever. By trying to help a potential customer, you instinctively do the following:

>> You're honest.

>> You demonstrate your expertise.

>> You listen a lot more than you talk.

When you focus on understanding a prospect's needs and genuinely helping them, you naturally guide them toward realizing that your solution is a great fit. That's why a sales process centered on helping people works so well.

Using social proof

When potential customers see that other people like what you do, they're more inclined to trust you. If those people remind them of themselves, their trust is even more powerful. This is where *social proof*, or influence from others, enters the sales process. Try to connect your prospects to social proof through testimonials or referrals, especially from people similar to them in terms of background or business needs.

Step 2: Create resonance

Trust is the foundation of sales, but connection makes people want to work with you. Think of it like a relationship with a neighbor, you may trust them, but that doesn't mean you want to have dinner with them. Resonance ensures your ideal customers feel aligned with you.

Use your value statement (from Chapter 13) to *qualify leads* (determine whether a potential customer will buy from you). Those with whom your message or product/service resonates (meaning people who feel aligned with what you're offering and how you talk about it) will be eager to engage, while others will naturally disengage. Whether it's through direct interaction or content (your website, videos, blogs), tailor your messaging to build this connection.

To create resonance, give these tactics a try:

>> **Do your homework.** Research prospects to understand their needs without overstepping.

>> **Manage your state of mind.** Your energy influences your interactions, so get into the right mindset before you talk with a prospect.

>> **Speak the prospect's language.** Mirror their concerns and desires to show you truly understand them.

>> **Make them feel understood and seen.** Validate their struggles. If you're a sales coach talking to a prospective client, you may say, "Selling is hard for most solopreneurs, and for good reason."

>> **Use their own words.** If the potential client says, "I hate begging for sales," respond with, "Sales shouldn't feel like begging; it should be natural. We can make that happen."

>> **Address unspoken objections.** Anticipate a prospect's doubts: "Many solopreneurs hesitate to invest in a sales coach, until they realize how much revenue they're losing."

>> **Show the prospect a better future.** Help them visualize success: "Imagine walking into a sales call with total confidence."

By creating resonance, you turn trust into real engagement, making it easier to close the sale.

Step 3: Establish desire (and ability)

What's the cost of doing nothing? Stress, lost revenue, missed opportunities? People ignore problems they don't know how to fix, but that doesn't make them disappear. Your job is to make potential customers feel the pain and then show them the way to ease it. Done right, this isn't manipulation; it's service. And if they don't feel that pain, they don't need your product or service, and you can move on to the next prospect quickly.

Qualifying for budget and authority

If people don't have the budget or the authority to buy what you're offering, no amount of selling skills will result in a sale. So, ask early to avoid surprises later.

If you're *qualifying for budget*, or determining the prospect's ability to buy your product/service, try this approach:

> "I want to make sure we're on the same page. If this solution is a great fit for you, do you have the budget to move forward?"

If they say no, offer alternatives like these:

>> **Payment plans:** Break the cost into manageable chunks.

>> **Smaller packages:** Scale down your offer to fit their budget.

If they say yes to one of your alternatives, you have the green light to continue. If not, redirect them; for example, guide them to another option from another provider. They may come back later when they can afford you.

When you're qualifying for authority, you confirm who the decision-maker is to ensure you're talking to the right person. Ask them:

> "Who else needs to be involved in the decision-making process for this purchase?"

If it's someone else, ask to set up a meeting with the decision-maker and/or get a formal referral to the decision-maker. If your contact is the decision-maker, reinforce their confidence:

> "Great! Let's make sure this is the right fit for you."

Timing matters, too. Even if the budget and authority check out, if the buyer's not ready to act soon, things can stall. Ask:

> "If we both feel this is a fit, when would you want to get started?"

This helps you gauge urgency and prioritize your follow-up accordingly.

TIP

If there's any question about the prospect's budget, authority, or timing, don't be afraid to ask. It's better to find out early in the process than to waste time trying to close a sale that isn't going to happen.

Driving action: Pain versus aspiration

When it comes to decision-making, pain is a far stronger motivator than aspiration. People act quickly to relieve discomfort but often hesitate to pursue improvements that seem optional. That's why, in sales, you start with the pain and help your prospect see the cost of inaction. Then transition to aspiration, showing them the rewards of taking action.

EXPLORING PAIN

Before someone is ready to move forward, they need to fully acknowledge what's holding them back. Instead of telling your prospect what their pain points are, ask the right questions so they articulate the problem themself.

Imagine a sales coach pitching a prospect. Instead of saying, "Boy, it must really stink losing every sales opportunity you go after," they should ask questions like:

>> What's the most frustrating part of your sales process?

>> What would it mean for your business if you could turn just half of those *noes* into *yeses*?

This helps your prospect internalize the problem rather than just nodding along to your sales pitch. When they verbalize their struggle, they feel the urgency to fix it.

ENVISIONING A BETTER FUTURE

Once a prospect recognizes their pain, shift the conversation toward what's possible. Help them see that a better future isn't just wishful thinking, it's an achievable result. Frame it in a way that feels personal and specific. For example, a sales coach can make the following pitch:

> "Imagine walking into every sales call with total confidence, knowing exactly how to handle objections and close deals effortlessly."

This vision of success makes the decision to move forward feel natural.

MAKING THE EMOTIONAL CONNECTION

Logic plays a role in buying decisions, but as you see in Step 4, emotions drive action. If you help prospects feel the impact of their struggles and see the transformation your solution offers, they'll be far more likely to commit. Start with pain to get their attention and end with aspiration to get their buy-in.

Step 4: Inspire action

People naturally hesitate to take any action. Your job is to give them a compelling reason to act.

Tapping into emotion and logic

People buy based on emotion and justify their decision with logic. For example, someone purchasing a luxury car may say it's an investment, but the real reason is the way it makes them feel. When closing a sale, tap into your prospect's emotions first and then reinforce with logic.

Employing urgency and scarcity

As a solopreneur, you've likely built some level of scarcity into your offering: You can help only so many people or make only so many products in a given amount of time. Did you know that a prospect's perception of scarcity is a great way to inspire action?

When people see something that they may not be able to get, they want it more. When an email blast says, "I currently have an opening for one new client," people know they need to act right away. Plus, the offer's scarcity causes it to be perceived as more valuable.

Here are some ways to convey urgency and scarcity:

>> **Cutoff date:** "This program starts on June 23. The next one starts in December."

>> **Deadline with reward:** "Join by Friday and get a private one-on-one strategy session with me ($500 value) at no extra cost!"

>> **Discounted price cutoff:** Enroll before March 3 or lose the $200 discount."

>> **Exclusive community:** "You need to show you have a business making at least $500K in revenue to join."

>> **Limited supply:** "Only 3 remain this month."

>> **Limited-time offer:** "This deal expires Friday."

>> **One-time offer:** "This is the ONLY time this workshop will be offered live."

>> **Wait list:** "Sign up now or wait 6 months."

WARNING

You should use urgency and scarcity only in an honest fashion. If you claim something is limited and it isn't, people will often figure that out and you'll lose credibility.

Reducing their risk so you close more deals

People hesitate to buy because they fear they're making the wrong choice. If you remove that fear, you remove their biggest reason to say no. Try these risk-reducing strategies:

>> **Action-based refund:** "Finish the course, and if you aren't satisfied, you'll get a full refund."

>> **Bonus retention:** "Keep the freebie, even if you don't buy."

>> **Fast-action refund:** "Cancel within 7 days, no questions asked."

>> **Money-back guarantee:** "If it doesn't work, you don't pay."

>> **Pay only after results:** "No charge until you see progress."

With no downside, why wouldn't a prospect say yes? Remove the risk, and watch your sales grow!

Closing the sale effectively

In high-touch sales, to get the deal, you have to convince the prospect to say *yes*. And to get them to say *yes*, you need to ask for the sale. This is difficult for many solopreneurs, but handling things right can make closing the sale a lot easier and more comfortable for you.

TEST CLOSING

One of the keys to closing is called the *test close*. Test closing involves getting people to say *yes* to your offer before you ask for the sale. You can ask questions like:

>> If I can solve [your pain point] and it only costs [$X], would it make sense for you to move forward?

>> On a scale from 1 to 10, how confident are you that this will solve your problem?

If they say *yes* or rate your solution highly, you're in good shape. If not, you need to respond to their objections . . .

HANDLING OBJECTIONS

At this point, assume your prospect's objections are misguided because you've done your homework and you know you can help them. When someone says *no* or claims your product/service isn't right for them, ask them to explain why. You should understand these two things about objections:

>> The prospect is telling you what you need to know to close the sale, so objections are a good thing.

>> You should never, ever disagree or argue with them.

Here's the step-by-step way to handle objections (have this list of steps in front of you when you make calls):

1. Acknowledge the objection and move on.

The prospect may have an automatic response like "I'm just looking." Say, "I hear you. A lot of people start out that way."

2. Listen without interrupting.

Give them space to resolve the objection on their own.

3. Repeat the objection as a question.

For instance, if they balk at the price of your product/service, you can ask, "So, you feel it costs too much?"

4. Get more information.

Dig a little deeper with a prompt such as "I know you have reasons for saying that. Would you be willing to explain them?"

5. Review the prospect's pain points.

It helps to remind them why they sought you out: "Let's take a step back. What made you interested in my offering in the first place?"

6. Align and reframe the connection.

You can use social proof to nudge them toward a decision: "I understand, and many people feel that way at first. But here's what they found after moving forward."

7. Remind them they need your help.

Underscore the fact that their issue will continue if they don't take action: "If we don't move forward, what's your plan to fix this?"

8. **Test close again.**

Conclude the discussion by saying, "So, it sounds like we've covered everything. Let's get this deal started." If they object, go back to Step 1. If they say, "Okay," go to Step 9.

9. **Close the sale.**

Sign the deal.

Step 5: Repeat Steps 1 through 4

This step is about leveraging your existing customer base. Successfully closing a sale isn't the end of the journey. In a sense, it's the beginning because the most profitable businesses know that repeat customers and referrals are the key to long-term success. The more you nurture your relationships, refine your sales process, and build efficiency, the easier it gets to generate consistent revenue.

Selling to past customers is less difficult and more cost-effective than acquiring new ones. If someone has already bought from you once, chances are, they'll buy again, but you have to stay on their radar. Follow these tips to do so:

>> **Step 1: Deepen trust.** Your job isn't done after the sale. Use onboarding (see Chapter 14) to reinforce the customer's decision and provide ongoing value. Check in, offer helpful insights, and position yourself as a trusted partner.

>> **Step 2: Increase your resonance.** If you're out of sight, you're out of mind. Maintain consistent, meaningful touchpoints like engaging emails, calls, or social media content to keep customers connected without always pitching to them.

>> **Step 3: Establish more desire.** Solving one problem often reveals another. If you build a bakery's website and they lack traffic, offer SEO services. Identifying their next challenge strengthens the relationship and drives new sales.

>> **Step 4: Inspire additional action.** Encourage repeat business by making it easy. Offer loyalty perks, exclusive services, or special pricing for returning clients. Referrals are gold, so create a simple, rewarding system to encourage them.

Satisfied customers are often happy to introduce you to others who need your services. Make it easy for them by offering a referral bonus or a simple way to share your business with others.

Prospecting for Customers

Sadly, customers won't just appear once you launch your website. If you don't actively seek them out, your sales pipeline will dry up fast. The good news? With the right prospecting strategy, you'll always have new leads coming in.

If you don't keep a steady flow of new leads, you'll wake up one day with an empty sales pipeline and zero revenue. Not fun.

Keeping your sales pipeline full

You can prospect for customers in lots of different ways. Some are appropriate for any touch level, and some make sense only for high-touch sales. Pick a few that work for you and your business, and do them religiously while constantly improving your approach. These lead-generation tactics can work regardless of the touch level of your sale:

>> **Referrals and introductions:** Leverage your network and existing clients to connect with potential leads. Ask for introductions and offer referral incentives when appropriate. This is the most powerful and effective way most solopreneurs get leads.

>> **Inbound lead follow-ups:** If someone downloads a resource, signs up for a newsletter, or engages with your brand, reach out personally instead of just relying on automated email sequences (see the next section).

>> **Social media selling:** Actively engage with prospects on LinkedIn, in Facebook groups, or on industry-specific forums by answering questions and starting conversations.

>> **Warm email outreach:** Send targeted, personalized emails to potential leads who fit your ideal customer profile.

In addition, high-touch sales can benefit from the following activities (which we also highlight in Chapter 17 when we talk about your marketing efforts):

>> **Event networking:** Attend live or virtual industry events, conferences, and networking meetups where you can engage directly with potential customers.

>> **Personalized LinkedIn outreach:** Connect with potential leads, engage with their content, and start value-driven conversations before pitching your offer.

>> **Strategic partnerships:** Identify complementary businesses and reach out to explore referral partnerships or co-selling opportunities.

>> **Warm calling:** Reach out directly via phone calls or social media to people you know in some way and can connect with through a mutual contact.

REMEMBER

Prospecting requires consistent effort. It's not a one-time task but an ongoing habit. The more you refine your approach and track your results, the easier it gets to maintain a steady flow of new leads and keep your sales pipeline full.

Following up with email sequences

Do you want to follow up with leads without spending all day in your inbox? That's exactly what *email sequences* do. Instead of firing off one email and crossing your fingers, you can use a well-planned automated sequence of emails to keep your business top of mind, build trust, and guide leads toward buying — without feeling salesy.

If you're not following up, you're leaving money on the table. Stay consistent, tweak your messaging, and keep testing it. Small improvements add up. Before you know it, you'll be turning more leads into paying customers on autopilot.

FIND
ONLINE

Get the Simple Email Sequence Formula at www.dummies.com/go/solopreneurbusinessfd.

Documenting, Tracking, and Staying Consistent

As a solopreneur, you wear all the hats, including the one that says *sales manager*. But as a solopreneur, you're busy; if you don't have a system to track leads, follow-ups slip through the cracks, deals get stuck, and your income seesaws. The good news? You have lots of ways to do this. You just need a simple but solid system that works for you. A solid sales-tracking system helps you

>> Capture every lead. (No more lost opportunities!)

>> Stay on top of follow-ups. (Because "I'll get back to them later" never works.)

>> Move deals through your sales pipeline.

>> Track proposals, contracts, and closed sales.

TIP

It's easy to get busy doing the work and forget about bringing in new clients. But a good system reminds you when to check in, so no potential deal slips away. Make it a habit to log every lead, track every conversation, and set follow-up reminders. See Chapter 16, where we discuss finding the right tools for every function of your business.

Managing Cash Flow

Large companies have an interesting approach to running their businesses. They want to get paid quickly but take their sweet time when paying their bills. They do this to optimize their *cash flow*. The concept of cash flow relates to the money that comes into your business (collected revenue) versus the money that goes out (paid bills). If you collect your money quickly and pay your bills slowly, you have more money in the bank. That's why large companies take this approach.

If you aren't paid upon delivery by using a shopping cart to sell your product/service, please pay special attention to this section. It may make the difference between failure and success.

Setting up a process for getting paid

You want to get paid as quickly as possible. It's not rocket science, but you need to do some things to optimize your process for quick payment. If you want to get paid on time, communicate the payment terms you establish in Chapter 13 up front when you're working with a new client. Here's how:

>> **Spell it out.** Define payment due dates, accepted payment methods, and any late fees in your contracts and invoices.

>> **Explain your terms early in the relationship.** Discuss your payment terms before starting work to avoid confusion later.

TIP

Clients are more likely to honor terms they've agreed to in writing. Include your payment policies in your proposals and contracts and, if appropriate, statements of work (see Chapter 13).

Invoicing for faster payments

The sooner you invoice your customers, the sooner you get paid. Follow these best practices:

>> **Send invoices immediately.** Get your invoice to the customer right after you deliver your product or service.

>> **Be clear.** Include details like payment due dates, itemized charges, and your contact info.

>> **Use a direct payment link.** Make it easy for clients to pay their invoice in one click by offering a digital payment option (see the next section).

Many accounting software tools allow you to automate your invoices. Use this feature to get paid more quickly.

WARNING

Like anything, avoiding a few simple mistakes can make a big difference. Don't make these mistakes:

>> **Creating confusing invoices:** Make sure they're easy to read and include all the necessary details.

>> **Forgetting to invoice:** Set reminders to send them out or use automated invoicing tools.

>> **Not enforcing payment terms:** If clients see you're lax about the rules, they'll take advantage.

Making payments easy

Although some customers may insist on paying you by using one of the more "traditional" ways, like a paper check or a bank wire, the fewer obstacles your invoicing system presents, the faster clients pay. That's why digital payments are a great idea. Yes, these payment options cost money, but they help you avoid customers' the-check's-in-the-mail excuses. Offer multiple payment options, such as:

>> **Credit/debit cards:** Most customers find this option fast and convenient.

>> **ACH transfers:** Electronic transfers between banks come with lower fees than credit cards.

>> **PayPal, Stripe, or other digital platforms:** Using a direct payment link is ideal for facilitating quick online payments.

WARNING

If your business only accepts checks, expect delays in receiving payment. Offering digital payment options can speed up your cash flow significantly.

Automating payment reminders

Late payments happen, but you can reduce them by setting up automatic reminders that follow a step-by-step process like this one:

1. **Send a friendly reminder a few days before an invoice is due.**

2. **Send another reminder immediately after the due date.**

3. **Check your accounts receivable weekly to identify overdue invoices.**

4. **Send a follow-up email.**

   A simple "Hey, just checking on this" message often works.

5. **Call if there's no response.**

   Get the customer to commit to a payment date. Keep calling until you get paid.

6. **Consider offering an installment plan.**

   If a client is struggling, offer a payment plan so you get something rather than nothing.

7. **Communicate that late fees are going to be charged.**

   It's important to remind them before you charge late fees so they don't claim they didn't know.

8. **Charge late fees if necessary . . . and then keep calling!**

TIP

If you have customers who pay for your product/service every month, automate your invoices so you never forget to send them. Lots of tools can be set up to do this.

Managing Financials

Staying on top of your finances is critical to keeping your solo business running smoothly. Managing your money effectively helps you avoid cash flow issues, make informed decisions, and ensure your long-term success. In this section, we cover key financial practices to help you stay in control.

Separating business from personal finances

One of the most important financial habits you can develop is separating your business and personal finances. Mixing your finances can lead to confusion, tax complications, and a lack of clarity about your business's financial health. Chapter 15 walks you through opening a business bank account, obtaining a dedicated business credit card, and setting up an invoicing/accounting system. If you haven't already done these things, do them now.

REMEMBER

Keeping your finances separate not only makes tax season smoother but also gives you a clearer picture of your business's performance.

Staying on top of your bookkeeping

Bookkeeping isn't just a year-end task; it's an ongoing process that helps you maintain financial stability. Falling behind on bookkeeping can lead to cash flow problems, missed deductions, and a stressful tax season.

Here are some best practices:

>> **Track every expense and income source.** Regularly log your transactions to avoid surprises.

>> **Reconcile accounts monthly.** Compare your financial records with your bank statements to catch errors early. If you integrate your accounting system with your bank accounts, this is usually painless.

>> **Save receipts and invoices.** Digital copies work fine, but keeping an organized record ensures you're prepared for tax audits.

By keeping your books in order, you'll always know where your money is going and how your business is performing.

Using financial statements

Financial statements help you understand your business's profitability, cash flow, and overall financial health. You should keep track of these two (or maybe three) key statements:

>> **Profit and loss statement (P&L):** Summarizes your revenue and expenses to show whether you're making a profit. (Flip to Chapter 9 for details on creating a P&L.)

>> **Balance sheet:** Provides a snapshot of your assets, liabilities, and equity at a given point in time.

>> **Cash flow statement:** If, for some reason, you decide to use accrual accounting instead of cash accounting, watch your cash flow statement to make sure that you're generating cash in your business. Most solopreneurs use cash accounting, and the P&L statement will do this.

Review these statements regularly to spot trends, make informed decisions, and plan for growth.

Watching your working capital

Working capital is the money you have available to run your day-to-day operations. If you don't manage it properly, you may struggle to cover basic expenses, even if your business is profitable. Maintaining a positive working capital balance ensures you can handle unexpected expenses and keep your business running smoothly. These tips can help you shore up your working capital:

>> **Monitor your cash flow closely.** Make sure you always have enough money to cover upcoming expenses.

>> **Invoice promptly and follow up on late payments.** The faster you get paid, the healthier your working capital balance will be.

>> **Control expenses.** Avoid unnecessary costs, especially during slow periods.

>> **Plan for seasonal financial fluctuations.** If your business has busy and slow periods, build up reserves when your cash flow is strong.

>> **Put aside money for taxes.** You don't want to be unprepared when the tax bill arrives.

WARNING

Surprisingly, businesses can fail because they grow too quickly. If your working capital flows out more quickly than your revenue comes in, you may wake up one day with an empty bank account. When things are going great, keep this in mind and plan ahead.

Operating Your Solo Business

Being your own boss sounds great, until you realize you're also the entire company. No employees, no safety net, just you keeping the wheels turning. That means managing your time, knowing when to work with service providers, investing in your growth, and staying ahead of risks that can make or break your success.

The good news? You don't have to hustle 24/7/365 to keep your business thriving. With the right systems and habits, you can work smarter, not just harder.

Managing your time

Time is your most valuable resource. Once it's gone, it's gone. Don't let distractions and mundane tasks steal it from you. Here's how to take control:

>> **Put money-making tasks first.** Sales, client relations, and marketing should be your top priority.

>> **Time block like a pro.** If you don't schedule focused work time, your day will vanish into a black hole of emails and random tasks.

>> **Create standard operating procedures (SOPs).** Document your processes so you don't have to remind yourself how to handle simple tasks. Setting up SOPs allows you to be more efficient and makes it easier to outsource basic tasks if you choose to.

>> **Automate what you can.** Use technology to automate repetitive or continuous tasks like invoicing.

>> **Outsource low-value tasks.** If a task doesn't require your expertise, pass it off to an outside service provider.

Outsourcing tasks to service providers

You don't have to do everything alone. The right freelancers or contractors can handle your bookkeeping, marketing, or admin work, which frees you up to focus on growth. But bad outsourcing? That's just more work for you in the long run. Here's how to do it right:

>> **Know what you need.** If you don't have a clear vision of the work to be done, your contractor won't either. Define success before you hire.

>> **Take the time to pick the right people.** A bad freelancer can make your life harder, not easier. Look for professionals who understand solopreneurs and can deliver the results you expect.

>> **Set clear expectations.** Be up-front about deadlines, *deliverables* (the finished product), and how you like to communicate.

>> **Stick with your SOPs.** This keeps things running smoothly, even when someone else is doing the work.

Good outsourcing isn't just about saving time; it's about making sure your business keeps running without running you into the ground.

Improving yourself

Your business grows along with you. If you stop learning, adapting, and experimenting, your business will follow suit. Here are some ways to improve and refresh yourself and your business:

>> **Keep learning about what you're doing.** Read books, take courses, and stay on top of industry trends.

>> **Build your network.** Solopreneurship doesn't mean isolation. Surround yourself with people who understand what you do.

>> **Test, refine, repeat.** The best business owners don't just set it and forget it. They tweak their practices, measure the results, and adjust.

You are your business's most valuable asset. Invest in yourself, and your business will reap the benefits.

Dig into Chapter 19 to see how to document issues with your business so you can improve it.

Looking for other risks

Risk isn't fun to think about, but neither is being unprepared for a crisis. A little planning now can save you from major headaches later. Here are two big risks to keep an eye on:

>> **Legal risks:** Contracts and policies (privacy policy, website terms of service, payment terms, and refund policies) aren't optional; they're your safety net. Get agreements with customers and service providers in writing.

>> **Client risks:** Not every client is a good client. Watch for red flags, enforce boundaries, and don't be afraid to say no to bad deals. Use statements of work (covered in Chapter 13) whenever appropriate.

Risk management isn't about being paranoid; it's about being prepared. By staying ahead of risks, you'll build a business that not only survives, but also thrives.

Chapter **19**

Documenting Problems and Solutions

This is Phase 2 of the Solopreneur Success Cycle, the doing (and learning) part, which solopreneurs often skip over with their busy schedules. We get that, but in this chapter we help you understand why it's important to take time to reflect and truly understand why things are or aren't going your way. In fact, out of the countless solopreneurs we've spoken to, a common thread across the successful ones is that they do a good job of stepping back and learning from their mistakes.

As you work through this chapter and begin to identify problems with your business and their solutions, keep your goals and your *why* in mind. Also keep track of how you feel running your business. Odds are, you started a solo business to take control of how you spend your days. If your days and your ideal life aren't what you thought they would be, take a step back and change a few things. The documentation process we outline in this chapter should help.

Knowing the Benefits of Taking a Step Back (and When to Do It)

Taking the time to step back and reflect on where your business is and where it's going has many benefits. Documenting your problems and solutions can help in areas you may not typically think of, including the following:

>> **Pattern identification:** Taking a step back allows you to spot overarching trends, recurring challenges, or emerging opportunities that might not be obvious when you're focused on daily tasks. These insights can inform high-level decisions around strategy, growth, and long-term planning.

>> **Time savings:** Knowing what you've done right or wrong in the past can help you streamline your decisions moving forward and avoid problematic activity without having to experience it time and time again.

>> **Confidence boost:** Knowledge is power. The more you can learn about what is and isn't working, the better your business will run, and the more resilient you'll feel as new conflicts come your way.

>> **Improved efficiency:** Creating scalable systems, such as documented workflows or repeatable onboarding steps, can help identify and solve recurring problems. These systems also support growth by making it easier to delegate or outsource tasks like customer service, content creation, or admin work to other contractors or virtual assistants. As you gather data and gain experience, refining these processes becomes simpler and more impactful.

>> **Easy transfer of knowledge:** To piggyback off of the last point, if you ever need to train a person, sell your business, or hand the business off, having a list of your problems and solutions handy will make the transition much easier and will assist in the longevity of your business, whether or not you're a long-term part of it.

TIP

How often you take stock of your problems and solutions depends on your business and what you're assessing. Use this list to help you determine when to check in on various issues:

>> If the problems are emotional (feeling burned out, for example, or doubting your abilities) or task-related, a weekly check-in may be appropriate.

>> If you're reviewing a sales or marketing process, give it a month or so between reviews to keep an eye on trends.

>> When it comes to strategic planning, do a quarterly check-in and make a plan for the next quarter.

Documenting What's Not Working

As you're planning your business, you have an idea in mind of how things will go. With your SMART goals (see Chapter 4) front and center, you're thinking about which metrics you'll track for marketing, the number of clients you want at any given time, how many hours per week you want to work, and so on.

When your business is up and running, you have some information (and if we're honest, gut feelings) about what's working and not working for you and your business. The purpose of documenting all of this isn't to put your failures in writing. Instead, it's a way to figure things out and explore new opportunities.

REMEMBER

Running your own business can be an emotional roller coaster, and reflecting on what isn't working can be tough mentally. We get it! Just remember, this kind of documentation is something all businesses should be doing, even if they're incredibly successful. If you're seeing that a bunch of things aren't going your way, that's okay. You're far from alone, and now you're simply putting the tools in place to change anything that's causing problems. So, don't shy away from this activity; instead, embrace it!

Because you're wearing multiple hats as a solopreneur, it's important to have a dedicated documentation system and process, whether you're using Google Drive, a note-taking app, or a pad of paper, so you don't misplace any of your records of what's working and what isn't. Have a separate document for each area of your business; that way, you can easily reference your past performance specifically for each category.

REMEMBER

Don't forget to update your Solopreneur Action Plan with how you will approach this and where to find your documentation.

The areas to consider tracking can include, but aren't limited to

>> Customer/client satisfaction

>> Finances

>> Operations

>> Personal/professional growth

>> Sales/marketing

>> Work-life balance

In each document, include the following:

>> **The issue:** Document what you were trying to do, when you did it, and what you thought the outcome would be. Then, write down what's currently happening and why it isn't what you anticipated.

>> **The impact of the issue on your business or your life:** Why is this a problem? How big of a problem is it?

>> **The cause of the issue:** Write down what caused the issue, whether you know for certain or just have guesses. Your hypotheses can turn into tests to gather data from moving forward. If you don't have any idea what's causing the problem, that's okay; if it's a big issue for your business, your lack of ideas should be your cue to problem-solve and figure it out.

>> **Your solutions:** If you've already solved the issue, note which solutions did and didn't work. If you haven't solved it yet, write down your ideas for a solution, and test them individually to see what works best.

>> **Your confidence:** How sure are you that your solutions will work?

>> **The level of effort required:** How difficult will it be to implement your solutions to the problem?

>> **How you'll move forward:** Write down your next steps, what you've learned from the experience, and what you'll do in the future to prevent the issue from happening again.

Implementing Solutions: Now or Later?

As a solopreneur, you need to get good at identifying which to-dos are urgent and important, important but not urgent, urgent but not important, and neither urgent nor important. We use the Eisenhower Matrix to help you organize tasks by urgency and importance. Figure 19-1 shows a version slightly adapted for solopreneurs.

	Urgent	Not urgent
Important	**DO or DELEGATE** Working IN your business	**SCHEDULE** Working ON your business
Not important	**DELEGATE** Find someone else to do this unless you like doing it	**DELETE** Unnecessary distractions

FIGURE 19-1: The Eisenhower Matrix can help solopreneurs with task management.

Use the following guidance to categorize your tasks from urgent to not important:

>> **Important and urgent tasks:** These are typically the tasks that you want to give high priority to. They are things that can really impact your business and are often deadline-driven. For example, submitting a proposal before a client's cutoff date or fixing a critical bug that's affecting your website functionality.

>> **Not important but urgent tasks:** These require immediate attention but don't necessarily contribute to the long-term goals of your business (for example, responding to emails or texts that need attention but aren't critical). They must get done, but aside from fostering client retention (which matters!), they're more of an interruption than something that moves mountains for your business.

Urgent tasks that aren't important may be good candidates for outsourcing to a virtual assistant (VA). A VA may be able to handle an urgent email response, for example, while you're working on strategy, something you can't outsource.

>> **Important tasks that aren't urgent:** These are things you need to do for the betterment of your business, like process documentation, analytics reviews, system development, and so on. They don't necessarily need to be done immediately.

Pushing these tasks off continually can be easy when there isn't a sense of urgency behind them, but it's important that you don't skip them. Put meetings with yourself on your calendar so you can conquer these tasks and stick to them as if they're a meeting with somebody else.

>> **Neither urgent nor important tasks:** Everyone has these tasks on their to-do list: attending unnecessary meetings, doing busywork . . . the list goes on. Ask why you're doing these tasks in the first place. If attending unimportant meetings gives you peace of mind that you won't miss anything and opens mental space to get other things done, then fine, keep them on your task list. But if you're doing them just because, what's the point?

As a solopreneur, your livelihood is dependent on which tasks you need to get done immediately and which can wait (no pressure). If anything impacts revenue or brings your operations to a standstill, address it first!

Plan to spend 75 percent of your work hours on must-get-done tasks. Leave the other 25 percent for unanticipated issues, which inevitably come up. Too often people load up their plates and then feel discouraged when they don't accomplish all their tasks, which can lead to a decrease in motivation and productivity. Completing just a handful of to-dos can be more attainable and will result in a sense of accomplishment. This can boost your mood and may give you a second wind to get even more than you had planned done that day. Your to-do list doesn't change, but how you approach and think about it can. It's weird, but hey, you're human.

Fixing what you can on the fly

David Allen, the mastermind behind the Getting Things Done philosophy, has a great two-minute rule that basically states that if you can accomplish a task in two minutes or less, just do it on the spot. There's no point in adding it to a growing to-do list or trying to figure out its priority.

These tasks can include things like fixing a broken link on a website, scheduling an appointment you've been putting off, and so on. Alternatively, consider batching a few of these quick tasks and knock them out in a focused Pomodoro session, dedicating 25 minutes to get through a handful of fixes all at once.

Prioritizing what to fix later

No matter how badly you want to work on something, it's important to realize that not everything is an emergency. As you look over your documentation of your problems and solutions (see the earlier section "Documenting What's Not Working"), pull out the to-dos you've come up with, put them in the important/urgent, important/not urgent, not important/urgent, and not important/ not urgent buckets (refer to Figure 19-1), and prioritize them from there.

If you like to put a number on things, the ICE Scoring Model, developed by Sean Ellis, CEO of GrowthHackers.com, is for you. ICE stands for Impact, Confidence, Ease, and it's a simple way to prioritize which problems to take on first. The idea is to assign each task a value from 1 (low) to 10 (high) for each category by asking yourself these questions:

>> **Impact:** How much will solving this problem benefit your business?

>> **Confidence:** How sure are you that this solution will work?

>> **Ease:** How easy is the solution to implement?

Then you use this simple formula:

ICE Score = Impact x Confidence x Ease

From there, you take on the highest-scoring tasks first.

TIP

No matter how much you love running your business, you'll encounter tasks you don't like to do; that's just the nature of running a business on your own. We find it helpful to get the tasks that cause mental blocks out of the way first thing in the morning (or at any other time when you're most productive). If you can get those types of tasks out of the way, you'll free up lots of mental space to conquer the rest of your to-do list for the day, and maybe even free up time for unexpected R & R! Dwelling on a task you don't want to do takes up a lot of mental energy. Save your energy and just get it over with!

Tracking Your Wins

You didn't think we'd end a chapter solely addressing everything you're doing wrong and what you need to fix, did you? Believe it or not, it's a lot easier to focus on what isn't working than what is, so tracking your wins may actually be harder than tracking your problems/solutions.

Because you're flying solo, you often don't have any external validation that lets you know you're on the right track and continues to motivate you, so you must provide that morale boost for yourself. Your wins don't have to be monumental. Celebrating the small victories, like receiving positive feedback from a client, sticking to your schedule for a full week, or completing a task you've been putting off, can be huge for your mental well-being and fuel for your motivation.

Tracking your wins is important for several reasons, including the following:

>> **Boosts motivation and confidence.** Patting yourself on the back can keep your momentum chugging forward and your determination to succeed high. Positive reinforcement is key to maintaining a consistent amount of effort and enjoying what you're doing.

>> **Builds a success-oriented mindset.** Mental health and well-being are critical to running a successful business. Keeping your mind in a positive place can give you an I-can-do-this attitude, rather than just an I-can-fix-this attitude.

>> **Helps you track growth.** Focusing on what you're doing right allows you to see real progress over time.

Documenting your problems, solutions, and wins shouldn't be viewed as a burdensome task, but rather as an important tool to use for growth, efficiency, and, honestly, overall happiness.

Many of you have heard the phrase *practice makes perfect*. But your business, and the way you run it, will never be perfect, and if perfection is your end goal, you're setting yourself up for failure.

TIP

Instead, recite *practice makes progress*. Every troublesome pattern you identify, every mistake you correct, and every success you celebrate is a win, and gets you one step closer to running the successful business you've always dreamed of.

REMEMBER

To help you stay organized, be sure to track your wins in your Solopreneur Action Plan.

5

Improving Your Business

Diagnose what's holding you back and decide whether to refine or reimagine your business.

Narrow your change list with the PRIORITY framework, choosing the right improvements without becoming overwhelmed.

Apply the SMOOTH Method to make meaningful business changes while avoiding burnout and managing risks.

Chapter **20**

Refining or Reimagining Your Business

I n this chapter, you find out how to review your business to make sure it's on track with your goals and identify any issues that are sidetracking your success. To help you do this, we walk you through the seven failure modes of a solopreneur business, which we've developed by working with many solopreneurs over the years. (Full disclosure: ChatGPT helped us refine two of the seven modes. We use every tool available to make our processes more effective.)

This is part of Phase 3 of the Solopreneur Success Cycle, Improving, which has three steps:

>> **Step 5:** Refining or reimagining your business

>> **Step 6:** Deciding what to change

>> **Step 7:** Adjusting your business

In this phase, you explore ways you can change your business to address the issues you've identified (this chapter). Next, you decide which things are worth changing (Chapter 21), and finally, you make those changes (Chapter 22). Then you go back to tracking what's not working as you operate your improved business because the Solopreneur Success Cycle is an ongoing process to ensure you and your business thrive.

REMEMBER

Chapter 19 takes you through the process of creating a list of issues you're having with your business. This list can help you identify what you may need to tweak or completely reimagine. You want to approach change in a systematic and productive way instead of flailing.

Evaluating Your Business: Why It Matters

If you want to build a solopreneur business that truly works for you, regular check-ins are a must. It's tempting to review things only when problems pop up, but even when everything seems great, stepping back to assess and refine your operations can keep your business strong and sustainable. Here's why regular reviews matter:

>> **The world is always changing.** Market trends, technology, and customer preferences shift. Staying ahead of change keeps you competitive.

>> **Your needs may evolve.** What worked for you last year may not fit your lifestyle or goals now.

>> **New opportunities arise.** You don't want to miss out on a smarter, easier, or more profitable way to run your business.

Improving your business doesn't always mean making more money and growing bigger. It may mean

>> Reducing stress by streamlining systems

>> Adjusting your business to better match changes in your industry

>> Finding more fulfillment by shifting your focus

>> Working fewer hours by automating or outsourcing

Think about it this way: Refining your business isn't just about fixing what's broken; it's about staying ahead of the game. If you wait for a crisis to force change, you're setting yourself up for lots of stress and missed opportunities. You've likely been tweaking your business as you go. But if you also track problems and issues as you go, you have a nice list to work through when it's time to choose what to change.

Even if you review your business and decide to change nothing, the process is worth it.

REMEMBER

When to do a review

How often you evaluate what you're doing depends on you and your business, but a yearly review is a great starting point. If you're in a fast-moving industry, consider doing a review every six months, or even quarterly.

The key is to schedule time to step back, reflect, and make adjustments so your business stays aligned with your goals and the world around you. You don't need a neon sign flashing "Fix This Now!" to tell you it's time for a change if you build the review process into your Solopreneur Action Plan. But if the neon sign is flashing, don't wait. Big problems need to be addressed ASAP.

TIP

Sometimes changes can wait. Other times they can't. Keep an eye out for these signals that you may need to adjust sooner:

>> You're serving customers with too many different needs and it's draining you.

>> You're fully booked but still aren't making enough money.

>> Customers aren't as happy as they used to be, and you have lower engagement and fewer repeat buyers.

>> Revenue is stuck in neutral (or worse, reverse).

>> You're losing money when you expected to be profitable.

>> You've spotted new opportunities.

>> Your list of issues is long enough to warrant review.

It's not a bad idea to schedule your review when you're planning your business: once per year, once per quarter, or something else. That way, you can build it into your Solopreneur Action Plan.

TIP

To refine or reimagine

Do you just need to refine your business, or do you need to reimagine it in some way? *Refining* means keeping the core of your business (what you do and who you do it for) the same, but you're adjusting how you operate. Maybe you edit your messaging, change your pricing structure, or switch which marketing channels you focus on. It's optimization. You're polishing, not pivoting. *Reimagining* means changing the business by changing what you do or who you serve, or both. It's a shift in identity, not just execution, like a coach who served burned-out professionals pivoting to serving Gen Z creatives.

Businesses can almost always benefit from refining. Nothing is ever perfect. Reimagining tends to happen either early in the business (when you haven't figured it out yet) or when either you or the world has changed, and you need to adapt to that change in a big way.

Sometimes, it's obvious that you need to completely reimagine your business: No one is buying what you're selling, you can't successfully deliver your offering, you're going broke, or deep down, you dread showing up for work because the model you've built is out of alignment with who you are or what the market wants.

Refining your business is a lot less work than reimagining it, so it may be tempting to start by refining some things because it's just easier. Sometimes this makes sense. In other cases, this can be like rearranging the deck chairs on the Titanic. If the business needs reinvention, it won't matter if you fix an inefficiency.

Reimagining a business can be a natural part of growing any company, big or small, and many solopreneurs and entrepreneurs do this. If you find that your business needs to be reimagined, you're going to want to start there. (But that's for Chapter 21.)

Before you dig in and start making changes, you need to understand the ways in which your solopreneur business can fail you and which issues require reimagining rather than refining.

Understanding the Seven Failure Modes of a Solopreneur Business

Some changes you identify in Step 4 of the Solopreneur Success Cycle will be straightforward. You might need a new email platform. Maybe your YouTube thumbnails need an upgrade. Stuff like that feels manageable and relatively easy to tackle. But others will be harder. The ones that sneak up on you. You are doing all the things, grinding it out, and are still stuck. You lose steam. Motivation disappears even though everything looks fine from the outside. Or worse, things blow up. Your launch tanks, your bank account hits zero, and you're left wondering what the heck happened.

That's usually the territory of what we call the *seven failure modes*. These are the most common ways solopreneur businesses stall out, flame out, or quietly fade away. You'll see them in signs like uneven income, overwhelm, constant overthinking, or just that persistent feeling that something's off. Spotting these patterns early and doing something about them isn't just helpful. It's how you stay in the game and keep your business working for your life.

Each failure mode represents a common way that solopreneur businesses drift off course. You may experience just one at a time, or multiple at once. They're not permanent or mutually exclusive, they're patterns. This chapter will help you recognize which ones you're dealing with and what to do about it.

TIP

Look at your list of problems and see if you can match them to one or more of the symptoms listed in the tables throughout the following sections. This can help you focus on solutions. Each section includes ideas for quick wins and suggestions for addressing the issues.

Whether your business needs a few smart adjustments (which we cover in this chapter on *refining* your business) or a bigger strategic shift (which we cover in Chapter 21 on *reimagining* your business), the failure modes help you identify what's really going on and then take action that moves the needle.

SURFACE-LEVEL OR ROOT CAUSE?

Some challenges show up across multiple failure modes, like burnout, low revenue, or launch hesitation. These are surface-level symptoms, not root causes. What matters is the underlying reason they're happening. Are you burned out because you're overloaded? Misaligned? Underearning? That's what these modes help you diagnose. If a symptom shows up in more than one mode, look for the explanation that fits your situation best and start there.

As you work through the modes, create a list and put it in your Solopreneur Action Plan. You'll have a (hopefully) short list of things to change in your business, which Chapters 21 and 22 can help with.

Failure mode 1: Misalignment

It's not always the big, dramatic problems that knock you off course. Sometimes it's the quiet stuff, the low-key misalignment (also known as the *burnout trap*), that slowly eats away at your energy.

Misalignment is one of the silent killers in solopreneurship. And if you don't catch it early, it can grind your business (and your enthusiasm) to a halt. Table 20-1 shows common symptoms of misalignment and whether they usually call for refining what you're already doing or reimagining your business to better align with who you are and what you want now.

TABLE 20-1 Failure Mode 1: Misalignment

Symptom	Approach
Loss of energy or enthusiasm	Refine your tasks and projects
	Reimagine if the feeling persists or worsens
Uneasiness with business	Reimagine your model, audience, or offer
Boredom / disengagement	Refine your focus or role
	Reimagine if energy doesn't return
Lifestyle conflict	Reimagine the structure of your business to support your life

Misalignment creeps in quietly

Misalignment usually doesn't show up with a flashing warning sign. Instead, it sneaks in like this:

» That subtle feeling that something's just . . . off

» Tasks that used to be fun feel like a slog

» A steady drip of "meh" around the work you're doing

From the outside, everything may look great. Clients are happy. Money's coming in. But inside? You're running low on fuel and losing interest fast. Here are a few examples:

» A solopreneur starts a drop-shipping business but ends up hating digital marketing and customer service.

» A life coach realizes they dislike working one-on-one with clients, and coaching begins to feel draining.

» An artist starts selling prints online but finds the transactional nature of the business unfulfilling.

You didn't go solo to feel stuck or drained. You're doing it for freedom, meaning, and control over your life. But when the work you're doing no longer lines up with your values, interests, or energy, it gets harder to stay motivated. And that leads to

» Burnout, even when you're technically successful

» Indecision or stalled-out progress

» A creeping sense that maybe this whole thing just isn't working

REMEMBER

If your business feels like a job you can never clock out of, that's not freedom. That's misalignment, and it's time to fix it. Here's a simple starting point, just a small move, that can jolt you out of the rut and help you reconnect with what matters:

» Write down what energizes you in your business: the stuff that lights you up, like working with specific clients or on certain projects, doing creative work, and so on.

» Then jot down what drains you: the tasks you dread, jobs that sap your energy, and things you avoid.

» For the next seven days, do more of the first list and less of the second.

Sometimes, small tweaks (refining) won't cut it. If that's the case, zoom out and make some bigger changes (reimagining) like these:

>> Pivot your offering to better reflect your skills, interests, or values.

>> Narrow your niche to work with the people you actually want to serve.

>> Redesign your weekly schedule so your business supports your life and goals.

TIP

You don't have to blow everything up. Often, a few smart shifts can change everything.

Bottom line: Catching misalignment early is key

Misalignment is sneaky but powerful. If you don't catch it, the business you wanted to run may slowly turn into something you want to escape. But the good news? You've got the power to fix it.

Stay curious. Check in with yourself. Make adjustments as needed. And keep building a business that works for you, not just one that looks good from the outside. Because real success for solopreneurs isn't just about income; it's about alignment, energy, and ownership over your life.

Failure mode 2: Overload

At first glance, everything looks good. You're busy. Clients are booking. Emails are coming in. Projects are getting done. It feels like you're making progress. But under the surface? Things are starting to crack. This is overload, or what we like to call life on the hamster wheel. And it's one of the most common ways solopreneurs quietly stall out.

Overload is often treated as a time management issue, but it's often a business issue. While many symptoms can be addressed through refinement, deeper or recurring burnout may mean it's time to reimagine how your business runs. Table 20-2 outlines which approach fits best for each common symptom.

TABLE 20-2 **Failure Mode 2: Overload**

Symptom	Approach
Burnout	Refine your workload and systems Reimagine the business if energy doesn't return
Overwhelmed by the workload	Refine your task load, delegation, or boundaries
No time for strategy	Refine your schedule to prioritize big-picture work
Health issues	Refine your pace and recovery habits Reimagine if stress remains chronic
Isolation	Refine by building regular connection (community, accountability, support)

The dangers of doing it all

When you're wearing every hat, CEO, service provider, marketer, bookkeeper, tech support, it's only a matter of time before something pushes you over the edge.

Here's what that usually looks like:

>> You're reacting all day instead of strategizing and making plans.

>> Your calendar is wall-to-wall client work.

>> Your time gets eaten up by emails, follow-ups, and random tasks.

>> You can't remember the last time you had a real break.

And here are a few examples:

>> A freelancer takes on too many clients and ends up working 80-hour weeks with no time to rest or strategize.

>> A solopreneur tries to manage every aspect of their business alone, leading to stress and eventual burnout.

>> An online course creator commits to frequent content updates and community engagement, but the workload becomes unsustainable.

If your business stops functioning the minute you stop moving, you're not building a business; you're building a burnout machine.

We know the instinct: You want to just push through. But spinning the wheel faster won't fix the wheel. Hustling harder isn't the answer because eventually your body starts throwing up red flags like fatigue, insomnia, or constant low-grade stress, even when things look fine on the outside.

The more overloaded you get, the harder it becomes to solve the problem. You don't have the energy to think about the big picture when you're stuck in the weeds.

You probably can't just hit Pause or cut your workload in half. But making these small shifts may start to tip the balance:

>> Set reasonable work hours and stick to them.

>> Use a basic task system like David Allen's Getting Things Done to keep your priorities clear.

>> Give yourself permission to walk away when you need a break.

A 20-minute walk clears more fog than two hours of panicked screen time.

Long term, the only way out is to start building a business that doesn't depend on you doing everything forever. Here are a few ways to begin doing refinements:

>> Automate the stuff you do the same way over and over.

>> Outsource tasks that drain you or slow you down or that someone else can do better or cheaper.

>> Create standard operating procedures for repetitive work so you're not reinventing the wheel every week.

>> Track your energy like you track your revenue, because both matter.

Your energy is your most limited resource. Protect it like it's your profit margin.

Bottom line: You can't scale chaos

You didn't go solo to work longer hours and burn yourself out. You did it for freedom, flexibility, and control, and so you'd have a business that serves your goals.

If your business doesn't allow you to have a life, it's time to rethink how you're running it. The sooner you let go of the idea that you can do everything yourself, the sooner you can build something that actually works for you.

Failure mode 3: When the money's not there

When the income from your business dries up or never really gets going, it's not just your bank account that takes a hit. It's your confidence. Your motivation. Your belief that the solopreneur path is even viable.

You launch something new . . . and you get crickets. You get leads . . . and they vanish. You hustle like crazy and still end up wondering what you're doing wrong. It's enough to make you question everything.

Table 20-3 shows common symptoms of market or income failure and recommends which approach to take for each.

TABLE 20-3 Failure Mode 3: Market or Income Failure

Symptom	Approach
Revenue crashes	Refine your offer and outreach
	Reimagine if deeper market fit issues persist
Can't close sales	Refine by improving your sales skills and process
Inconsistent income	Refine your marketing and delivery systems
	Reimagine if problem doesn't improve
Lack of leads	Refine your visibility strategy
	Reimagine if audience targeting is off
Plateauing revenue	Refine your positioning or offers
	Reimagine if growth doesn't return

When great offerings still flop (or diminish over time)

You care about your work. You're putting in the effort. You know that you can help people. So why aren't they buying?

Here's the truth: Having a great product or service isn't enough. If your offering isn't hitting the right *pain point* (customer need) in the right way, the market won't respond, no matter how good it is.

If people don't immediately get how your product or service helps them, they'll scroll past, close the tab, or walk away. Every time. Signs of market failure aren't hard to see; they look like this:

>> Inconsistent (or zero) revenue

>> Leads that disappear

>> A launch that lands with a thud

>> Feeling like you're talking to an empty room

It's easy to blame the economy. Or the algorithm. Or the fact that everyone and their cousin seems to be offering the same thing. But the root issue is usually a fuzzy message, a niche that's doesn't match the pain point you solve, or nonexistent, or a lack of clear value.

And it isn't just a revenue problem. It's a mental one, too, which can make you second-guess everything. You start asking yourself questions like these:

>> Should I lower my prices?

>> Should I completely change my offering?

>> Maybe I just need to run ads and hope for the best?

And suddenly, instead of running a business, you're running in circles, chasing attention instead of attracting the right people. Examples include the following scenarios:

>> A coach launches a profitable service but fails to adapt to changing customer expectations, leading to a slow decline in revenue over time.

>> A handmade goods seller initially thrives but struggles when mass-produced competitors enter the market.

>> A subscription-based business gains early traction but fails to keep users engaged, causing high churn rates (you get a lot of people subscribing, followed by lots of people unsubscribing).

What's missing for most solopreneurs is one or both of these:

>> A real marketing strategy
>> A real sales system

A business that lasts and supports your life needs a few key components:

>> A well-defined niche and personas (Chapters 8 and 10)
>> A clear market position (Chapter 10)
>> A compelling value statement (Chapter 13)
>> A lead generation plan (not just "be active on social media," Chapter 12)
>> A way to stay in touch with people who show interest (Chapter 12)
>> A follow-up process that turns curiosity into commitment (Chapter 13)

Without these, you're just hoping someone stumbles across your product or service and is ready to buy on the spot. That's not sustainable.

You can get out of the revenue rut by taking these two steps:

>> Find the weak link.
   ● Are the right people seeing your offering?
   ● Are you solving a clear pain point that resonates with these people?
   ● Are you following up with the folks who already expressed interest?

Talk to three people who didn't buy from you and ask why. If you need help with this, refer to Chapters 7 and 8 (which cover your competition and your customer, respectively).

>> Build a simple, repeatable sales system.

- Get clear on your niche (Chapter 10).
- Sharpen your message so the value of your offering is obvious (Chapter 11).
- Create a lead magnet or intro offer that solves a real problem (Chapter 16).
- Set up a way to regularly connect with new people: ads, email, partnerships, and the like (you don't need all of them, just one that works).

Bottom line: Consistency beats charisma

You don't need to go viral. You don't need thousands of followers. You need a clear message, a defined audience, and a strategy and tactics that continuously put you in front of the right people even when you're not grinding away nonstop. That's how you go from barely scraping by to building a business that supports your life.

As Jay Acunzo, a solopreneur who teaches marketers about storytelling, puts it, "Don't be the best; be their favorite."

Failure mode 4: External risks

Solopreneurs are pretty great at focusing on what they can control: getting clients, tightening up offers, cranking out content. But here's the part most folks don't think about until it's too late: Your business doesn't exist in a bubble. It lives in the real world. And the real world is full of curveballs. Don't get blindsided by external risks (highlighted in Table 20-4) because you weren't looking.

TABLE 20-4 Failure Mode 4: External Risks

Symptom	Approach
Legal/tax issues	Refine your compliance setup
	Reimagine if these risks threaten your core business
Data loss	Refine your security and backup systems
Platform dependency	Refine to collect email addresses from prospects
	Reimagine if your current approach doesn't allow for this
Competitor pressure	Refine your positioning and customer retention strategy

The hidden threats you don't want to deal with

We aren't talking about burnout or overwhelm here. Those creep in. External risks? They hit fast and hard. You can see what we mean with these examples:

>> Instagram *shadow bans* your account (suppresses your content so other users can't see it), and suddenly your engagement is down by 90 percent.

>> A handshake deal with a client goes south, and so does your payment.

>> You click a sketchy email, and now your files (or your client's) are locked up.

>> You fail to file tax returns or other important government reports.

>> A sudden change in tax law messes with your finances.

>> A payment processor freezes your account for "verification."

These aren't rare horror stories. They're happening every day to smart, capable solopreneurs who just didn't see them coming.

WARNING

If you're running your business without contracts and statements of work (see Chapter 13), if you're relying on social media contacts instead of collecting email addresses, if you're not using basic security on your computer setup, you may feel scrappy. But that's not scrappy; it's risky.

You don't need to live in fear of every *what if?* But you do need to be proactive and set up some simple guardrails. Once things go sideways, it's too late to wish you had, so do these things first:

>> *Turn on two-factor authentication* for every account.

>> *Use written contracts and possibly statements of work* even with your clients. And make sure the words match the deal.

>> *Back up important files* to the cloud and a local drive.

>> *Don't rely solely on social media* for your connection to your prospects. Capture their email addresses.

>> *Watch out for single sources* of products or services. What happens if they go away?

>> *Make the easy fixes* to solve issues that can kill your business.

Many of these things are free or supercheap, and you can knock them out in an afternoon.

Once the basics are in place, it's time to think a little bigger. Resilient businesses aren't just protected; they're adaptable. Start thinking about these issues:

>> *Collect as many email addresses* as possible from your prospects.

>> *Make sure you've set policies and boundaries* around scope, payments, and availability.

>> *Get insurance* if your work has any liability risk.

>> *Create a list of required government filings.*

>> *Set unique and complex passwords* for all online accounts.

>> *Securely track* contracts, accounting data, and other important information.

Prioritize these issues from most risky to least, and get them done as soon as you can. This may feel like a distraction, but it's nothing compared to getting hit by an unexpected disaster.

Being prepared doesn't mean you're preventing all possible disasters. It means you're building something strong enough to survive one.

Bottom line: Stuff happens, so be ready

You can't stop every problem from showing up. But you can decide whether it knocks you down for an hour or a month or shuts down your business entirely. Solopreneurs who think ahead don't just recover faster; they build more resilient businesses. Because when something goes wrong (and it eventually will), they've already put the pieces in place to bounce back.

Mode 5: Stagnation

Like misalignment, stagnation is sneaky. Everything looks fine. Clients are coming in. You're paying the bills. You're not constantly putting out fires. But under the surface? Something's off. You're busy, but you feel like you aren't getting anywhere. Your growth has stalled. Your product/service seems . . . dated. Meanwhile, you see others in your space evolving, experimenting, and pulling ahead. You're still moving, but you're going in circles, not forward.

Welcome to stagnation. As Table 20-5 shows, most symptoms of this mode require reimagining.

TABLE 20-5 **Failure Mode 5: Stagnation**

Symptom	Approach
Flat revenue	Refine your offers or pricing Reimagine if the plateau is persistent
Falling behind	Refine by updating your offer Reimagine if it no longer fits the evolving market
Stale product	Reimagine the product to meet current demand and client expectations
Resistance to change	Reimagine your mindset and business model to support innovation

The trouble with stagnation and what causes it

The problem with stagnation is, it's quiet. It doesn't crash your business. It just slowly drains the momentum out of it.

Here's how it shows up:

>> Revenue has been flat for a while, and it isn't meeting your goals.

>> Your offerings haven't changed in years.

>> You're constantly busy but not getting ahead.

>> Nothing's broken, but nothing's all that exciting either.

Usually, it comes from these two places:

>> **Comfort zone mode:** You've found something that works. Great. But now it's your default, and it may be keeping you from trying anything new.

>> **No margin for growth:** You're so deep in client work that you have zero time (or energy) to think strategically, test new ideas, or sharpen your skills.

The market's usually not standing still. If you're not adapting, someone else is, and they might take your spot. Don't let yourself live out these examples:

>> A content creator **consistently produces the same type of content without adapting** to audience preferences or industry trends, leading to a slow but steady decline in engagement and relevance.

>> A consultant offers **the same services for years without updating their approach**, causing clients to flee to more innovative competitors.

>> A niche blogger who **relies on outdated SEO tactics** sees traffic steadily decline as search engine algorithms evolve.

Breaking out of stagnation doesn't require you to blow up your business. But you do need to treat growth strategy as part of your job, not something to work on when everything else is done. Try these approaches to get out of comfort zone mode. You can explore refining first, but you may need to do some reimagining depending on the specifics of the problem:

>> Look at your customers' current pain points. Have they changed since you defined your product/service? If so, update your offering to address those pain points more effectively.

>> Present your updated offer in a way that clearly addresses the new pain points and what you do to solve them.

>> Block out 30 minutes a week for researching, brainstorming, or testing a new idea.

Try these approaches to create time to focus on growth:

>> **Outsource a noncrucial task** and use the time to work on growth strategies.

>> **Automate processes that are repetitive** to free up time for brainstorming.

Try approaches like these to break out of the time-for-money trap (where you're charging by the hour, possibly requiring you to work more hours than you want to):

» Create a product that doesn't require a big chunk of your time to deliver, like a recorded course.

» Provide an online *paid community* (a members-only group that clients pay to join) for your target market.

Bottom line: Stagnation is a signal

Stagnation doesn't mean you've failed. It just means your business is ready for something new. Stagnation is the whisper in your ear that says, "Hey, this isn't broken. . . but it can be better." So, listen. Then, make changes that get things moving again.

Failure mode 6: Execution failure

You're working hard. You're full of ideas. You've got the drive. But for some reason, things just aren't clicking. This is execution failure. Your effort doesn't lead to traction, income, or business growth, not because you're not trying hard enough, but because your efforts aren't aligned with what the business needs. It's not because you're lazy. It's because something in the execution chain is misfiring, like strategy, messaging, offer structure, or product/service delivery.

Table 20-6 shows that you can either refine or reimagine your execution efforts to correct course.

TABLE 20-6 Failure Mode 6: Execution Failure

Symptom	Approach
Leads engage but don't convert	Refine your messaging and sales flow
	Reimagine if offer is misaligned with value
Always busy, but no growth	Refine your focus and systems
	Reimagine if the pattern persists
No feedback loop	Refine to find feedback
Skills don't match offer	Reimagine the offer to match your current skill level
Idea, but no traction	Refine your value statement and outreach
	Reimagine if there is no demand for your product or service

Spotting skill misalignment and other execution breakdowns

One common form of execution failure is building a business around something you haven't quite mastered yet. This shows up a lot for creative solopreneurs (designers, coaches, writers) who jump in fueled by passion but still need to sharpen their craft.

How do you know if this is your issue? Watch for things like clients canceling or not renewing, vague or noncommittal feedback, and a lack of *social proof* (good reviews and testimonials from happy clients). To start solving the problem, try these fixes:

>> Adjust your offering to match your current skill level. For example, a newly certified coach launches with a high-ticket, 12-week transformational program aimed at "executives seeking life-altering clarity" and get crickets. They then scale back to 3-session "Reset & Refocus" coaching packs. This usually involves reimagining your offer.

>> Refine your business by developing your skills through courses, coaching, or good old-fashioned practice.

>> Refine your focus to emphasize client results, because great work is the best marketing tool you have.

But not every execution issue comes down to skill. You may be missing the mark because of how you're planning (or not planning) your business. Here are a few more reasons execution stalls:

>> **No market validation:** You launched something without checking if anyone wanted it.

>> **Unclear messaging:** You're talking about your offering's features, not its benefits.

>> **Lack of prioritization:** Your to-do list runs your day, and it's running you in circles.

>> **Working in a vacuum:** You're not getting feedback, testing your product/service, or refining your offering.

Busyness doesn't equal progress. You need to be working the right way on the right activity to move forward.

TIP

Here are a few small-but-mighty shifts that can quickly sharpen your execution:

>> **Validate your offering.** Ask your audience if they're interested before you build your product or service.

>> **Clarify your messaging.** Highlight the results your clients get, not just what you do. Speak to their pain points and the results you produce.

>> **Get real feedback.** Share your work in progress with peers, mentors, or past clients.

Review your offering, content, or plan with someone outside your bubble. One honest opinion can save you months of spinning your wheels.

Bottom line: Put your effort into executing what matters most

Execution failure isn't about how much effort you're putting in. It's about how aligned, focused, and skillful that effort is.

If you can tighten up your delivery, be clear about what you're offering, and create systems that support consistent progress, you'll move from being busy and stuck to becoming focused and profitable.

Failure mode 7: Psychological barriers

You've got the idea. You've got the skills. So, what's stopping you? If you're stuck but can't figure out why, the real problem probably isn't tactical. It's internal. These aren't business problems; they're mindset patterns. These invisible mental blocks can quietly sabotage your business from the inside out.

The good news? You usually don't need to rework your whole business, you just need to rework the way you relate to fear, risk, and visibility. Table 20-7 outlines the inner work that can help you move forward. These aren't signs of weakness; they're signs your nervous system is trying to keep you safe. But in business, staying safe often means staying stuck.

TABLE 20-7 **Failure Mode 7: Psychological Barriers**

Symptom	Approach
Avoiding sales	Refine the sale process so you view as a service then build confidence through low-stakes practice
Charging too little	Address self-worth; gather evidence of value (testimonials, results)
Overthinking	Set boundaries on decision loops; practice "good enough" mindset
Isolation	Seek connection; get regular external input and encouragement
Launch paralysis (unease with your business idea)	Identify underlying fear; clarify alignment; take small public steps, or adjust your business idea to align better with your "gut"

Common barriers: From sales to pricing, isolation, and fear of launching

We start with a big one: avoiding sales. You can't build a successful business if no one gives you money. Solopreneurs usually avoid sales for the following reasons:

>> Fear of rejection

>> Lack of confidence in knowing how to sell

>> Fear of being judged

>> Not wanting to come off as pushy or sleazy

Even the most capable solopreneurs can freeze up when it's time to sell their product/service. A quick fix? Try role-playing a sales conversation with a friend to get the nerves out of your system. But the real shift comes from changing how you think about selling. Look at it as less *convincing* someone to buy from you, and more as *helping* them solve a pain point. Ethical selling isn't about pressure. It's about connection and service, as we explain in Chapter 13.

Another big psychological barrier is pricing (specifically, underpricing). If you're charging way below market value, it's usually not just a math issue, but a confidence issue. You may be thinking

>> Who would pay that much for this product/service?

>> I'm not experienced enough to charge high prices.

>> I just want to make my offering accessible.

Although generosity is great, the sustainability of your business matters too. A small price bump can be a win, but if it freaks you out, pair it with some work on your mindset. Try journaling your wins, gathering testimonials, or reviewing your results to remind yourself of the value you bring.

Another psychological barrier is based on the fact that solopreneurs are often flying solo. Too much solo time can become a psychological trap. Without outside input, it's easy to

>> Spiral into self-doubt.

>> Get stuck in indecision.

>> Second-guess every move.

Fixes include joining a mastermind (a peer mentoring group of like-minded people), accountability group, or online community. In the long term, you'll get the most value by doing regular check-ins, discussing shared goals, and receiving honest feedback from people who get what you're doing.

So, now you've created the thing. You've edited, refined, and rebuilt it. You've rewritten your sales page on your website for the twelfth time. And yet . . . you still haven't launched. That's not laziness; it's *launch paralysis*. From the outside, it may look like perfectionism. For example, your website is ready to go live, but you're still tweaking font colors or rewording headlines. Under the surface it's often about something deeper: self-protection. Your nervous system is wired to avoid risk, and launching something new is full of risk. So, your brain throws up all kinds of roadblocks with warning signs like

>> What if no one buys?

>> What if people judge me?

>> What if I mess this up?

That's the fear side. But there's another, sneakier reason launches stall out: misalignment. You may be hesitating because something foundational isn't clicking. Common signs of misalignment include

>> Your offering doesn't feel exciting or meaningful.

>> Your niche is vague, forced, or doesn't fit your offering.

>> Your business model sounds good on paper but drains you.

Procrastination isn't always the problem; it's often a signal. And "just hit publish" won't solve it if the work doesn't feel right.

If launch paralysis is preventing you from moving forward, the answer isn't brute force; it's reflection. Take a step back and ask yourself these questions:

>> Am I proud of this offer?

>> Is it helping the right people in a way that feels energizing?

>> Will I want to be running this version of the business five years from now?

If the answer is *no*, or even *I'm not sure*, you don't need more motivation. You need realignment (so check out "Failure mode 1: Misalignment" earlier in the chapter).

When your offering, your audience, and your values are in sync, maintaining your momentum gets a whole lot easier.

Bottom line: Your mindset is everything

No strategy, system, or hack will help you move forward if your brain keeps pulling the emergency brake. There's an old saying in business: Culture eats strategy for breakfast. As a solopreneur, your culture is your clear mindset.

Psychological barriers don't make you unqualified to run your business. They make you human. But if you want your business to grow, you need to look at mindset mastery as part of the job. Think of it this way: Your mindset is your most important business tool. Keep it sharp, support it with honest feedback, and make sure it's aligned with your goals, and everything else will get a lot easier.

Chapter **21**

Getting Strategic About Change

W elcome to Step 6 of the Solopreneur Success Cycle: Deciding what to change. You've got a list of potential improvements for your business longer than your arm, and it keeps growing. Exciting? Sure. Overwhelming? Definitely. But here's the truth: Trying to do everything at once is a recipe for failure. The key to success isn't doing more; it's choosing better.

That's where this chapter comes in. We walk you through a tool we've developed called the PRIORITY framework because working business concepts and procedures into catchy acronyms is a time-honored tradition. Regardless, this framework will help you sort through your options for improving your business and make confident, well-timed decisions. We also offer guidance on how to narrow down your ideas for change so you can actually implement them.

Weighing Changes with the PRIORITY Framework

The PRIORITY framework isn't a rigid formula. It's designed to help you weigh your options when you're staring down a dozen different potential directions for your business. Review each change you're considering against the following categories in the order they're presented. Each category begins with the question or questions to ask that will help you evaluate each change.

Peril

Is this change critical to your business's survival? Ask yourself: If you don't make the change, are you in big trouble?

If the answer is yes because you're about to lose a major client, run out of cash, hit full-on burnout, or face another existential threat, then the change goes straight to the top of your to-do list.

WARNING

If any of your Peril = Yes changes aren't doable (because you lack the resources or capacity to make them), you have a deeper problem. This isn't just a change issue; it's a business design issue. Don't power through. Step back, revisit Chapter 20, and rethink the way your business is structured so you can address the threat. You may need to reimagine things to reduce your risk to a reasonable level. In startup culture, this is called a *pivot,* and it's resulted in some of the greatest companies in history. This is your chance to build something sustainable and resilient.

Resources

Do you have what you need to pull this change off?

Resources include money, time, energy, and *emotional bandwidth* (the mental capacity you need to accomplish something). Looking only at this specific change, ask yourself if you have the capacity to do the work. If not, can you scale the idea back or roll it out slowly? You may have to table it until you have the resources to implement it.

Implementation

Can you actually make this change now?

A great idea doesn't mean much if you can't execute it. Do you have the skills to implement this change? The tools? The time? If not, can you outsource any part of it? Lacking the ability to make a change means you'll have to put it off until it's doable.

Opportunity

What's the upside of making this change? Will it increase revenue? Serve your customers better? Make your life easier? Align better with your values?

If a change helps you move toward your goals, you need to give it real weight to get it implemented.

Relevance

Is this change aligned with what you're building?

Relevance is your shiny object filter, which shows you just because something is trending, that doesn't mean it's right for you. Ensure the change fits your business model, vision, and goals. If it isn't aligned with what you're doing, it's not worth your resources.

Impact Risk

What can go wrong if you make this change? Will it confuse your audience? Dilute your brand? Overwhelm your systems?

We're not saying you should never take risks, but you should know what the risks are. You also need to know what the consequences of taking those risks are, so make sure you're moving forward with your eyes open to the impact of this change on your business.

Threats of Execution

What can go wrong when you execute this change and how bad would it be?

Consider the following scenarios:

>> **Failing to make the change successfully:** What are the chances that you try but fail to implement the change? Which parts of your business will be affected?

>> **Doing harm to your business:** How likely is it that the change will have a negative impact on revenue, customer trust, or operations?

>> **Passing the point of reversibility:** How difficult will it be to undo this change if it doesn't work as you hoped?

How bad would the consequences of these scenarios be? If they're bad, think about how you can test the change on a small scale first.

Yes, No, or Not Now

After you walk through the framework for each potential change, it's time to decide if you can make it happen. Ask yourself, "Should I make this change?" Each idea goes on one of the following lists, depending on how your evaluation trends for the categories as a whole:

>> **Yes:** This change goes on the *Consider Doing Now* list.

>> **No:** This change doesn't serve you, so it goes on the *Trash* list.

>> **Not now:** Good idea, bad timing. This change goes on the *Someday/Maybe* list.

Paring Down and Ranking Your Changes

Now that you have a list of changes that are feasible on paper, you need to consider reducing the number of changes you make this cycle. We encourage you to think about limiting your changes because you have only so many resources (including your own bandwidth) to get things done.

Not only does the PRIORITY framework help you identify which changes to make, but it also helps you prioritize those changes. (See what we did there?) Figure 21-1 shows the entire process.

After you evaluate your possible changes, put the doable ones on your Consider Doing Now list in order from most desirable to least. Obviously, any changes addressing existential challenges (Peril = Yes) need to go to the top of the list. From there, rank the rest of the changes based on how much of a positive impact they will have on your business. This is your Ranked Changes list. Now you're ready to pare down the list even further.

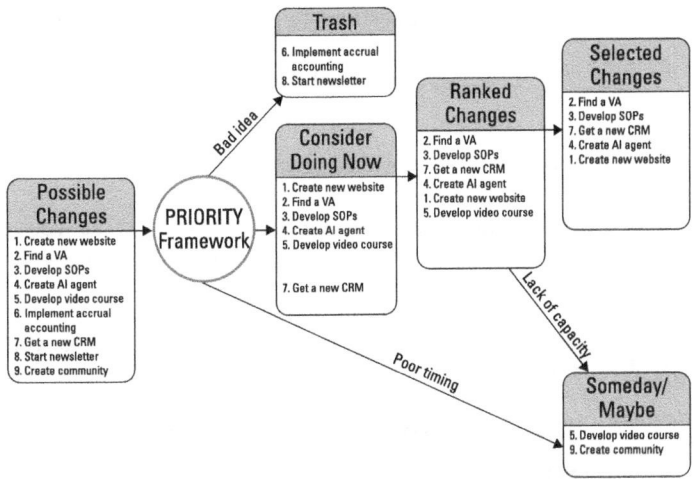

FIGURE 21-1: Paring down your change list to what makes the most sense for you.

Listening to your gut

Sometimes a change checks all the boxes on paper, but something still feels off. Or maybe an idea seems wild, but it lights you up inside. Your intuition is built from experience, the ability to recognize patterns, and subtle signals your brain has picked up, even if you can't explain them logically.

TIP

Remove any items that feel wrong from your Ranked Changes list. Put them on the Someday/Maybe list. Keep the ones that light you up.

Getting feedback from people

Even when you're flying solo, you don't have to figure everything out alone. Run your ideas past some of the following people:

>> A mentor or coach

>> A trusted peer or fellow solopreneur

>> A loyal customer or client

Here are a few questions to guide the conversation:

>> Does this change feel aligned with where I'm headed?

>> Would you implement this change in my shoes?

>> What am I not seeing here?

Rearrange your Consider Doing Now list as you process the insights you gain from other people. This helps you create your Ranked Changes list.

Feedback is *input,* not instruction. Your business, your call. Take the input that makes sense to you. Ditch the rest.

REMEMBER

Reviewing your capacity to make changes

Now you have the changes you're considering ranked from best to worst or most important to least important. But you don't have unlimited resources. You most likely need to consider how many resources you can devote to the change process.

Given that you're a solopreneur, you're probably optimistic by nature, which is a good thing . . . until it isn't. Optimism makes you dream big. But it can also trick you into biting off way more than you can chew. As you work your way down your Ranked Changes list, look at each item and ask the following questions:

>> Do you have enough time to accomplish this change?

>> Do you have enough money to see this change through?

>> Do you have enough emotional energy to get this change done?

When you hit a *no,* don't just stop. Look at the next item. It may require less time, money, or energy than the previous one and therefore be more feasible. You should move any changes that you can't do now to the Someday/Maybe list. After you've narrowed down your ideas based on your capacity to implement them, you'll have your Selected Changes list.

Smart solopreneurs are conservative with their bandwidth, not because they're lazy, but because they know the cost of burning out halfway through a project. Instead of launching five new changes and dropping them all, launch one and finish strong. Progress beats scattered effort every time.

REMEMBER

Making a Plan

Once you've said yes to a change, don't just leap. Instead, you need to plan. Open up your Solopreneur Action Plan and, for each change on your list, record the following information:

>> The change you're making

>> Why you should do it now (Use the PRIORITY logic!)

>> First step to take

>> Resources or support you'll need

>> How you'll know if it worked

REMEMBER

Writing down a plan makes the changes real and far less intimidating. You're not aiming to fix everything. And you're definitely not aiming for perfection. Instead, you're choosing changes that help serve your life and business as best you can. That's how you create a business that energizes you, instead of one that eats you alive.

» Applying the SMOOTH method to navigate change

» Managing change without burning out

» Keeping customers and partners in the loop

» Learning from every change to make the next one easier

Chapter **22**

Making Changes to Your Business

Change isn't just inevitable in business; it's essential. But change can also be disruptive, risky, and overwhelming if you don't have a solid process to follow. Enter the SMOOTH method, a cleverly named step-by-step system, which we designed to help you make meaningful changes without breaking what's already working.

In this chapter, we take you through this method to help you make adjustments to your business. This chapter falls under Step 7: Adjusting your business, the final step of the final phase of the Solopreneur Success Cycle, where you improve your business. Congratulations on making it to this step!

Introducing the SMOOTH Method

Here's what SMOOTH stands for:

» **S**equence smartly.

» **M**anage your load and energy.

>> **O**pen lines of communication.

>> **O**wn the risks before they own you.

>> **T**rack success with clear metrics.

>> **H**arvest lessons and lock them in.

We bring these steps to life by following solopreneur Sarah Sypniewski through a set of business changes. We introduce Sarah in Chapter 5 and follow her throughout the book. Sarah built a successful career as a professional writer, providing freelance content services to clients across many industries.

After years of project-based work, she realized she wanted to offer something more lasting and meaningful: a structured service to help people turn their personal stories into published books. This vision became The Legacy Authors Society. But Sarah had to make the following changes before her idea turned into a reality:

>> Redesign her website to reflect her new offering.

>> Launch mid-tier service packages to appeal to more price-sensitive customers.

>> Switch to a new marketing platform to improve email deliverability and employ automation.

Sarah was excited, but she knew this major shift needed careful execution. In the following sections, we show how she applied the SMOOTH method to make it happen.

Sequence smartly

Smart change doesn't happen randomly. You need to prioritize and organize your changes so they build upon each other logically. Ask yourself these questions:

>> What are the dependencies? Does one change need to happen before another?

>> Can you group similar tasks to reduce wasted effort?

>> What's the best timing based on customer activity and business cycles?

So, Sarah decided to make her changes in this order:

>> Switch marketing email platforms, ensuring her messages would reliably reach her community without a lot of effort on her part.

>> Launch The Legacy Authors Society membership program, using her refreshed email capabilities to spread the word.

>> Redesign her website, reflecting the new service, testimonials, and branding.

Sequencing this way helped Sarah avoid wasted effort and positioned her for a smoother rollout.

Need help mapping out your changes? Download the Change Plan worksheet at www.dummies.com/go/solopreneurbusinessfd.

FIND ONLINE

Manage your load and energy

Big changes demand time, focus, and energy. Trying to do everything at once can lead to burnout or sloppy execution. Protect yourself by pacing the work. Answering these questions can help:

>> Can you continue serving customers while making these changes?

>> Do you have enough time, energy, and *emotional bandwidth* (mental capacity for the task)?

>> Will the change impact your cash flow, and do you have a buffer if it does?

Sarah paced herself by spacing the email platform switch and membership launch a month apart. This gave her time to manage client commitments while building her new offering without burning out.

Open lines of communication

Change affects your customers, partners, and audience. If you don't communicate clearly, you risk damaging trust. For each change, answer the following questions:

>> Who needs to know?

>> What do they need to know?

>> When and how will you tell them?

Sarah crafted this communication plan:

>> **Email platform switch:** She sent a personal note to the people on her email list, explaining the change and asking them to put her new email address on their "not spam" list.

>> **Service launch:** She used email, social media, and personal outreach to announce The Legacy Authors Society and invite early members to join.

>> **Website relaunch:** She sent an email sequence highlighting the fresh design and new services.

These proactive updates kept her community engaged and in the loop.

Own the risks

Every change carries risk. Don't wait until something breaks to fix it. Proactively manage risk by revisiting your earlier risk assessment and asking these questions:

>> What can go wrong?

>> What's the impact if it does?

>> How can you test it yourself, vet it with customers, or roll back the change if needed?

Sarah knew her changes carried risks. Would her audience respond? Would the tech transition go smoothly? Would the new service resonate? She tackled these risks in the following ways:

>> Testing the new email platform with a small group before doing a full rollout

>> Soft launching The Legacy Authors Society to a select group of trusted clients and friends for early feedback

>> Previewing the new website with a few loyal supporters to catch any issues before going public

These steps allowed Sarah to refine her approach and build confidence before releasing it to the world-at-large.

Track success with clear metrics

If you don't define success, you won't know when you've achieved it. Set measurable targets and gather real customer feedback. Here are some questions to help you gauge your success:

>> Which key metrics (leads, sales, engagement) will tell you if your change worked?

>> What qualitative feedback can you gather to validate the experience?

Sarah defined what success would look like for each step with these metrics:

>> **Email platform:** Improved open and click-through rates

>> **Membership launch:** A steady flow of new members and positive testimonials

>> **Website relaunch:** Increased engagement and recognition from her audience

She set review checkpoints to assess these metrics two weeks and one month after each change went live.

Now it's your turn to make some SMOOTH changes to your business!

Harvest lessons and lock them in

Once your change has settled, capture what you've learned by asking these questions:

>> What worked better than expected?

>> What didn't go as planned?

>> What would you do differently next time?

>> What new ideas or improvements emerged?

TIP

Document these insights and update your systems so you aren't reinventing the wheel next time.

After implementing her changes, Sarah garnered the following takeaways:

>> Soft launching allowed her to refine her messaging and build confidence.

>> Testing the email platform prevented a deliverability disaster.

>> Feedback about the website from her accountability group inspired small but impactful adjustments.

She then documented these lessons and updated her internal processes (see the next section), making sure future changes would build on these successes. She also noted future opportunities, like offering bundled services, to add to her road map for the new venture.

Documenting Your Change

Once you've applied the SMOOTH method and completed your change, it's important to document it properly in your Solopreneur Action Plan. This ensures you capture what worked, what didn't, and what's next. It also helps you build a personal playbook you can reuse and refine over time. Here's what to record for each completed change:

>> **Change summary:** What was the change? Why did you make it?

>> **Execution timeline:** When did you start? When did you complete the change?

>> **Key actions taken:** What steps did you follow to implement the change? (Use your SMOOTH checklist as a guide.)

>> **Metrics and results:** Which success metrics did you track? What were the outcomes?

>> **Outside feedback:** What did your audience, clients/customers, or partners say about the change?

>> **Lessons learned:** What worked well? What would you do differently next time?

>> **Future opportunities:** What new ideas or follow-up actions did the change uncover?

>> **Updated systems and processes:** Which documentation, tools, or workflows did you update as a result of the change?

Taking the time to capture these details ensures you build on your experience, improve with every change, and move forward with greater clarity and confidence.

Understanding That the Cycle Never Ends

The SMOOTH method can help you manage change without breaking what's already working. But understand that this isn't just a single-use playbook. It's part of a bigger picture, the Solopreneur Success Cycle, which this book is based on.

Implementing a change isn't the end of the process. You're making an ongoing effort to keep your business in sync with a changing world and a changing you. The Solopreneur Success Cycle is designed to help you build, run, and improve your business over time. Every time you complete a round of change, you don't just move forward; you loop back into the previous phase of the cycle with greater clarity, deeper experience, and better tools at your disposal.

After you finish documenting a change in your Solopreneur Action Plan (see the preceding section), take a moment to reflect on how you're feeling.

>> Have your goals shifted based on what you learned?

>> Have you revealed new customer needs or opportunities you didn't see before?

>> What's the next priority that deserves your focus?

At this point, you're reentering Phase 2 of the Solopreneur Success Cycle: Doing and learning (see Chapter 2). This is the key to running your business, where you put plans into action, deliver value, and learn from the results. Every change you implement feeds new insights into your business. Those insights make your next round of doing smarter, more focused, and more aligned with the future you're building. But know that you'll always be learning about your business and finding new things to change in the future.

By treating change as part of a continuous improvement cycle, you build resilience, develop adaptability, and foster long-term success. The best solopreneurs aren't the ones who avoid change or chase every new idea. They're the ones who use a repeatable process to make intentional, meaningful progress again and again.

TIP

So, when you finish this round of changes, don't just close this book. Go back to Phase 2 and run your business while learning which additional changes you can make. You've already done this, and every time you do it again, it gets easier and your business gets better.

When you're ready, come back to Phase 3: Improving your business, because the cycle never ends, and that's what makes your business stronger at every turn.

6

Living the Solopreneur Lifestyle

Preserve your energy, motivation, and well-being by setting clear work-life boundaries and prioritizing self-care.

Remain relevant, adaptable, and prepared, whether you stay solo, scale, or sell.

> » Setting and honoring boundaries
>
> » Prioritizing self-care, mentally and physically
>
> » Preventing isolation and burnout
>
> » Designing a productive routine for yourself
>
> » Enjoying your wins and staying motivated

Chapter **23**

Balancing Your Work and Personal Life

ongratulations! By following each phase of the Solopreneur Success Cycle, you have all the business-related components of your venture in place, as well as ideas for how to assess whether things are working and pivot if need be. As wonderful as it feels to have each piece of your business in place, you still need to address something else: your well-being.

We note throughout the book that one of the main things differentiating solopreneurs from standard entrepreneurs is the desire to have a strong work-life balance. It's often the primary motivator for many one-person business owners. So, the life part of that balancing act deserves its own chapter (and a longish chapter at that).

Balancing your work and your life can be a delicate dance, and it doesn't come easily for everybody. It takes consistency, practice, and dedication to get everything to fall into place the way you want it to. This chapter provides tools and insights to help you find that balance while still running a successful business.

Establishing Boundaries Between Work and Personal Time

As you start your solopreneur journey and set your goals, you may be dreaming of the ideal work-life balance and what it will look like as you run your business.

No matter how well-intentioned you are, the reality is, things can get busy, and it can be easy to push your personal time to the back burner. It's important that you don't do that. Establishing boundaries between your work and your personal time is essential for the success of your business and your quality of life.

REMEMBER

You'll find, as you continue through this chapter, that almost everything you do to achieve work-life balance comes back to setting the right boundaries for yourself and sticking to them. Establish your boundaries early on so you don't suffer the consequences of not having them when your business is up and running.

Creating a work schedule

People often talk about how important it is to separate your work life from your personal life . . . because it is. We discuss building a routine for yourself later in this chapter (see "Building a Routine That Works for You"); here, we cover why a routine is important from a boundary-setting standpoint.

First, creating a set work schedule helps you prevent burnout. Trust us when we say that if you don't establish clear boundaries between work hours and playtime, you'll likely fill your personal time with work. Many solopreneurs fall into this trap. Setting firm starting and stopping times for your workdays can preserve your mental energy and keep you more present when you're working and fully engaged in your personal life when you're not.

Additionally, if you think you can work around the clock, you'll be more likely to procrastinate or get distracted throughout the day. But if you set a time to put the work away, you'll be motivated to stay productive because you're up against a deadline.

Most of the solopreneurs we meet want to build a business that serves their lives. No matter how well-intentioned you are, old habits die hard. If you were a workaholic in the past, you may find it difficult to break that habit. So, to achieve the work-life balance you desire, set a reasonable work schedule early on in your solo journey.

Setting expectations with your clients and customers

You want to provide good customer service (we get that and encourage it). However, there's a difference between taking care of your clients and being available for them around the clock. That's exhausting. And not even necessary.

Instead, inform clients/customers of your working hours at the beginning of your engagement and give them an idea of how long it typically takes you to respond. Tell them how to reach you in an emergency, but emphasize that if they abuse your after-hours accommodation, there will be consequences. These could be additional fees for off-hours communication, a temporary pause in work, or, in repeated cases, a reevaluation of your contract and working relationship.

Don't be afraid to enforce your business hours policies and stand by them confidently if you get any pushback. You'll find that either people respect you for setting boundaries or they don't. If it's the latter, you probably don't want those people as your clients or customers anyway.

TIP

One way you can enforce your boundaries is by turning off your email notifications and putting your phone on Do Not Disturb after business hours. In the professional world, it's reflexive to react to customer needs and requests as quickly as possible. If you aren't aware of a communication from a client until the next workday, you can head off your automatic urge to respond. This gives you a sense of control over your business and allows you the freedom to fully achieve the work-life balance you're striving for.

Focusing on Self-Care

Prioritizing self-care can be hard, especially if you need to focus on an upcoming deadline. And while a client meeting can be difficult to reschedule, a hike with a friend may seem like something you can postpone until the following week. However, we strongly encourage you to take breaks from your work and prioritize self-care, not only for your mental well-being, but also for the success and longevity of your business.

You need to remember that you *are* your business. If your physical and mental health start to suffer, your business's health will also begin to decline.

Maintaining your physical health

Physical health is more than just toning up your muscles so you look good in your clothes; it's about taking care of the incredible machine that is your body and making sure all your parts are operating correctly. Like a car, your body needs regular maintenance and proper fuel to function at its best.

After speaking with many solopreneurs who focus on their physical health as a part of their business's overall success, we compiled this list of key takeaways:

>> **Schedule physical activity.** Add exercise to your work calendar and treat it like an important client meeting so you don't skip it. Just 30 minutes of daily physical activity can do wonders for your body and mind.

>> **Consume healthful foods.** When you have a busy schedule, it can be easy to resort to takeout or fast food, but the better you eat, the better you feel. If possible, prep your meals for the week each Sunday so you don't have to cook during the workweek. Focus on foods that nurture your body and give you energy. Reduce your caffeine and alcohol consumption to test whether limiting those substances has any impact on your performance.

>> **Find accountability buddies.** We've said it once and we'll say it a million more times: Flying solo in business doesn't mean you're alone. Meetup with other solopreneurs for walks or workouts at the gym. If it helps, you can compete to see who can get the most exercise in a week. You'll feel more motivated to fit physical activity into your schedule if somebody else is along for the ride.

>> **Use your schedule to your advantage.** You're the boss, which means you don't have to cram your workouts in before 8:00 a.m. or after 5:00 p.m. You can work for a few hours, go to an exercise class for a quick break, and then

get back to your desk. Think about how you can make your flexible schedule work for you for peak performance, with both work and exercise.

>> **Find fun ways to sneak in physical activity.** Need to take a call? Talk while you're on a walk. Stuck in a virtual meeting? Do some strength training with resistance bands while you participate. Park in the farthest spot away from the door to increase your steps. Be creative about adding more physical activity to your day without investing too much time and thought in your exercise regimen.

If you aren't used to setting aside time for physical activity, it may take some getting used to. Stick with your exercise plan for a few weeks, and you'll find it becomes part of your routine. Stick with it even longer, and you'll forget what life was like before.

Protecting your mental health

Your mental health needs to be a top priority if you want to run a successful business. It truly impacts every area of your life: creativity, productivity, happiness, stress management, decision-making . . . you name it.

It's imperative that you put effort toward your mental health every day. Working on your physical health can certainly impact you mentally, but you need to be doing more. Here are a few ways you can make your mental health a focus and part of your routine:

>> **Start the day off with "me" time.** Too often people wake up to their alarm and immediately grab their phone or laptop. We challenge you to not touch any of your devices for at least the first 30 minutes of your day (ideally an hour). Use this time to enjoy a cup of herbal tea, read a book, or walk your dog. Doing something quiet and relaxing and focusing on yourself in the morning will help set the tone for the rest of the day.

>> **Check in with yourself.** Before you go to bed at night, check in with how you're feeling. If you're feeling positive, reflect on that feeling and savor it. If your mood is negative, think about why you're feeling down and prioritize how you can change course for the next day.

>> **Meditate.** We know some of you may resist this suggestion, but meditation has become more mainstream in recent

years for a good reason: It's incredibly beneficial for your mental health. Even if it's just for a few minutes, sit still and focus on your breath, or go through a guided meditation on an app. Regularly giving your mind a rest can really improve your focus and help you stay calm when your solo journey becomes a bit overwhelming.

» **Avoid doomscrolling.** Why has it become such a habit for people to scroll through their phone looking at negative news from all over the world or comparing themself to others on social media? Doomscrolling may seem harmless in the moment, but it can be incredibly detrimental to your overall mental health. Be selective about the type of information you're consuming and ask yourself if you feel better or worse after you read something online. It's one thing to know what's going on in the world, but it's another thing altogether to let a constant stream of negativity impact your thinking and your well-being.

» **Get plenty of sleep.** We know we're not the first people to recommend a good night's sleep, and we also know it's easier said than done, especially when you have a million things running through your mind. However, you'll find that if you take care of yourself and follow some of our suggestions in this chapter, better sleep may come more naturally. Rest is productive because it's a way to recharge your energy, so look at it that way if you feel like you should be doing something else.

The moral of the story is, the better you care for yourself, the more successful your business will be, so consider your mental health an essential part of your business plan and add self-care to it. Many solopreneurs start seeing the benefits to their business almost immediately.

Please note: We aren't mental health experts. If you're facing challenges you aren't able to resolve on your own, consider reaching out to a qualified professional for support.

Dealing with Isolation

Whether you're an introvert or an extrovert, and regardless of which phase of the solo journey you're in, having a plan to deal with isolation and loneliness (should they rear their ugly heads) ensures you can face these feelings head-on without missing a beat.

You may think you can do everything on your own and be successful in a silo, and maybe you can, but it'll be a much harder journey. We have a couple of ideas for combating these feelings, which we discuss in this section.

Feeling isolated as a solopreneur is totally normal. It doesn't mean you're not cut out for the job; it simply means you need to put a plan in place to overcome any distress you're feeling.

When you're putting together your business plan, include a plan for making connections with ideas like *meet for coffee with a new person once a week*, or *join an adult soccer league*, or *attend a monthly virtual networking event*. If you see it in your business plan, you're more likely to follow through with it.

Finding a community

Whether you do it virtually or in person, finding (or building) a community can do wonders for both your mental health and your business growth. Interacting with people in a community can help you with the following:

>> **Idea generation:** Your thinking will be limited (and biased) if you're working in a vacuum. Talking things over with others can lead to new ideas and revelations.

>> **Collaboration opportunities:** It's incredibly beneficial to collaborate with others to expand your footprint and reach new audiences, but you can't do that if you're alone all day. People are more likely to join forces with someone they know, like, and trust, rather than someone who approaches them out of the blue. Building solid relationships increases your odds for new collaborations.

>> **Accountability:** Many people think they're very self-motivated when they're not, and they often don't realize this until they're a solopreneur. Having an accountability group provides a host of benefits, including increased motivation, access to feedback, better deadline achievement, and an overall boost in productivity and personal happiness.

>> **Mental health:** Being around like-minded individuals can really impact your mental health. You have people to vent to,

so you don't hold all your negative thoughts and feelings in. You have a sense of belonging, which may have gone missing when you left your corporate job. And that feeling of community can increase your *endorphins* (those mood-boosting chemicals your brain releases when you feel pleasure), which can lead to more happiness and more enjoyment of running your own business.

Your community doesn't have to be work-related. In fact, it's often more beneficial if it isn't. Find people with whom you share hobbies and passions, so you can get away from the grind for a bit.

Doing regular social check-ins

Social check-ins are intentional conversations with people who "get you," and you should make a point of doing them regularly. They're like accountability groups, but for your mental well-being. Think of them almost like therapy sessions with a peer, where you discuss what's going on in your business and your life, what's working and what isn't, how you're feeling, and so on.

This is your chance to get honest feedback as well as support from people who understand what you're going through. Although social check-ins can be with friends or mentors, we've found that it's helpful to do your check-ins with other solopreneurs, who understand the journey and the ups and downs of running a company of one.

Look at social check-ins as part of your necessary operations to keep your business running and build them into your routine.

Talking to a professional

If you follow our tips and still struggle with feeling isolated, consider therapy or coaching. A professional can work with you to address the issues you're grappling with and guide you through them. Again, having a hard time with isolation is normal for solopreneurs, yet for some reason it can be a taboo topic. We want to help change that: Get counseling when you need it and know you're not alone in feeling lonely and isolated.

Avoiding Burnout and Decision Fatigue

Do you know how many decisions you have to make through-out the day as a solopreneur? A lot. And that can lead to *analysis paralysis* (when you think about an issue so much that you can't make any decisions about it) and eventually *burnout* (a state of exhaustion due to prolonged stress) from using so much of your mental capacity. *Decision fatigue*, a condition related to analysis paralysis, occurs when you're able to make decisions, but you're faced with so many in such a short time that you may start to make poor choices.

REMEMBER

At the beginning of this chapter, we mention that almost every-thing related to work-life balance ties back to setting and stick-ing to clear boundaries. This is a case in point. The better you are at adhering to your boundaries, the less likely you'll be to face burnout and decision fatigue.

If you do start to feel decision fatigue, repetition is key to getting past it. Focus on your systems and routines until they become effortless because they're second nature. Far too often solopre-neurs feel like they need to reinvent the wheel or try something new every day or every week, and that simply isn't true or sus-tainable. Make familiarity your friend.

We also recommend that you focus on the toughest decisions when you're at peak energy, so you can tackle them more effi-ciently and they won't bog you down for the rest of the day.

REMEMBER

When your to-do list gets lengthy, it can be quite intimidating. Select just a handful of tasks you want to get done every day. Anything you do beyond that is a bonus. Even the tiniest achieve-ments can give you the momentum to get more done, so what may seem like taking care of just a few small tasks can end up feeling like you've accomplished some big wins.

Understanding the Power of No

Being able to say *no* is arguably the most important thing you need to master as a solopreneur. Saying *no* to the wrong projects and clients can be the key to building a thriving and fulfilling business.

Take a look at everything you're doing in your business. If you find that you're becoming a people pleaser, experiencing burnout, or taking on work that doesn't align with your goals, then odds are, you need to be saying *no* to more things.

REMEMBER

This can include turning down things that may seem like good opportunities. You may be offered the role of a lifetime as the CEO of a Fortune 500 company, but if taking that on requires you to stray from your life and career goals (work-life balance, flexibility, stress reduction), is it worth it?

TIP

Practice makes progress. Start saying *no* to small things in your life, like when a friend offers you a second cup of coffee or your spouse insists you take the last cookie. If you can get the hang of refusing these small things, you'll soon master the ability to say *no* to the bigger stuff.

Building a Routine That Works for You

When you work for another person, you're often following their routine and schedule, which may not always be conducive to being your most productive self. Take Lewis, for example.

Lewis is a solopreneur software developer who used to work for a company that required him to be in the office every day by 8:00 a.m. But he isn't a morning person. His most productive work hours are in the middle of the day and late at night. Was he able to work those hours in the corporate world? Of course not! As a solopreneur, not only can he create a schedule and a routine that allow him to work when he's most productive, but he can also enjoy life on his terms.

Lewis now sleeps in until 9:00 a.m., has breakfast and goes for a run, works from 11:00 a.m. to 3:00 p.m., picks his kids up from school, enjoys time with friends and family until everybody (including his wife) goes to bed at 8:00 p.m., and then works until midnight or 1:00 a.m., when his brain is on fire! It's not conventional, but this routine makes him far more productive than his old setup ever did.

Not all solo businesses allow for the kind of schedule Lewis follows, especially if you work with people during normal business hours. Brainstorm how you can fit your routine within your business schedule and plan from there. The following sections offer some suggestions.

Time-blocking techniques

Time blocking (scheduling your day in blocks of time on your calendar and focusing on one thing during each block) is a fantastic way to find a routine and stick with it. Schedule your time blocks like meetings on your calendar so you honor them. The key is to be realistic, not aspirational.

TIP

In a perfect world, you'd spend time at the beginning of the week strategically blocking out all your time and then follow your plan. The reality is that things change. We recommend reevaluating your schedule at the end of every workday so you still have the next day planned but can adjust as necessary. And intentionally schedule some open time blocks during your day to either take a break and recharge (for your physical and mental well-being) or accommodate tasks that take longer than anticipated.

Daily and weekly planning

If your business allows, consider assigning themes to your workdays so you wake up in the morning knowing what you need to focus on. For example, Mondays are client meeting days, Tuesdays are dedicated to marketing, Wednesdays are for client work, and so on. Being able to give your full attention to one task for an entire day can help keep you focused.

We realize not all businesses can function that way, which is when time blocking can be beneficial (see the previous section).

TIP

From a bigger-picture point of view, you can plan your operations and marketing calendars in 90-day increments. This allows you to plan into the future so you know what's coming and have goals to work toward, but you're not scheduling tasks so far out that you can't pivot if unforeseen circumstances arise.

Setting Up an Ideal Workspace

As you daydream about your solopreneur business, you may have images of what your workspace will look like. Some of you may want a big office with a cushy chair, and others may picture a comfy beach chair under a shady umbrella. The important thing is, you should set up a workspace that makes you productive, and there isn't a one-size-fits-all description of this. Here are some things to consider when you're setting up your workspace.

Ergonomics for your home office

Have you heard the warning that sitting is the new smoking? It stems from research showing that sitting for long periods can be harmful to your health. So, it's important to take frequent breaks to do something physically active away from your desk (as we note in "Maintaining your physical health" earlier in the chapter). But it's also important to factor in how your workspace impacts your focus and productivity. In a nutshell, you want your work setup to be comfortable and reduce your risks of strain and injury while also improving your efficiency and ability to concentrate.

So, how do you accomplish this? Set up your workspace with ergonomics in mind. The biggest things to focus on for your physical health and comfort are solid back, neck, and elbow support. Place your computer screen on your desk so the top is around eye level. Your mouse and keyboard should be situated so that your elbows are bent at a 90-degree angle when you're typing. Use an adjustable chair with lumbar support to help maintain proper posture; if you can, make a conscious effort to sit up straight rather than slouching.

It's amazing how lighting can play a huge role in getting ergonomics right as well. Natural light is ideal, but if your office doesn't have windows, you can mimic sunlight with cool blue or white light bulbs. If you're lucky enough to have windows, keep in mind when you're setting up your space that natural light changes throughout the day, so don't position your computer screen in a place where you'll get a glare for an extended period.

TIP

Consider purchasing ergonomic tools and equipment for your workspace. A standing desk may reduce back pain and improve your posture. Blue light glasses can protect your eyes if you spend lots of time in front of a computer screen. You can get an adjustable monitor stand to ensure your computer screen is at the correct height. And a riser or tray with support for your wrists can create the right angle for typing and allow you to use your keyboard and mouse comfortably. Make sure that any office tools and equipment designed to be beneficial for your health and comfort foster productivity as well.

If you aren't used to an ergonomically correct workstation, the adjustment may feel a bit uncomfortable at first. Stick with it. Your body will thank you in the long run!

Organizing your space for maximum focus

You need to become the Marie Kondo of your workspace. In other words, you should declutter and tidy up your workspace in an intentional, and hopefully joyful, way.

Keeping your digital workspace organized is just as important, if not more so, than tidying your physical workspace. Nothing is more stressful than not being able to find files or having too many tabs open in your browser. You can waste a lot of time and mental energy trying to locate a particular piece of information. Have a process for organizing your digital files and tabs so you can quickly find what you're looking for and keep your sanity.

Nailing Productivity Hacks

Who doesn't love a good productivity hack? We can geek out on these hacks, but if you can find a better way to get more done, don't you want to use it?

The Pomodoro Technique is one of our favorite productivity hacks for solopreneurs, so we've given it a section of its own, but other hacks we enjoy include these:

>> **Get dressed.** Dress the part of a business owner. Take a shower, put on regular clothes (not sweatpants), and act like the boss you are. It's weird, but putting on some clothes really does cause a mental shift that helps you accomplish more.

>> **Implement the two-minute rule.** If you can get something (like paying a bill) done in two minutes or less, just do it. Otherwise, it becomes one more thing on your endless to-do list and adds to your overwhelm. If it takes a minimal amount of time, get it off your plate.

>> **Eat the frog.** This saying basically means you should do your hardest or most frustrating task first. If you can achieve that, you'll feel like you can conquer the rest of the day with ease.

You have tons of tried-and-true productivity hacks at your fingertips. Test some out and see which ones work best for you. Feel free to tweak them so they support your work style.

Trying the Pomodoro Technique

One productivity hack that seems to get a lot of attention is the *Pomodoro Technique.* This is the way it works: You pick one task and set a timer for 25 minutes (one *pomodoro*). During that time, you focus on that task and nothing else. When the timer goes off, you take a 5-minute break to recharge and then get back to your task (or another task) for 25 minutes (and so on). Once you've completed four pomodoros, you treat yourself with a 15- to 30-minute break.

We love this approach because it gives you mini breaks through-out the day that allow you to recharge while also encouraging the uninterrupted focus you need to tackle your to-do list.

TIP

For maximum impact, consider grouping similar tasks into back-to-back pomodoros. For example, you can do this with content creation. Brainstorm a social media strategy during the first pomodoro, create the content during the second, come up with a design in the third, and schedule your post during the fourth. That way, your thinking isn't too scattered, and you can break one seemingly large task into shorter sprints.

Using task prioritization tools

Many technological tools can help you prioritize tasks (see Chapter 16), but here we focus on a couple of mental tools you can add to your tool belt. One of them is the Eisenhower Matrix, which we introduce in Chapter 19.

You can use the Eisenhower Matrix (see Figure 23-1) to prioritize tasks based on their urgency and importance (it's also referred to as the *Urgent-Important Matrix*). This should be your go-to method for deciding how to prioritize tasks and be productive. Wasting your time on low-value tasks should become a thing of the past.

	Urgent	Not urgent
Important	**DO or DELEGATE** Working IN your business	**SCHEDULE** Working ON your business
Not important	**DELEGATE** Find someone else to do this unless you like doing it	**DELETE** Unnecessary distractions

FIGURE 23-1: The Eisenhower Matrix helps you prioritize your work.

TIP

Another task prioritization tool is the *Pareto principle*, or the *80/20 rule*. According to this principle, you focus on the 20 percent of your tasks that bring in 80 percent of the results. This allows you to really see what's worth your time and what isn't. Take time to assess which tasks propel your business forward, so you can focus more time and energy on those. It'll help you make smarter business decisions.

Celebrating Wins, Big or Small

Gone are the days of merit-based promotions or high fives from your cubicle mate when you win an account or meet a deadline. Now, it's up to you to give yourself the congratulations you deserve.

This may seem silly at first, but celebrating your wins, no matter how big or small, can do wonders for your motivation and productivity.

It can be easy to ignore milestones as you focus on your business and your clients. We encourage you not to do this. Tracking your wins helps you see how far you've come and gives you the necessary momentum to keep going. It's much easier to dwell on your mistakes and bring yourself down. But acknowledging your achievements can make you realize how much is going right.

Tracking wins can be fun on its own and bring a little lightness to your day. Here are some ideas for keeping tabs of your wins:

>> **Keep a wins diary.** It'll feel good to write them down, and you'll have something to reference on down days when you need a boost and want to reflect on everything you've been doing right. In addition to a physical or digital journal, consider creating a folder in your email where you save testimonials and positive client feedback. It's an easily accessible collection of accomplishments you can revisit anytime.

>> **Have a celebratory routine.** Whether it's doing a victory dance, getting a fancy drink from your favorite cafe, or indulging in some other treat, reward yourself with something you only get when you've completed a real achievement.

>> **Create an achievement jar.** Perhaps treating yourself after every little milestone isn't your thing (or it breaks the bank). If that's the case, write each achievement down as it happens and put the folded paper in a clear glass jar. When the jar is full, reward yourself with something you've been waiting for. (And read the notes for an extra boost!)

REMEMBER

You've already promoted yourself to CEO of your business, so you may as well celebrate everything that comes along with being the boss. You are your company's most valuable asset. Treat yourself like a precious resource.

Combating Slumps

This shouldn't come as news to you, but as wonderful as solopreneurship is, it's not always rainbows and unicorns. You'll have some down days. Heck, you may have a lot of down days, but the way you bounce back from them is what ultimately determines how successful you'll end up being.

Some days, you'll simply lack motivation. Other days, you may have a client crisis that affects your mood in a very negative way. The key is to reflect on what's causing your slump and address the issue appropriately.

Recharging with breaks

Sometimes, all you need to do to get out of a slump is press the Pause button. Here are some ways you can do that:

» **Take a break from technology.** Do something that doesn't involve your phone or computer. And don't even think about scrolling through social media. As great as tech is, it can distract you from what's important, which may add to your slump. If you're in a mood and need to lighten up, don't engage with things that can make it worse.

» **Do something that makes you feel good.** This doesn't have to be work-related. Listen to your favorite song, call an old friend, or soak up some sunshine. Take a break and do something you know will put a smile on your face.

» **Distract yourself with an activity that's unrelated to your work.** Perhaps feeling isolated is contributing to your slump. Try signing up for a midday workout class or an in-person workshop that doesn't have anything to do with work. Focusing on something other than what's waiting for you back at your desk can recharge your batteries. We often hear people (ourselves included) say they find the big-picture thinking occurs when they get their mind off work for a while.

» **Take micro breaks.** If you don't want to take a long midday break, consider giving yourself 5-minute micro breaks throughout the day, ideally every 30 minutes or an hour. We talk about this as a way to increase your productivity in the earlier section "Trying the Pomodoro Technique." If lack of productivity is your biggest hurdle, giving yourself some mini breaks can turn your slump around and boost your motivation.

» **Do nothing.** Take 15–20 minutes to shut off your brain and allow your mind to wander. Just a small amount of time spent decompressing this way can reenergize you for the rest of your day.

Shaking up your routine

Sometimes all you need to do to get out of a slump is mix things up. Maybe your routine has grown stale. You don't have to change things up forever, but trying something new may provide the boost you need right now.

For example, consider a change in scenery. If you work in a home office all day, try working from a coworking space or a library for a few days. Or, just work from a different room in the house. Here are some other ideas:

>> **Start the day with something that lights you up.** Instead of reaching for your phone when you wake up, do something that energizes you and gets your creative juices flowing.

>> **Identify what feels stale.** Often, people don't realize their routine has become stale because they haven't taken the time to think about it. Which parts of your day do you dread? When does your energy flag? Which tasks feel tedious or inefficient? Take a look at your routine and see how you can reinvent your day.

>> **Focus on personal/professional growth.** When kids act out, people say it's because they're bored. Adults are the same way. Challenge yourself by learning new things, even if they aren't work-related. Stimulating your mind in different ways can spark your creativity and shake up your day-to-day habits.

>> **Do your day in reverse.** If you usually do something in the morning, do it in the afternoon instead, and vice versa. You may find that changing up the timing of your tasks is enough to get you out of a rut and give you renewed energy to get things done.

Chapter **24**

Looking into the Future of Solopreneurship (and Your Business)

Wouldn't it be nice if everything outside your business stayed the same forever and you only ever had to run it the way you currently are? It's a great thought, but it's not reality.

Solopreneurship is an exciting journey of ups and downs. You just have to be ready for them! Embrace a resilience mindset and figure out how to keep going if things get hard, pivot calmly, and find opportunities in unexpected places. Because no matter how well things are going in your business, you always need to be prepared for shifts and changes that may impact you.

In this chapter, we address what some of these changes are and how to stay ahead of them.

Keeping Up with Trends

We live in a fast-paced world, and as soon as you think you've gotten the hang of something, it changes. You need to do your best to predict trends or understand them early on so you can catch the wave at the perfect point.

Before you can stay on top of trends, you need to have a hunch about the types of trends and shifts that impact your business so you can properly monitor them. Say you run an omelet stand. You probably know it's a good idea to keep track of egg prices and other factors that impact the egg market so you can adjust your prices and operations as necessary. Put time on your calendar to consistently check in with the current trends, so you know which ones are relevant to your business.

WARNING

Monitoring trends is one of the easiest things to put off, but how silly would you feel if something that totally impacts your business came along and you could've done something about it, but didn't? This isn't something you want to procrastinate on.

REMEMBER

Some businesses are so authentic and unique that trends may not necessarily impact them. If that's you, great! But, for the vast majority of mainstream solopreneur businesses, shifts and trends are definitely something to pay attention to.

Lastly, be aware of shiny objects, those things that are appealing and may get your attention but ultimately don't do anything for you in the long run. For example, a TikTok trend is often just a hyped-up video format (such as a dance or challenge) that dies after a week. It's fun, but is it worth paying attention to and will implementing it into your marketing strategy make any real impact on your company?

Monitoring industry news and resources

You're constantly flooded with news and information, so it can be hard to home in on the things you should be paying attention to. You need to make space to allow the relevant information to get through and try to ignore the rest.

Before you do anything else, we highly recommend decluttering your news feeds. Be honest — you follow people or companies on social media that you scroll right past and never pay attention to. Unfortunately, they still tend to pull your focus away from the people you should be following to stay current for your own business. So, unfollow people and organizations that don't serve you and your business, and start following people who do.

Consider having a personal and a professional account on social media. If you absolutely have to follow that one fashion influencer, that's fine, but keep your guilty pleasure separate from the accounts that impact your business so you can more easily track the news coming out of them.

In addition to getting a better grip on your news feeds, set up alerts based on relevant keywords that notify you when news comes out about something that may impact your business. A plethora of social media monitoring tools can help you track, listen to, and analyze conversations on social media platforms and online channels in real time.

You can also use monitoring tools like Google Alerts, which sends you an email when content about a given topic you've flagged is published. Competitive intelligence tools, news aggregators, relevant online forums, and trend discovery platforms are also savvy ways to stay on top of what's happening in your industry.

For a list of recommended tools and platforms, visit www.dummies. com/go/solopreneurbusinessfd.

Networking to stay current

Along with monitoring social media, you want to be active in social media groups that relate to your business and where your audience hangs out. You can certainly be a fly on the wall and observe conversations for data-gathering purposes, but you should also interact and engage with community members to get more of the information you're seeking.

Be in the know about what's going on around you that may impact how you run things. You'll find that you'll gain access to far different information in social media groups than you'd get in a formal report. Listening to the chitchat on the ground level can be just as important to your decision-making as an industry overview.

Additionally, virtual events and webinars that pique your interest and are relevant to your business should be on your calendar regularly. These online resources can be directly or indirectly related to what you do. They can be industry-specific gatherings or presentations covering topics of interest (such as marketing trends that work for small businesses). This is a great way to hear what your peers and other businesses are doing and, depending on the event, a great opportunity to ask questions about how you can best use the topic at hand to improve your business.

REMEMBER

It's imperative to schedule time to enlighten yourself on what's happening in your field and the world around you. If you focus only on your business, and not on the external things that can impact it, you're falling behind.

Future-Proofing Your Solo Business

We understand that unpredictable things happen, but that doesn't mean you can't be as prepared as possible should a curveball come your way. Here are some ways to prepare for the unexpected.

Diversifying income streams

Diversifying *income streams* (a buzzword that simply means sources of income) is one of the smartest things a solopreneur can do. Expanding your sources of income can save you financially if client work slows down or demand shifts suddenly. This list highlights ways to increase the number of income streams flowing into your business (it doesn't include external income streams like real estate investment on the side and so on):

>> **Affiliate marketing:** This is when you share a link for another company on your website and earn a commission when somebody buys the affiliate's product/service using the link you provided.

>> **Digital product creation:** Examples include selling e-books and digital courses so you don't have to worry about physical fulfillment of each purchase.

>> **One-to-many services (group coaching versus one-to-one):** For example, instead of coaching 10 people separately, you can host a group session and get paid by all attendees at once which maximizes your time and earning potential.

>> **Service productization:** This involves turning custom services, such as coaching, into a repeatable standardized product that you can sell to more people (like a coaching course).

>> **Subscription model:** Under this payment model, you charge a recurring monthly fee for your product/service.

TIP

Strategize around the lowest-hanging fruit and move forward from there. Start with one additional income stream at a time and master it before moving on. If you don't intentionally focus your efforts, you can become overwhelmed and spend all your time looking for more sources of income.

Developing new skills

As a business owner, you should always be learning new things and expanding your abilities as a survival tactic. Continuing education is imperative for the success of your business and can help you better adapt to change, stay competitive, innovate further, and build resilience.

You can sign up for digital courses and tutorials, gain expertise through online communities, or just listen to an audiobook or podcast while you're on a walk. Exercising while educating yourself? It's a win-win. Making skill development enjoyable and something you look forward to will help you prioritize it.

TIP

The skills you're working toward should be either something you enjoy doing or some talent or ability you need to develop for your business. Don't hone a skill because you think you should because others are doing it. Go back to your *why* and ask yourself how the new skill truly benefits you personally and professionally in the long run.

Using Artificial Intelligence and Automation in Solopreneurship

When it comes to the future of your solo business, you must have the ability to thrive and adapt in a fast-paced world. One of the best ways to stay on top of a constantly changing landscape is by using artificial intelligence (AI) and automation.

If you've been resisting AI, we have bad news for you: You're falling behind. Once upon a time we were hesitant about using it, but now we can't imagine running our business without AI. It's the epitome of the idea of working smarter, not harder. The vast majority of your competitors are likely running and improving their businesses with help from AI and automation, so don't get left behind. Figure out how to incorporate these tools into your business and embrace them.

Your clients/customers demand personalization, speed, and consistency, and fulfilling those expectations can be difficult, if not impossible, to pull off as a one-person show. The following sections explain how AI and automation can help.

Relying on AI tools to save time

If you want to streamline your operations and save time, the first place you should look is AI. Now, when people hear the term *AI* (at least at the time of this writing), their brains may immediately conjure up ChatGPT. While this is a wonderful tool, we encourage you to think outside the box when it comes to AI. Other tools are available to help you manage your time, deal with your inbox, handle marketing, and so on. So, do some research on the AI tools that can assist you in the areas you need the most help with and start there first.

A few ways AI can help you include these:

>> **Content assistance:** Whether it's writing emails, creating social media posts, or coming up with other types of communication, AI can generate content in a matter of seconds, making your life much easier. While you can always train AI to mimic your tone and personality, it's still a good idea to review every piece of content it generates. It's helpful, but not perfect! AI can also assist you with ideas for new content (or brainstorming in general) when you find yourself in a rut.

>> **Research:** AI is great for analyzing trends, evaluating your competition, giving you feedback on the state of your industry . . . you get the idea. Type in a specific prompt into a tool like ChatGPT or another AI assistant to get the information you need.

>> **Skill development:** AI can act as an on-demand tutor. Whether you're diving into marketing tactics, video editing, or pricing strategy, AI can guide you through concepts, explain jargon, and answer pressing questions immediately.

>> **Meeting prep:** AI can summarize past interactions, review your meeting attendees' websites or social media profiles, and highlight what matters to the person you're meeting with. This allows you to enter the conversation confident and informed without spending a ton of time preparing.

You can find AI tools that provide a variety of benefits and help with many different business needs, like analyzing data, improving customer service, or streamlining marketing. Identify the areas you need help with, research how AI can help you in those areas, and implement the tools that will allow you to more effectively run your business.

Incorporating automation throughout your business

The sole purpose of automation is to take things that don't require *your* time and energy off your plate. Time is money after all, and the more time you have for the strategic work, the better off your business will be.

Automation can be a real game changer, and it's a proactive way to keep your business humming along (and your sanity intact). Your success with using automation in your business is correlated to your ability to run a business without a team while continuing to provide the stellar experience your clients/customers have come to expect.

How cool would it be to be on a vacation with your family while the automated systems you've set up are sending emails, publishing social media posts, and checking off admin tasks in the background? Our answer: Very cool!

We can write an entire book dedicated to automation, but here are a few places to get started if you're new to the concept:

>> **Scheduling:** Stop wasting time on endless back-and-forth emails just to set up a meeting. Automate your scheduling process with tools that let clients or collaborators book time from a list of options based on your real-time availability.

>> **Sales and marketing:** The automation sweet spot! There are tools that can automatically send emails to people who show interest in your services, helping to build trust over time (a process known as *lead nurturing*). Various platforms can track how people interact with your website or emails and send follow-ups to those who are most likely to buy. Some even support *retargeting,* which means showing ads to people who visited your site but didn't take action. This helps you stay top-of-mind and close more sales without manual follow-up.

>> **Invoicing:** Who wants to spend their time sending invoices and following up with payment reminders? Let tools do these tasks for you.

>> **Customer service:** There are platforms that can send client onboarding emails. A chatbot can answer common questions posed by customers, and software exists that can prioritize requests for service or support.

Find a list of automation tools and platforms at www.dummies. com/go/solopreneurbusinessfd.

FIND ONLINE

The trick is to start small. Begin by automating one or two processes until you have them down to a science. Then, grow your automated processes gradually from there until you have enough of the small stuff off your plate that you can focus on the big-picture, future-proofing items.

Outsourcing is another way to get tasks off your plate. You should absolutely consider outsourcing tasks and processes if you're having trouble finding an automated solution.

REMEMBER

Planning for the Long Term

To create a sustainable long-term business, you need to be intentional and realistic. Be aware that you'll be forced to pivot when unexpected issues arise, so you'll need to master the ability to be flexible.

Setting long-term goals

Yep, we're back to talking about your goals again. As your business grows and evolves, your long-term goals likely will expand and change too. What do you want your business and your life to look like in 5 to 10 years? Do you even want to be a solopreneur at that point? (You can find more on that in "Leaving Solopreneurship" later in the chapter.)

You can't plan for the long term if you can't envision what you want it to look like. Having an end goal in mind will help you guide your business's growth, prioritize what matters for your business, stay motivated, and decide which steps are necessary to achieve your long-term aspirations.

Scenario planning

Scenario planning is a great way to prepare for uncertainties in the future. It's like playing the *What if?* game and having a solution for every situation that may arise. A few common *What if?* scenarios include

>> **A recession:** Are you financially secure enough that you can weather the storm if a recession strikes? What can you do now to set yourself up better financially in the future? If you're struggling to understand how to recession-proof your business, meet with a financial professional who can guide you.

>> **A new, larger competitor entering your space:** Just when you think you have a handle on your market, a new business may show up in your space. What will you do if this happens? Will you see it as healthy competition that can strengthen your business, or will it rattle you and make you want to throw in the towel?

>> **Personal life changes:** Whether your family responsibilities increase, you're given the opportunity to take the trip of a lifetime, or some other significant change to your personal life comes up, your focus on your business may shift. Because you have a one-person business, your personal life impacts your professional life, so figure out ways your business can run if you need to reduce your involvement.

>> **Sudden increase in demand:** Not all scenarios are bad! Some excellent developments can be detrimental to your business if you don't address them properly. For instance, you need to make a plan to handle a sudden increase in demand for your product or service (or risk losing clients, your credibility, and revenue).

>> **Contractor becoming unavailable:** We talk about outsourcing throughout this book because it's a great way to help you focus on what really matters. But what happens if a virtual assistant or contractor you rely on to do administrative tasks suddenly becomes unavailable? What's your plan B? Are you able to handle the workload, even if it's only for a short time?

This isn't an exhaustive list, and the *What if?* scenarios will change from business to business. Try to think of all the uncontrollable situations that may impact your business and plan out how you'll respond if they arise. You can't predict everything, but some of the plans you put in place may help you lessen the impact of unforeseen circumstances on your business.

Leaving Solopreneurship

Most people don't go into marriage thinking about divorce. But, as everyone knows, divorce is an outcome for many marriages. Likewise, many solopreneurs intend to run their one-person business for the rest of their career. No more bosses or employees to worry about forever! But no matter what your intentions are at the beginning, you may encounter situations that derail your plans and take you off the course of a lifetime of solopreneurship.

Hiring employees

Sometimes, the only way to truly *scale* your business, or grow it beyond your original plans, is to bring on employees. Going from running a solo business to leading a team can be quite the shift. It may be exhilarating and terrifying at the same time. If you think your business is headed in that direction at some point, keep the following in mind:

>> **Understand why you need employees instead of contractors.** Ask yourself if hiring employees is a knee-jerk reaction to a temporary situation or something that's truly necessary for the longevity and sustainability of your business.

>> **Prepare financially.** One of the benefits of being a solopreneur is that you have lower overhead costs than when you're managing others. You'll need to budget for payroll, taxes,

benefits, office equipment, or workplace tools, just to name a few expenses. Hiring employees typically implies that you don't have an end point in mind, so you'll need to make sure you can cover all these costs indefinitely. No pressure, but other people's livelihoods will now depend on you.

You'll need to prepare financially if you decide to hire contractors, too, but that list is generally confined to budgeting for their fees.

>> **Know how to let go.** You'll be moving from the doer role to the manager (and doer) role. Tasks that were once yours alone now need to be entrusted to somebody else. Are you able to let go of things, even the tasks you love doing? Remember to hire for your desired outcome, which means hiring qualified people you don't need to micromanage. Having to constantly look over somebody's shoulder won't serve the reason you hired employees.

>> **Lead by example.** When you started out as a solopreneur, you had your ideal lifestyle in mind. If you still value that work-life balance, consider passing that culture down to your team. For example, allow them to work hybrid schedules, let them wear jeans to work, give them unlimited paid time off. Figure out how you can maintain your original core values and goals as you scale your business with employees.

>> **Put systems and processes in place before you hire.** You need to think long and hard about how the systems and processes you set up for your one-person business relate to new employees — and go beyond what you may have done if you'd opted for contractors. Understand how operations will run and be managed *before* you bring on an in-house team. This can help eliminate bottlenecks and the constant need for your attention and intervention to get things done. Be as thorough as you can so employees have clear direction from the start.

Selling the business

Solopreneurs may want to sell their business for any number of reasons: unforeseen life circumstances, an offer they can't refuse (insert Godfather tone of voice), market changes, and so on. If selling your business is the best step for you, here are some questions you should ask yourself (and be able to answer) before proceeding:

>> **Is your business transferable?** Do people support your business because your products and services are stellar or because they like *you*? If you take yourself out of the equation, where does your business stand? Is your business even worth purchasing or acquiring? How will you determine its value?

>> **Are your finances in order?** Have you ensured that your personal and business expenses are completely separate? Do you have all the necessary financial documents (including cash flow statements, tax returns, and so on) ready for the sale? That list can be long. If you decide to sell your business, be sure to understand the financial metrics potential buyers prioritize and ensure your records clearly reflect them.

>> **Do you know what you're actually selling?** Are client lists included as part of the purchase? Will the new owner be able to take over your website, domain (your unique web address), email, and social media accounts? Will they have access to the equipment you used? What about your systems and processes? Be clear about what you're selling and don't leave any room for dispute to avoid messy legal battles post-transaction.

>> **Are you mentally prepared to let go?** This may be the hardest question of all. Giving up your business is a big shift, and not a scenario many solopreneurs ever planned for. Have grace with yourself and try to take it all in stride. Know the legacy you want to leave and sell your business to someone who will continue it.

TIP

When it comes to selling your business, we highly recommend getting a professional, such as a business broker, accountant, and attorney, who can guide you through the financial, legal, and logistical aspects of the sale.

7

The Part of Tens

Avoid ten common solopreneur mistakes so you can build a business that lasts.

Keep your mindset strong as you work your way through the solopreneur journey.

Find practical answers to the most common questions solopreneurs ask.

Chapter **25**

Avoiding Ten Common Solopreneur Mistakes

As a solopreneur, you'll make mistakes. It's just the nature of the game and the way you'll figure things out and grow. But wouldn't it be nice to avoid some of the most common mistakes solopreneurs across all industries make and learn something from their failures? That's exactly what we strive to help you do in this chapter. Here are the ten most common mistakes we see in the world of solopreneurship, with some tips for how to avoid them.

Not Fully Understanding Your Audience

Everything you do in your business comes down to one thing: solving your audience's problems and giving them what they want. That's it. A big thing that gets solopreneurs in trouble is *assuming* they know what their audience wants instead of taking the time to research and actually *know* what their audience wants. You must do what you need to do to understand your audience inside and out. Don't just rely on an image of them from the perspective of your business.

Lacking a Plan or Direction

Far too often solopreneurs are working so hard to keep up with their competitors that they neglect to have their own plan, direction, and unique brand and strategy. This often results in burnout, wasted time, and inconsistent income. Without a clear plan, you'll constantly be spinning your wheels and chasing after shiny objects that won't do you any good in the long run.

REMEMBER

Tie everything back to your *why* (Chapter 4), your goals (also Chapter 4), and your audience's pain points (Chapter 8), and how you can solve them. Use those as your compass to create a strategy that makes sense for your business.

Failing to Get the Word Out

Tell people what you do. Sounds simple enough, right? Unfortunately, even the most successful solopreneurs sometimes struggle to spread the word about their product/service, especially in the beginning. We have a great story about a solopreneur who overheard her parents telling their friends that she's a creative director for an advertising agency. The funny thing is, she had never been a creative director, and she had left the ad agency a couple of years prior. After initially being frustrated with her parents, she quickly realized their misunderstanding of her livelihood was nobody's fault but her own. She hadn't actually told her parents what she does for a living. She just assumed they knew!

Many solopreneurs don't like to discuss what they do because they're afraid they'll come off as salesy, but that simply isn't true. If you approach the topic in an informative and educational manner, you're simply introducing a new concept or idea to another person. And this approach is authentic, so people will likely take an interest in what you're building and want to hear more about it. If you have this conversation with the right people (your target audience), you're one step closer to closing your next deal.

Trying to Do Everything on Your Own

Everyone say it together: Flying solo in business doesn't mean you're alone. You'll burn out faster than you can say *solopreneur* if you try to carry the weight of an entire business on your own. We get it. This business is your baby, but you need to figure out how to automate and outsource tasks early on. Otherwise, you may end up resenting a business you once loved, becoming the bottleneck that slows the momentum of your business.

TIP

Use AI technology and tools, implement automated systems, and outsource. You may think lightening your workload is a luxury, but it's a necessity for the longevity and success of your business.

Neglecting Self-Care

Consider this a warning to put your mental and physical health above everything else in your life, personally and professionally. You want your business to run like a well-oiled machine, right? Then you need to make sure your body is a well-functioning machine first. If you don't take care of yourself, you risk experiencing burnout, decreased productivity, reduced creativity and innovation, health issues (see Chapter 23 on self-care), and falling out of love with your business.

TIP

Treat self-care like it's a part of your business. You have your operations, your marketing, your finances, your client work . . . and your personal fitness. Don't look at your mental and physical health as something separate from the health of your business. For a solopreneur, everything ties together, so nurture all aspects of you.

Ignoring Feedback

Feedback can make you uncomfortable. While everyone loves hearing how incredible their business is, listening to criticism can be a bit of a gut punch. But you know what? Critical feedback is necessary for growth, and it's often the fastest way to improve something. Don't look at feedback as failure. Look at it as a road map for improvement. We recommend that you seek feedback early and often. To overcome any resistance to feedback, try the following:

>> **Separate yourself from your business.** Remember that critics aren't attacking *you*; they're genuinely trying to give you their input on your product or service.

>> **Get feedback anonymously.** If you're worried about how you'll react to a certain person's comments, use an anonymous survey to get feedback.

>> **Change one thing at a time.** You can't fix everything overnight. If you want to respond to feedback properly, take time to process it. Then, think strategically about how you can change things.

>> **Take some feedback with a grain of salt.** If you receive a comment that doesn't make any sense or a suggestion that you know won't work for your business, ignore it. Just make sure you're ignoring it for the right reason.

Not Having an Emergency Fund

WARNING

One of the most common mistakes solopreneurs make is not having an *emergency fund* (money you've set aside for unexpected expenses, a dry spell, or other financial hardship). In a perfect world, you'll never need it, but your income can fluctuate from month to month. And if you don't have the money when you do need it, you're in for tough times.

It might take time to build up your emergency fund, especially if your budget is already stretched. We recommend aiming for at least three to six months of both living and business expenses (more if you can swing it). And put your emergency fund in a savings account separate from the rest of your business and personal accounts. That way, you'll be less likely to pull money from it when you don't need it.

Managing Your Time Poorly

Many solopreneurs grapple with time management because they simply have so much to do and don't know how to handle all of it. We want to make one thing very clear: Being *busy* isn't the same as being *productive.* Many solopreneurs struggle to manage their time because they're doing things they don't need to be doing themselves. Or things they don't need to be doing at all. Getting time management right is essential for the longevity of your business, and to help you prevent burnout and improve your stress management.

So, repeat after us, "Automate and outsource, automate and outsource." Figure out which tasks you can hand off to a contractor or virtual assistant (consider trading services if money is tight), as well as things you can automate (maybe tasks like scheduling meetings and social media posts). This helps you trim your workload down to the big-picture items and other tasks only you can perform.

Overcommitting to Clients and Customers

Nobody goes into a customer meeting thinking they're going to over-promise and under-deliver, but it happens. One of the first things you should do when you engage with a new client or customer is set clear boundaries and explain the processes you expect them to follow. Many solopreneurs overcommit simply because they cater to customers' every desire. If you're clear about what you will and won't do from the get-go, you can make that less of a problem. This allows you to focus on what you've committed to rather than diverting your attention to endless free add-ons.

TIP

Not every client is going to be a good fit. If a client pushes the boundaries you've set, consider if they're the type of person you want to work with in the long run. If you respect your own limits, most clients will respect them as well. If this is difficult for you, just remember the wise words of Harvard Business School professor Michael Porter: "The essence of strategy is choosing what not to do."

Underpricing Your Product or Service

In Chapter 10, we mention that we don't think it's a good idea to use price to win clients over your competition. In fact, when we talk to solopreneurs, we often encourage them to *increase* their prices so they can free up more time while making the same income (or more). As a solopreneur, you must understand your worth.

If you charge too little or only for your hours, you don't have additional funds to invest in tools and technology that help your business run efficiently (or build an emergency fund). You may think you're doing yourself a favor by keeping your prices low, but you're really doing yourself a major disservice. People often perceive lower cost as lower quality. If price reflects perceived value, be sure your prices portray a confident and highly qualified individual who can transform clients and help them find success in the areas they're struggling with.

WARNING

Lower prices may get you more clients at first, but are they the type of clients you want? Plus, if you keep adding more clients to your roster because your prices are low, you risk work overload and total burnout. It's an unsustainable model.

» Reconnecting with your purpose

» Committing to lifelong learning

» Knowing you don't have to go it alone

» Building resilience and adaptability

» Celebrating progress and staying aligned

Chapter **26**

Ten Important Reminders for Solopreneurs

Solopreneurship can be a bumpy road, but it's one worth traveling. You don't have to have it all figured out (nobody does), but you do need to continue learning, adapting, and showing up for yourself. We provide the reminders in this chapter as tools to help you build a thriving and meaningful business that serves your goals.

Keep Your Why Front and Center

As a solopreneur, you'll likely encounter stressful deadlines, unreasonable client requests, industry curveballs, and basically a variety of things that can make you question why you're even running this business in the first place. Many solopreneurs experience self-doubt from time to time; when you do, keep the *why* for your business front and center. Not only can focusing on your purpose help you when the going gets tough, but it can help you maintain momentum when things are going well. It's the North

Star that guides your journey and takes you back to your center when you feel lost.

Embrace Continuous Learning

The number of research inquiries you'll type into search engines, and the number of people you'll have to call for advice, is mind-boggling. You'll watch educational YouTube videos at odd hours and listen to informative podcasts while driving. You'll expand the number of business-related books you read and watch webinars like they're the hottest thing on your streaming service.

You'll constantly encounter unfamiliar territory, so prime your brain for steep and frequent learning curves, but also get excited about all the new information you'll acquire! What an opportunity it is to be able to discover so much while pursuing something you love. Along the way, you'll gain technical and operational skills, but you'll also master boundary setting, communication, resilience, and other necessary talents to thrive in your solo business.

Remember You Don't Need to Do Everything Alone

People have the idea that if you decide to fly solo in business, you'll need to do everything on your own, but that's not so. Make outsourcing, automation, and AI your friends, all of which can free up time so it doesn't feel like the weight of an entire business is always on your shoulders (even though it technically is). Relying on other professionals as well as technology is a superpower, not a weakness.

REMEMBER

The goal of going solo is to create your dream business and your ideal life, which is hard to do when you're in constant burnout mode from taking on too much. Although your business is like a baby to you, you need to figure out how to delegate and let go to maintain a solid work-life balance.

Stay Flexible

You have to maintain flexibility in every aspect of your business: from dealing with scheduling snafus, to adapting to shifts in the market and demand for your product/service, to handling curveballs clients throw at you . . . the list goes on. Welcome change with open arms and become familiar with the unknown. Being able to adapt and experiment will serve your business well. A resilient mindset will allow you to conquer shifts and changes that come your way.

Let Customer Pain Points Drive Decisions

We can't say this enough: Your clients and customers don't care what you sell. They care about how you make them feel and whether you solve their *pain points* (the issues they need to resolve). Making decisions for your business based on what you want or what you think is right can be the easy option, but your decisions should be based on your customers instead.

Celebrate Your Achievements

It feels good to celebrate your wins, big or small, but acknowledging your achievements also fuels your solo journey. You're building something from the ground up, and that's no small feat, especially when you're doing it alone. You deserve to give yourself a pat on the back occasionally because what you're accomplishing is hard! Whether you land a new client, hit a big deadline, or just survive a stressful workweek, take a moment to congratulate yourself. In the world of solopreneurship you won't get any promotions or office accolades; you must provide them for yourself.

Plan for the Potential Feast or Famine Roller Coaster

Preparing for the ups and downs of running a business requires strategic planning and a resilient mindset. As you're likely aware, the best thing you can do is have a financial cushion for yourself and avoid touching it unless it's an emergency. We recommend keeping three to six months of savings in your emergency fund so you can survive financially even if your client pipeline is at a standstill.

On that note, be aware that it can be easy to work *in* your business, but you have to work *on* it as well. Even in peak times, make sure your networking and marketing efforts remain strong so you always have warm leads to nurture.

It's also smart for solopreneurs to diversify income streams so that if one area of your business takes a hit, it won't impact all areas of your business. For example, if you're a coach who typically does one-on-one coaching, consider adding digital courses covering topics you discuss frequently in sessions that people can purchase on-demand if they'd prefer to receive guidance on their own time.

Lastly, with the understanding that your income will ebb and flow, plan for downtime in advance. Average out how much you bring in monthly and save extra during the more lucrative months to cover the slower months.

REMEMBER

This is why retainers can be a nice payment model. You get paid the same amount every month even though you'll have more work some months than others. Flip to Chapter 6 for details on using retainers as your form of payment.

Figure Out How to Say No

Solopreneurs often tell themselves that they need to say *yes* to everything. Declining a potential paycheck seems silly, right? That isn't necessarily the case. The most important assets a solopreneur has are their time and energy. And if you want to be successful as a solopreneur, you need to guard those things fiercely. If you say *yes* to everything, you don't leave room for the opportunities that truly matter (or are more lucrative). Saying *no* isn't a negative thing. It actually gives you power and, in turn, the confidence to go after what you really want. Think of the types of clients you want to work with and how much you want them to pay. Then do what you can to stay aligned with those dream scenarios. Your business will grow when you take on the *right* clients, not the *most* clients.

Review and Refine Regularly

As a solopreneur, it's easy to have blind spots without another person looking over your work and giving you feedback, so you need to do regular check-ins to assess your results (see Chapter 19) while also getting external input. Get feedback from somebody you trust to be honest and not just tell you what you want to hear. Review what works and what doesn't and put a plan in place to adjust. The survival of your business depends on your ability to adapt.

Enjoy the Journey

You can get so caught up in keeping your eyes on the prize that you forget to stop and smell the roses along the way. Solopreneurship isn't about the destination; it's about the journey, and it's important to take the time to reflect and appreciate the small wins as well as embrace key discoveries and insights. If you spend your time always thinking about tomorrow rather than today, you're in for a potentially miserable experience as a solopreneur.

REMEMBER

Lots of people are sitting at their corporate desks wishing they were taking the chance that you are, so be grateful for the opportunity.

» Knowing how to sidestep common solopreneur mistakes

» Building your customer base and finding affordable health insurance

» Saying *no* with confidence

» Understanding what it takes to be a solopreneur

» Scaling your one-person business

Chapter **27**

Ten FAQs About Solopreneurship

The frequently asked questions (FAQs) in this chapter address common hurdles or misconceptions people may have about solopreneurship. By addressing them, we hope to give you the confidence you need to get started (or to continue plugging away).

What Are Some of the Biggest Mistakes Solopreneurs Make?

As a solopreneur, you'll inevitably make mistakes; it's part of the learning process. We cover ten of the most common mistakes we've seen solopreneurs make in Chapter 25, but here are a few more:

>> **Abstaining from outsourcing and helpful technology:** Make outsourcing, automation, and AI your best friends to avoid burnout and help you run a more efficient business.

- >> **Overplanning before starting:** If you wait for everything to be perfect, you'll never launch your business. Release your product or service when it's good enough, and make changes and improvements based on feedback over time.

- >> **Failing to niche down:** Narrow down your target audience and build everything around them. You always have time to expand to other audiences and markets, but make sure you're really good in one area first.

- >> **Neglecting to pursue new business opportunities:** Many solopreneurs focus on working *for* their business rather than growing their business.

- >> **Not learning from mistakes:** You need to learn from your mistakes quickly and make changes when needed. Your business is constantly evolving, so get used to the cycle of implementing, reviewing, and revising.

What Are the Best Ways for Solopreneurs to Find Clients?

Traditional marketing and sales tactics don't always work for solopreneurs because they may require a lot of time and resources you simply don't have. Consider these ideas instead:

- >> **Tell people in your life what you do.** Friends, family, former coworkers, and professional connections all can be a powerful referral source, especially if they understand how to help (and they probably want to!). This isn't about pitching; it's about making them aware your business exists.

- >> **Reach out to niche communities.** Become a familiar presence on the online platforms and spaces your audience visits. It establishes credibility with these communities; when they need help with problems you solve, they'll think of you.

- >> **Be active in your local community.** Establishing relationships with people outside work (for example, by playing in a tennis league) allows you to broaden your network. The people in these groups may not be clients, but they can be excellent referral sources.

- **》 Partner or collaborate with complementary businesses.** Collaborations and partnerships often mean half the work with twice the exposure because you're being introduced to the other business's audience.

- **》 Establish yourself as an authority.** Set up speaking engagements, teach workshops, or do podcast interviews. The more knowledgeable you appear to others, the more likely they'll be to choose you over your competition.

How Can Solopreneurs Find Healthcare Insurance?

Many people worry that if they leave their corporate job, they won't have access to affordable health insurance. Health insurance coverage is accessible for solopreneurs in the United States. Be aware that things may change around this topic, so do your own research and find what works best for you. Here are some options to consider:

- 》 Affordable Care Act marketplace plans

- 》 COBRA coverage from your previous job

- 》 Insurance coverage provided by your spouse or partner's employer (Some businesses don't require employees to be legally married to qualify for dependent/family coverage.)

- 》 Healthcare sharing plans (noninsurance alternatives in which members share healthcare costs)

- 》 Insurance offered through professional or trade organizations

- 》 Supplemental and gap coverage for out-of-pocket medical expenses

- 》 Medicaid and Children's Health Insurance Program (commonly known as CHIP) plans

How Should Solopreneurs Approach Tax and Legal Matters?

The short answer? Hire a professional. Throughout the book, we mention the importance of outsourcing some parts of your business. Unless you have extensive legal and tax knowledge, you should consider outsourcing these matters to the pros. However, you can take control of some basic tasks within these categories.

Taxes	Legal
Keep your personal and professional finances separate.	Register your business and trademark your name (trademarking isn't mandatory, but it's recommended).
Set aside funds for your tax bill throughout the year and pay quarterly taxes.	Understand your obligations regarding insurance coverage, compliance requirements, industry-specific licenses, and so on.
Track your business expenses.	Get an address that isn't your home address. Separating personal and business details helps you look more credible and safeguards your personal information.
	Create service agreements and contracts to use with clients and contractors.

Can Anybody Be a Solopreneur?

We don't want to be dream squashers, and technically anybody can pursue solopreneurship. But the honest answer is, not everybody is cut out for this type of business, and that's okay. Some people thrive when they have structure, external accountability, and coworkers. If you have a hard time working independently, problem-solving, and forging your own path, you'll likely struggle as a solopreneur.

If uncertainty makes you squirm, you should think long and hard about whether solopreneurship is right for you. When a mistake occurs, you're the one at fault. When income isn't coming in, it's on you to figure out how to shore up your finances. These responsibilities can (understandably) be a lot for some people to handle.

How Can Solopreneurs Dabble in Outsourcing and Automation?

Solopreneurs can incorporate automation and outsourcing into their business in countless ways, but the sheer number of options you have can be incredibly overwhelming. If you want to start small, consider dipping your toes in the water in the following areas.

Automation	Outsourcing
Emailing and onboarding customers	Bookkeeping
Meeting scheduling with clients or leads	Administrative tasks
Invoicing and collecting payments	Marketing content creation

Is It Easy to Make Money as a Solopreneur?

We'll go with the answer everybody loves: It depends. With intention, strategy, and hard work, you can make your business profitable. In addition, you don't have the overhead costs that come with employees, tech makes many tasks much easier for one-person businesses, and many people prefer the personal touch of solopreneurs over the impersonal approach of larger companies. Frankly, your ability to make money depends on how well you *niche down* (narrow your focus), how expansive your skill set is, how in demand your services are, how flooded (or not) with competition the market is, and how well you're able to stand out in your market.

How Can Solopreneurs Avoid Loneliness?

When you're running a one-person business, it's hard to not feel isolated from time to time. Chapter 23 offers tips for dealing with isolation, but here are a few reminders:

>> **Work from a coworking space.**

>> **Join professional communities.**

>> **Pursue interests outside work.**

>> **Strengthen your relationships outside work.**

>> **Find an accountability partner.**

REMEMBER

Even though you no longer have coworkers to chat with throughout the day, that doesn't mean you'll end up lonely. Through strategic partnerships, client interactions, collaborations, networking, and non-work-related activities, you may find you interact with more people than you did in a traditional office environment. You just need to put some effort into making that happen.

What's the Difference Between a Solopreneur and an Entrepreneur?

Solopreneurs are considered a subset of entrepreneurs — individuals who run a company of one without the desire to scale with traditional employees. While solopreneurs tend to value autonomy and lifestyle flexibility, entrepreneurs may aim to build teams, pursue larger scalability, and position their businesses for larger market impact or eventual acquisition.

The line between solopreneur and entrepreneur isn't always clear-cut. The core difference often lies in intention: solopreneurs typically aim to create a business that supports the lifestyle they want, while entrepreneurs are more likely to design businesses that exist beyond themselves. For example, a fractional chief marketing officer might choose part-time solo work for schedule freedom, rather than launch a full-service agency with staff and long-term growth goals. That same solopreneur might still chase big profits or even plan to sell one day, only with a business built to match their personal vision.

How Can Solopreneurs Scale Their Business Without Hiring Employees?

If we had a nickel . . .

It's hard for people who are unfamiliar with solopreneurship to imagine efficient ways to *scale* (grow revenue and/or impact) without adding employees. Sure, adding employees is the best way to scale *if* you want to scale exponentially. If you're just trying to build a business that supports your lifestyle, this list offers some great ways to achieve that:

>> Outsourcing tasks you don't need to do yourself

>> Automating repetitive tasks

>> Productizing services (turning your expertise into standardized, packaged offerings) so you're not trading time for money

>> Using AI to streamline tasks

>> Increasing your rates or prices to escape the burden of having to say *yes* to every project

>> Partnering and collaborating with others to get exposure to new audiences while sharing the workload

Index

A

A/B testing, 91
accountability, 53–55, 314, 317
achievements. *See* wins
Acunzo, Jay, 142, 282
adaptability, cultivating, 16–17
adjusting your business (Step 7 in
    Solopreneur Success Cycle),
    31, 301–308
  Change Plan worksheet, 303
  documenting change, 306–307
  never ending cycle, 307–308
  SMOOTH method, 301–306
  harvesting lessons, 305–306
  managing your load and
      energy, 303
  opening lines of
      communication, 303–304
  owning risks, 304
  sequencing smartly, 302–303
  tracking success with metrics, 305
affiliate marketing
  defined, 228
  as marketing tactic, 150
  overview, 228–229
AI. *See* artificial intelligence
Allen, David, 262
Ammari, Zaid, 124
analysis and analytics
  blue ocean strategy, 127–128
  Competitor Analysis Sheet, 85
  paralysis defined, 319
  quadrant analysis, 126–127
  standing out, 126

  tools for, 153, 210
  website metrics, 233
Angelou, Maya, 179
app recommendations, 204
artificial intelligence (AI)
  bots, 212
  effective use of, 208
  finding customers with, 90–91
  productivity tools, 207
  sales chats, 164
  saving time with, 334–335
  scaling with, 9
Atelier LKS, 80
audience
  determining, 88–89
  engaging through websites, 232
  failing to understand, 343
  identifying with personas, 93–95
  resonating with, 143
  visual branding for, 135
authority principle, 144
automation
  incorporating throughout business,
      335–336, 359
  marketing, 147
  scaling, 9
  tools for, 204
awareness phase, of buyer's
    journey, 97–98

B

balance sheets, 252
banks, 189–190
blue ocean strategy, 127–128

O

P

About the Authors

Joe Rando started his first business in 1990 as a solopreneur real estate developer, combining a real estate-focused MBA with the programming skills he picked up while earning his physics degree. He developed almost 1 million square feet of commercial real estate using software he created to assess locations for retail space. He then grew that software into a tech company he cofounded called Trade Area Systems, which he and his partner sold in 2020. Since then, Joe has been working on AI technology, earning several patents along the way. Recently, his focus has been on LifeStarr, where he helps solopreneurs build businesses that serve their lives and goals.

Joe lives in Western Massachusetts with his wife and their golden retriever. He loves cycling, hiking, and playing the guitar in a style he currently describes as "rusty." His favorite gig of all? Being goofy with his granddaughter.

Carly Ries has been immersed in the marketing world for nearly two decades, bringing her expertise to businesses ranging from local mom-and-pop shops to global Fortune 500 companies. Since 2014, she has embraced the remote work lifestyle as a solopreneur, including years as a digital nomad. Carly joined LifeStarr in 2020 as the fractional chief marketing officer and cohost of The Aspiring Solopreneur podcast. She has dedicated her career to helping solopreneurs create businesses and lives they love. She's found that while she initially set out to educate other solopreneurs, they have taught her just as much.

In her downtime, Carly is usually back home in Colorado, spending time with friends and family, exploring local trails, uncovering hidden gems around town, and soaking up everything her community has to offer.

Dedication

To Licia, my wife and best friend, who taught me what it really means to be brave and to stand up for what's right.
-Joe Rando

To my Nana, who always believed in helping others and reminded people you'll never be lonely if you have a good book in your hand.
-Carly Ries

Author's Acknowledgments

Writing *Solopreneur Business For Dummies* was no small feat, and while it may have our names on the cover, this project also belongs to the many people who helped bring it to life.

First, we'd like to thank the incredible team at Wiley, especially Nicole Sholly, whose steady guidance kept us on track, and Tracy Boggier, who got the ball rolling from the very beginning.

We are deeply grateful to our LifeStarr team: Stacy Blette, Tricia Harvey, and Shelley Rapoza for their constant dedication to helping solopreneurs thrive. You've been the heartbeat behind our entire mission.

Thank you to George B. Thomas and everyone at Sidekick Strategies for your strategic wisdom and unrelenting energy. You helped us think bigger and deliver better.

A heartfelt shoutout to Sarah Sypniewski, not only for the example you set as a rock-star solopreneur featured throughout this book, but for your encouragement and belief in this project from day one.

To the LifeStarr Community, you are the reason this book exists. Your courage, your passion, and your entrepreneurial spirit inspired every page. Here's to your continued journey of going solo together and to doing business *your* way.

And last, but certainly not least, a huge thank-you to our wonderful families. Without your support (and patience), this book never would've been written. We love you with all of our hearts.

Publisher's Acknowledgments

Executive Editor: Tracy Boggier
Project Manager: Nicole Sholly
Copy Editor: Kelly Brillhart
Technical Editor: Jessica Lackey

Production Editor: Magesh Elangovan
Managing Editor: Sofia Malik
Cover Image: © Marko Cvetkovic/ Getty Images

Printed and bound by CPI Grou~ ~rdon, CR0 4YY

18/0

14719741-0001